Table Of Contents

CD Track #	Song Title	Sheet Music	Chord Charts	Cut Capo Charts
1	A Greater Song	3	196	239
2	Adoration	8	197	240
3	Amazing Grace (My Chains Are Gone)	24	198	241
4	Be Lifted High	14	199	242
5	Be Praised	18	200	243
6	Beautiful News	29	201	244
7	Captivated	34	202	245
8	Carried to the Table	38	203	246
9	Closer	43	204	247
10	Created to Worship	62	205	248
11	Everything	48	206	249
12	Forever Holy	52	207	250
13	Give Me Jesus	58	208	251
14	Give You Glory	67	209	252
15	God of Justice	72	210	253
16	Great God of Wonders	77	211	254
17	Here and Now	82	212	255
18	Highest and the Greatest	86	213	256
19	How Can I Keep from Singing	91	214	257
20	I Stand for You	96	215	258
21	I Will Remember You	100	216	259
22	Join the Song	105	217	260
23	Let God Arise	110	218	261
24	Love Came Down	115	219	262
25	Made to Worship	122	220	263
26	O Church Arise	128	221	264
27	On the Third Day	130	222	265
28	Resurrection Day	134	223	266
29	Shine	138	224	267
30	Sound of Melodies	144	225	268
31	Speak O Lord	150	226	269
32	Tears of the Saints	152	227	270
33	The Wonder of the Cross	160	228	271
34	To the Only God	164	229	272
35	Unwavering	167	230	273
36	We Remember	182	231	274
37	Yes and Amen	172	232	275
38	You Are God	178	233	276
39	You Are My God (Like a Whisper)	187	234	277
40	Your Glory Endures Forever	190	235	278

Chords Used in This Song

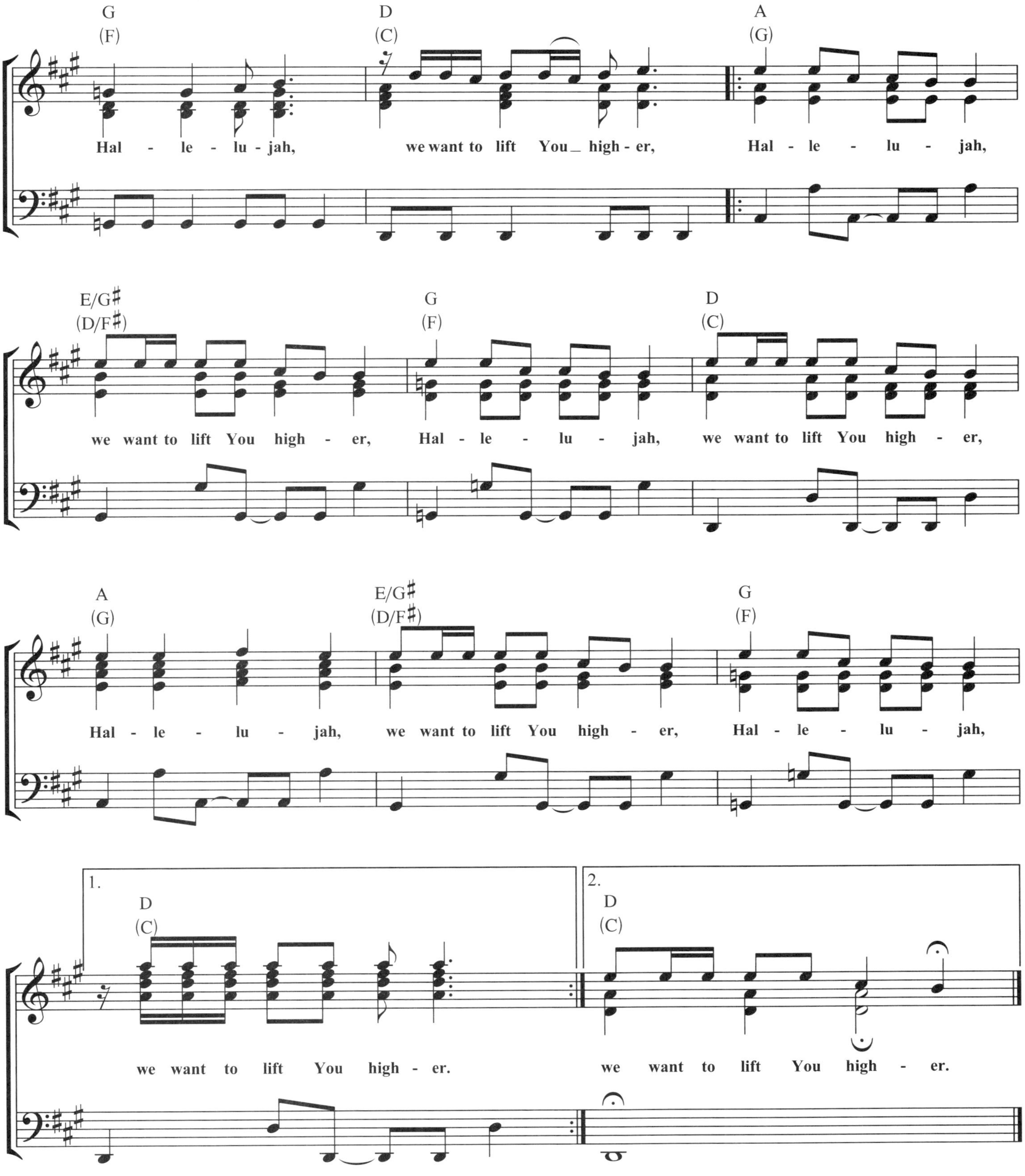

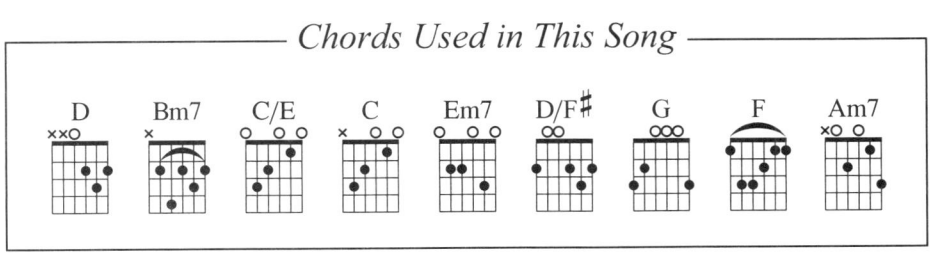

Adoration
(Down In Adoration Falling)

Copyright © 2003 Thankyou Music (PRS) (adm. worldwide by EMI CMG Publishing,
excluding the UK and Europe, which is adm. by kingswaysongs.com/spiritandsong.com (BMI) (adm. by EMI CMG Publishing)
All rights reserved. Used by permission. CCLI Song No. 4729949

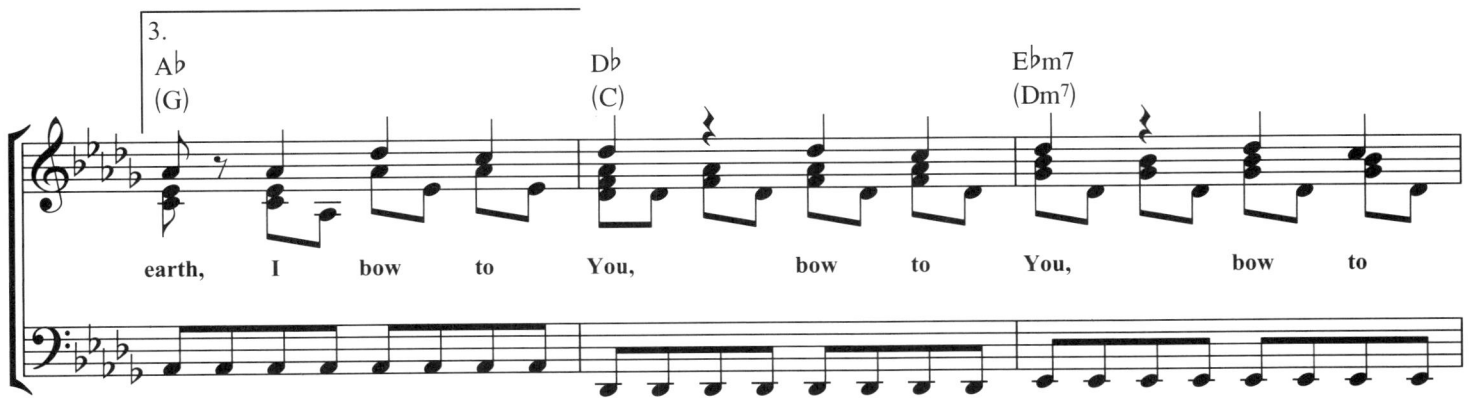
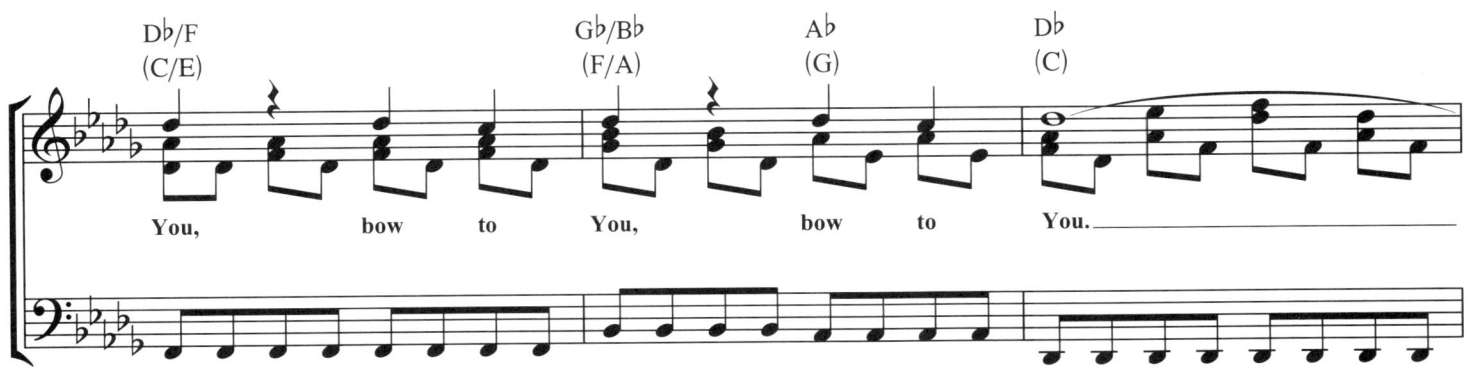

Chords Used in This Song

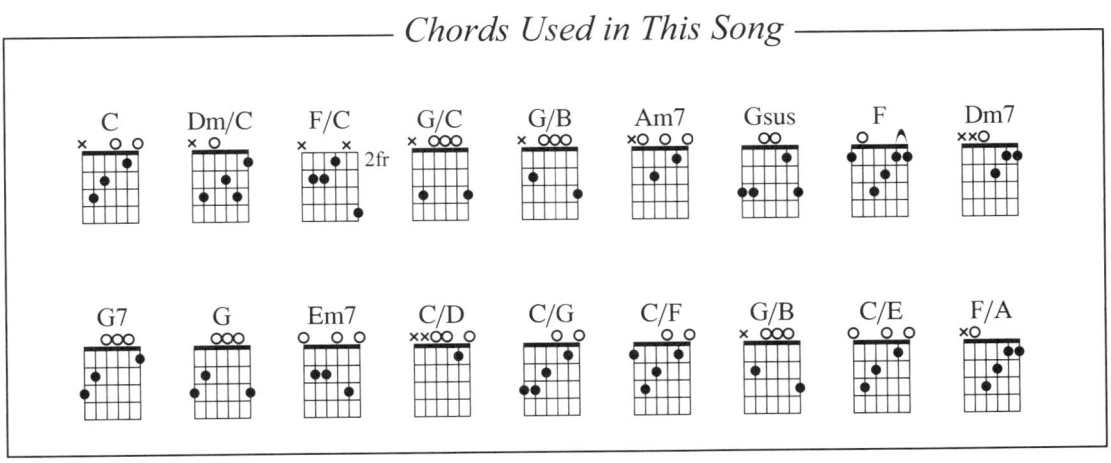

Be Praised

Chords Used in This Song

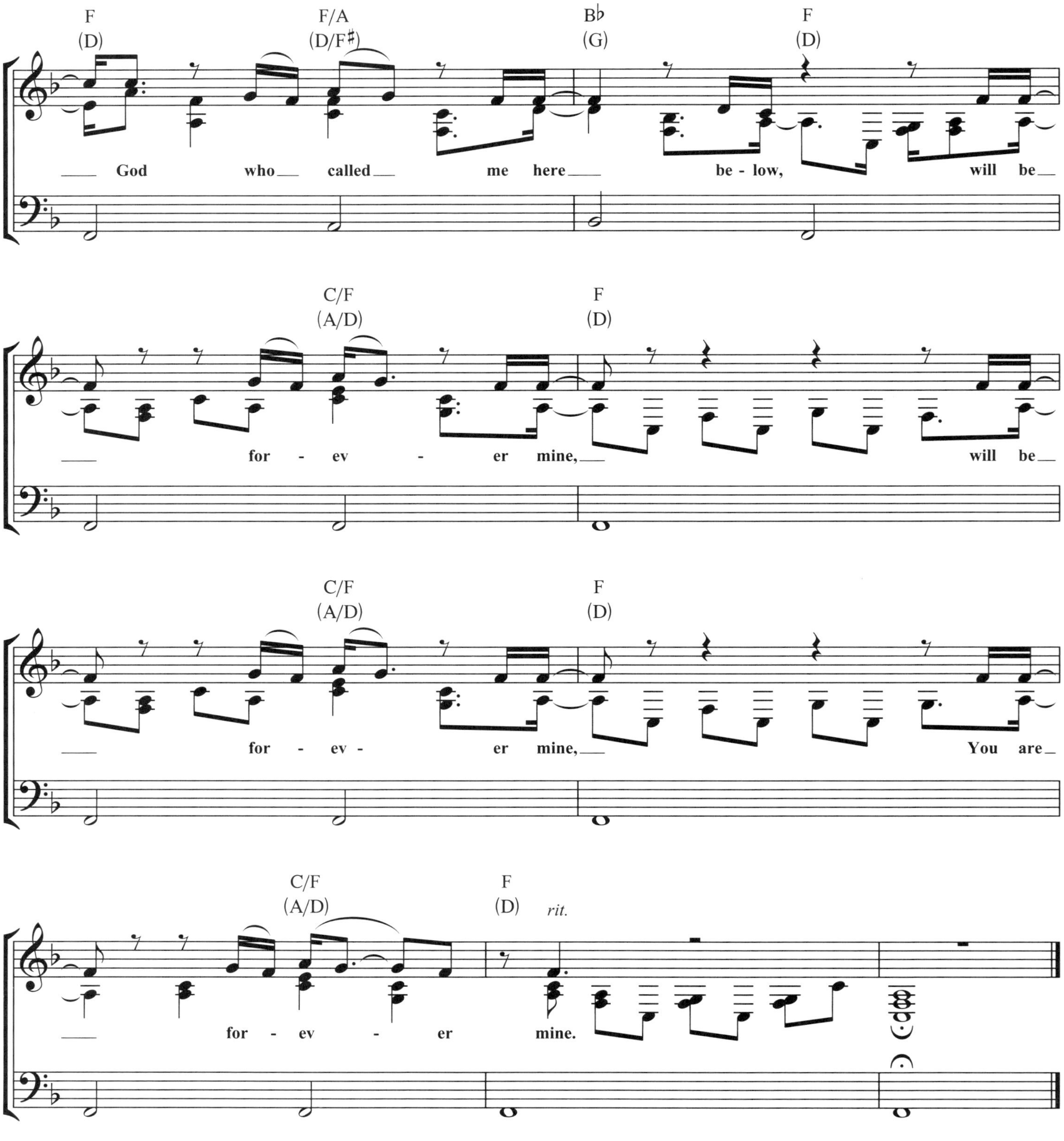

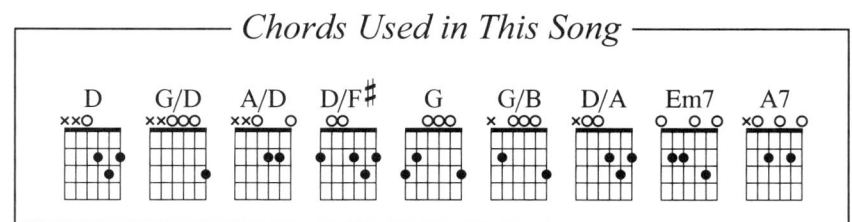

Captivated

**Words and Music by
VICKY BEECHING**

Moderately slow ♩ = 72

1. Your laugh-ter it ech-oes like a joy-ous thun-der,
2. Be-hold-ing is be-com-ing, so as You fill my gaze,

Your whis-per it warms me like a sum-mer breeze.
I be-come more like you and my heart is changed.

Your an-ger is fierc-er than the sun in its splen-dor,
Be-hold-ing is be-com-ing, so as You fill my view,

You're close and yet full of mys-ter-y. And ev-er since the
trans-form me in-to the like-ness of You. This is what I

Copyright ©2005 Thankyou Music (PRS) (adm. worldwide by worshiptogether.com Songs excluding
the UK and Europe, which is adm. by kingswaysongs.com).
All rights reserved. Used by permission. CCLI Song No. 4673703

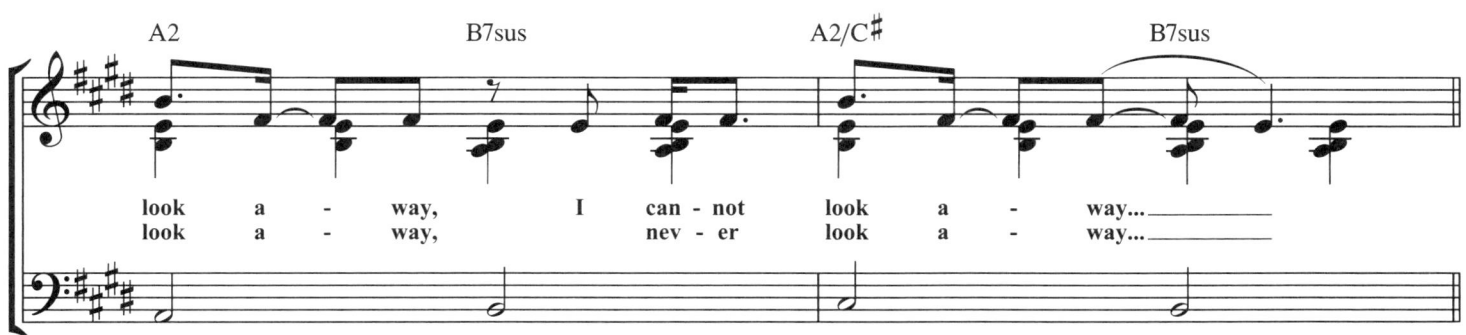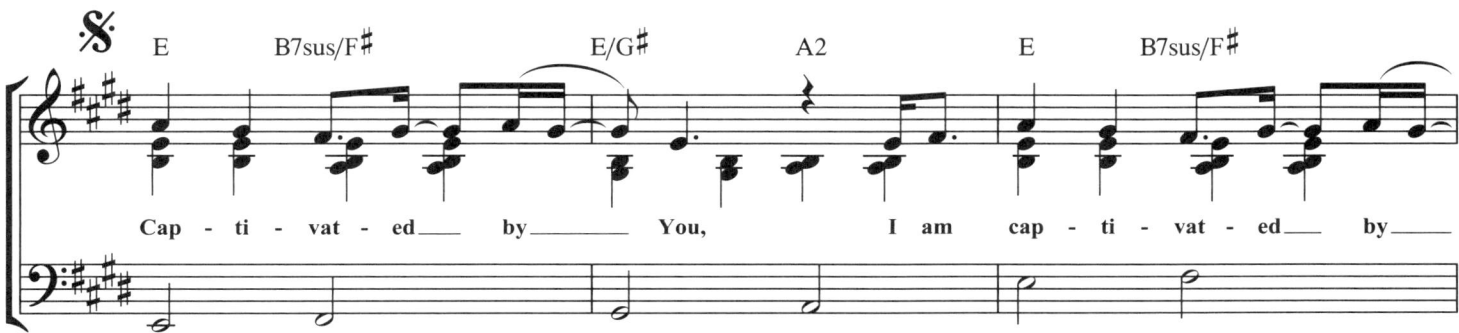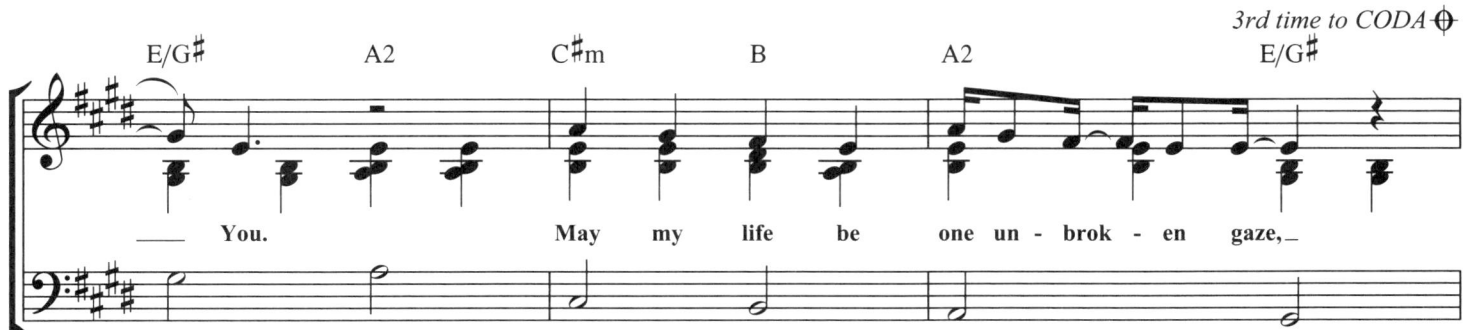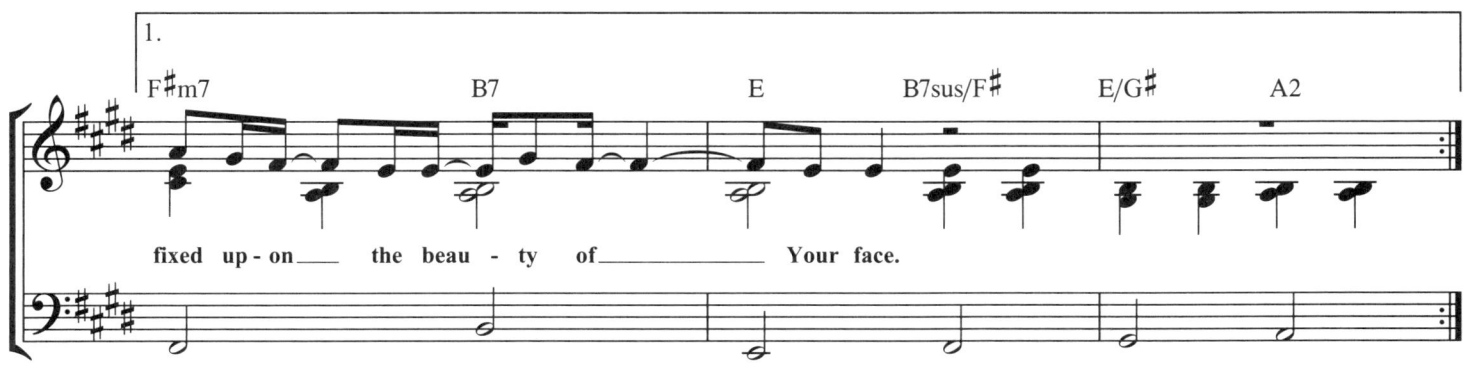

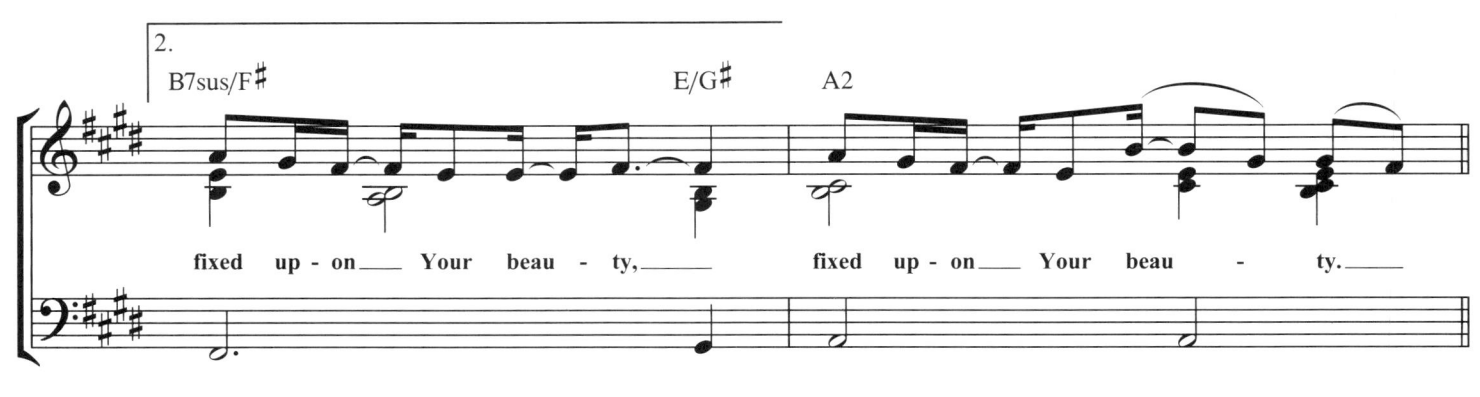
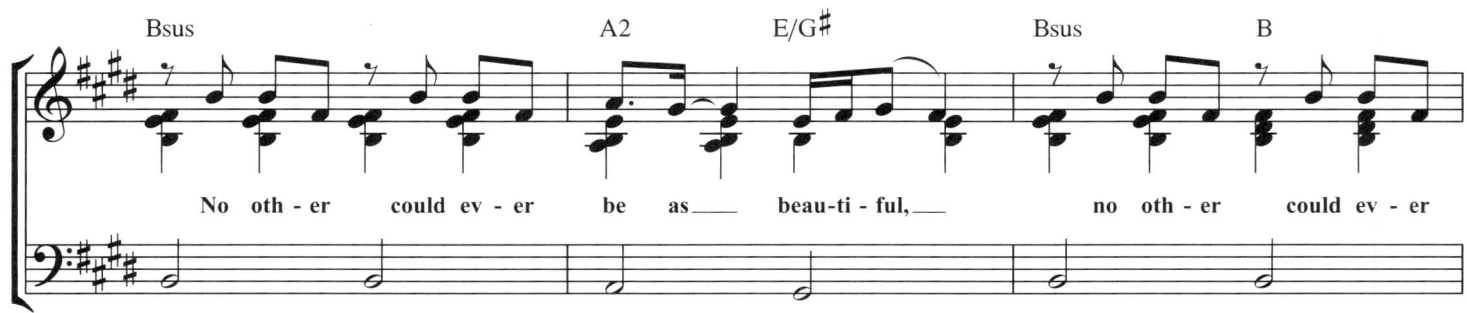

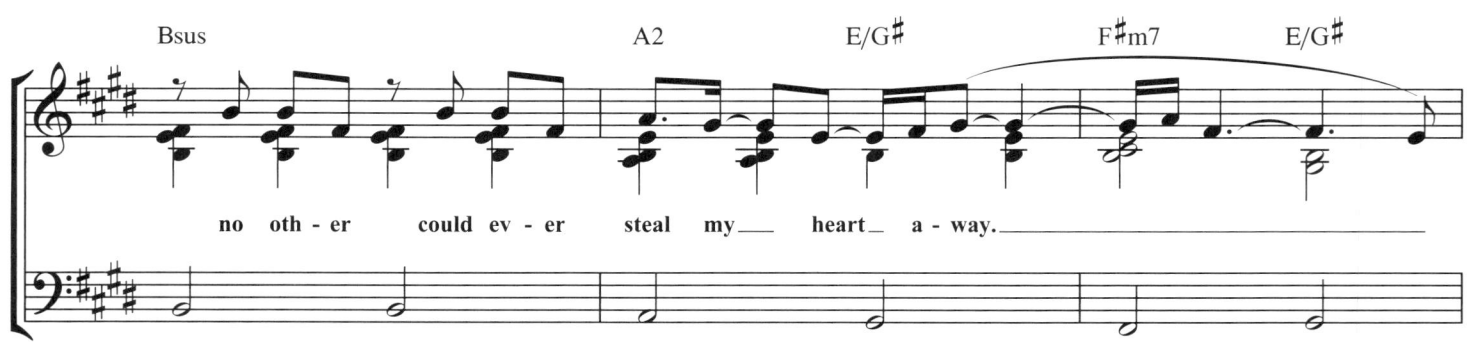

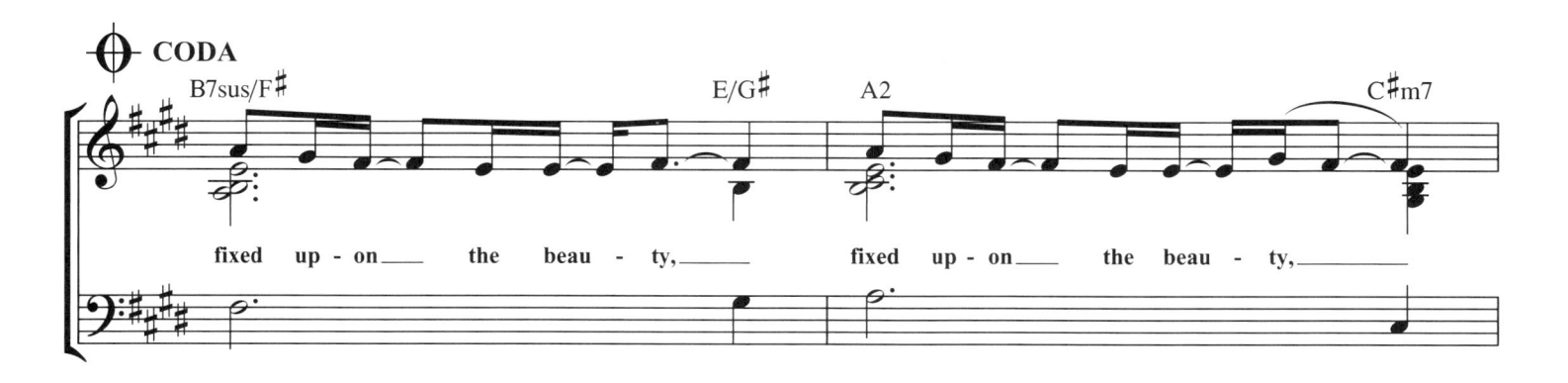

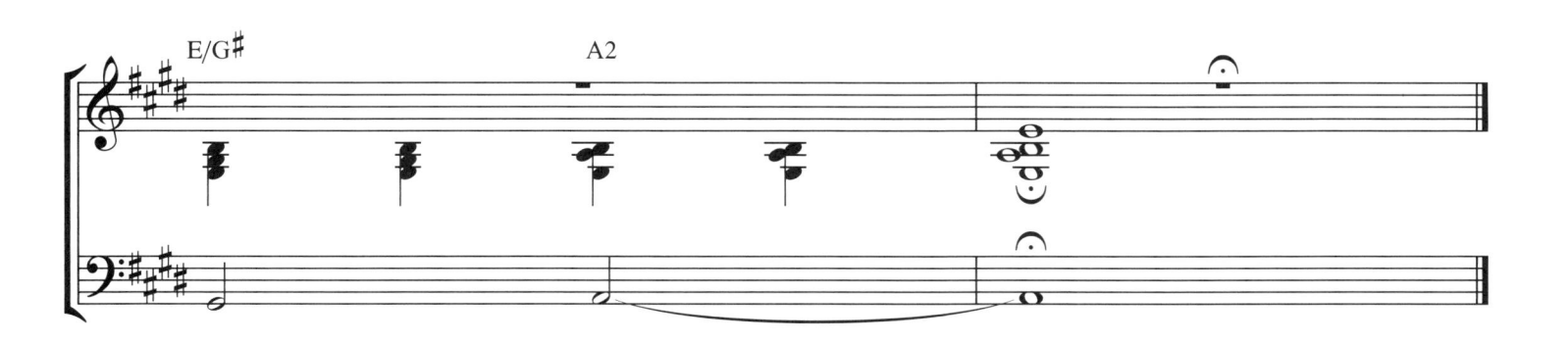

fixed up-on the beau-ty, fixed up-on the beau-ty,

fixed up-on the beau-ty of Your face.

The beau-ty of Your face.

Chords Used in This Song

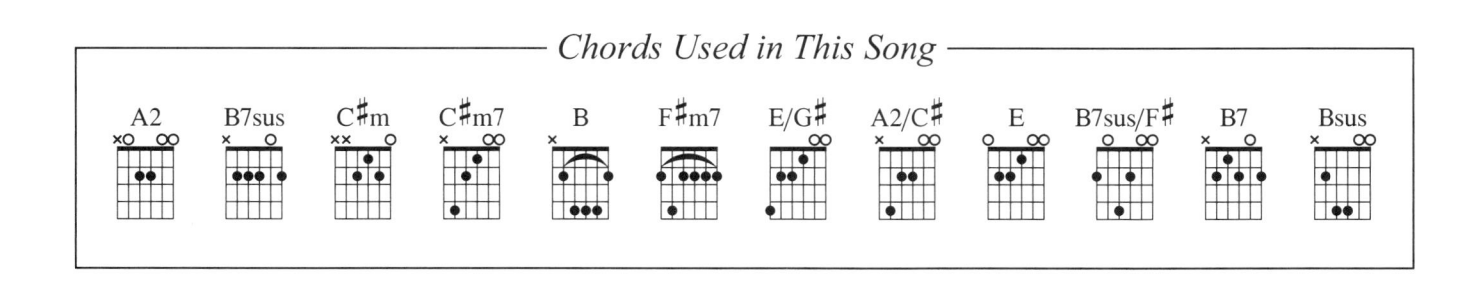

A2   B7sus   C#m   C#m7   B   F#m7   E/G#   A2/C#   E   B7sus/F#   B7   Bsus

Carried To The Table

Words and Music by
LEELAND MOORING,
MARC BYRD and STEVE HINDALONG

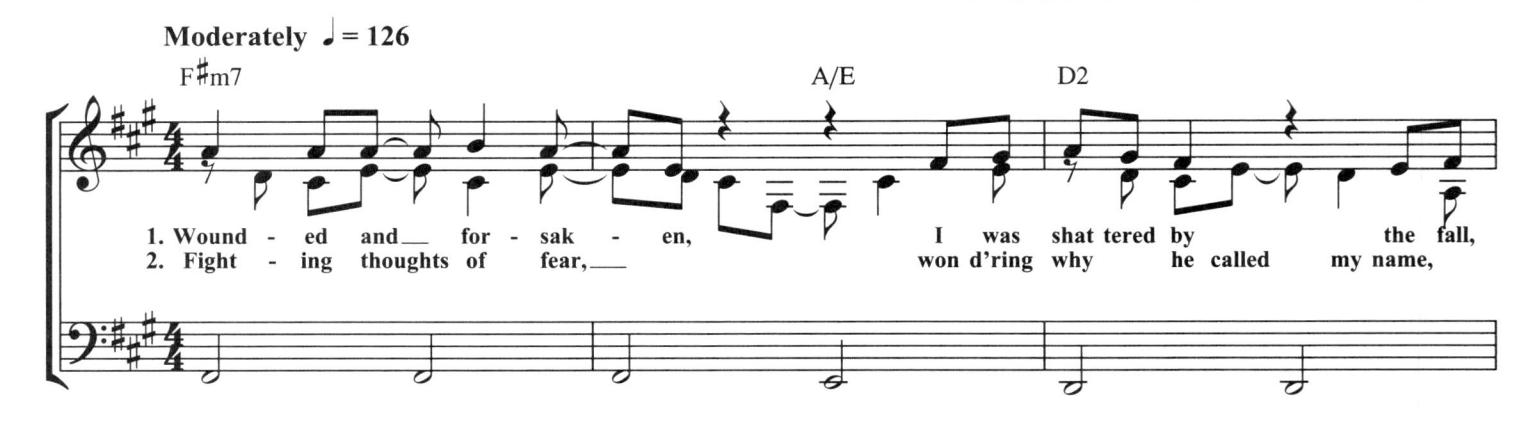

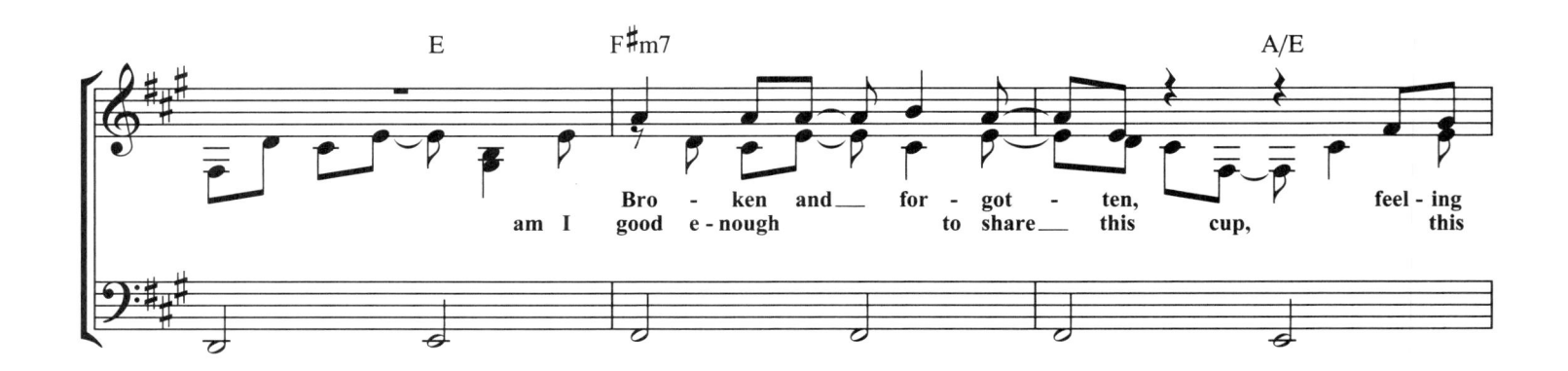

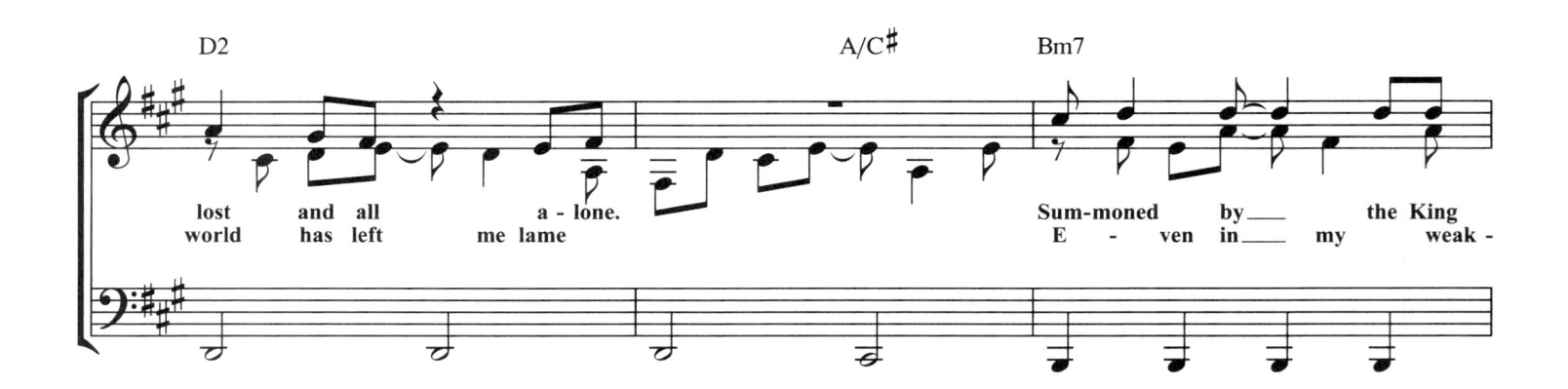

Moderately ♩ = 126

1. Wound-ed and for-sak-en, I was shat-tered by the fall,
Bro-ken and for-got-ten, feel-ing lost and all a-lone. Sum-moned by the King in-to the mas-ter's courts,

2. Fight-ing thoughts of fear, won-d'ring why he called my name, am I good e-nough to share this cup, this world has left me lame E-ven in my weak-ness, the Sav-ior called my name,

Copyright © 2006 Meaux Mercy / Blue Raft Music (BMI) / Meaux Hits / Colorwheel Songs (ASCAP) (adm. by EMI CMG Publishing)
All rights reserved. Used by permission. CCLI Song No. 4681678

39

swept a - way by___ His love.__

And I don't see__ my bro - ken - ness an - y - more, when I'm seat - ed at__ the ta - ble__ of the Lord._ I'm car - ried to the ta - ble,

41

CODA

Lead vocal ad lib.

You car-ried me my God, You car-ried me.

Play 6 times and fade

You car-ried me my God, You car-ried me.

Chords Used in This Song

F#m7 A/E D2 A/C# Bm7 Esus E A D2/F# Asus A/G# D2/A

Closer

Words and Music by CHARLIE HALL,
KENDALL COMBES, DUSTIN RAGLAND
and BRIAN BERGMAN

Slow Rock ♩ = 138

Capo 3 (G)

44

45

46

47

Come in___ close,___ come clo-ser to me.___

Come clo-ser to me,___

clo-ser to me.___

Chords Used in This Song

G G2/F# G/B C2 Em D/F# C Dsus D

Everything
(God In My Living)

Words and Music by
TIM HUGHES

Moderately ♩ = 80

1. God in my liv-ing, there in my breath-ing. God in my wak-ing, God in my sleep-ing,
(2. God in my hop)-ing, there in my dream-ing. God in my watch-ing, God in my wait-ing,

God in my rest-ing, there in my work-ing. God in my think-ing,
God in my laugh-ing, there in my weep-ing. God in my hurt-ing,

God in my speak-ing.
God in my heal-ing.

Be my ev-'ry-thing, Be my ev-'ry-thing,

Be my ev-'ry-thing, Be my ev-'ry-thing.

2. God in my hop-

Copyright © 2005 Thankyou Music (PRS) (adm. worldwide by EMI CMG Publishing excluding the UK and Europe, which is adm. by kingswaysongs.com)
All rights reserved. Used by permission. CCLI Song No. 4685258

2.
C F G
- thing. Christ in me, Christ in me,
Am F G Am
Christ in me the hope of glo - ry, You are ev - 'ry - thing.
F G Am
Christ in me, Christ in me, Christ in me the hope of glo - ry,
F G Am G/B Fmaj7 G
Be my ev - 'ry - thing. Be my ev - 'ry - thing, Be my ev - 'ry -
Am G Fmaj7 G C
- thing. Be my ev - 'ry - thing, Be my ev - 'ry - thing. Be my ev - 'ry -

to CODA 2
Fmaj7 G Am G Fmaj7 G
- thing, Be my ev - 'ry - thing. Be my ev - 'ry - thing, Be my ev - 'ry -
D.S. (verse 2) al CODA 1
C
thing. God in my hop -
CODA 1
G6 Fmaj7 G Am G
- ing. Be my ev - 'ry - thing, Be my ev - 'ry - thing. Be my ev -
D.S.S. al CODA 2
Fmaj7 G C
'ry - thing, Be my ev - 'ry - thing. Be my ev - 'ry -
CODA 2
C F G
thing. Christ in me, Christ in me,

Am F G Am G/B
Christ in me the hope of glo - ry, You are ev - 'ry - thing. You are ev - 'ry -
Fmaj7 G Am G Fmaj7 G
- thing, You are ev - 'ry - thing. You are ev - 'ry - thing, You are ev - 'ry -
C Fmaj7 G Am G
thing. Je - sus ev - 'ry - thing, Je - sus ev - 'ry - thing. Je - sus ev - 'ry -
Fmaj7 G C
- thing, Je - sus ev - 'ry - thing.

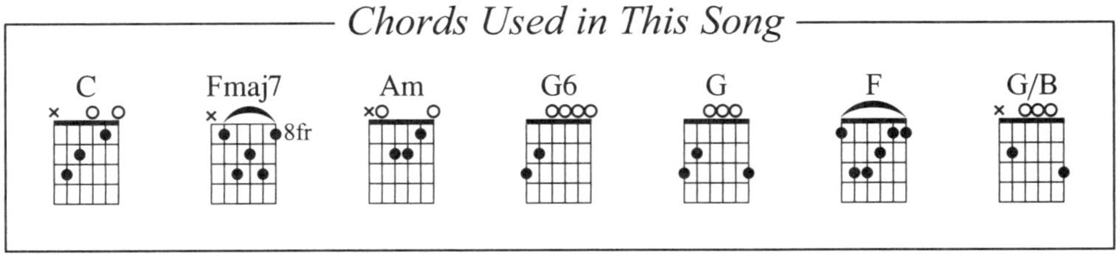
Chords Used in This Song
C
Fmaj7
8fr
Am
G6
G
F
G/B

Forever Holy

Words and Music by
BEN CRIST

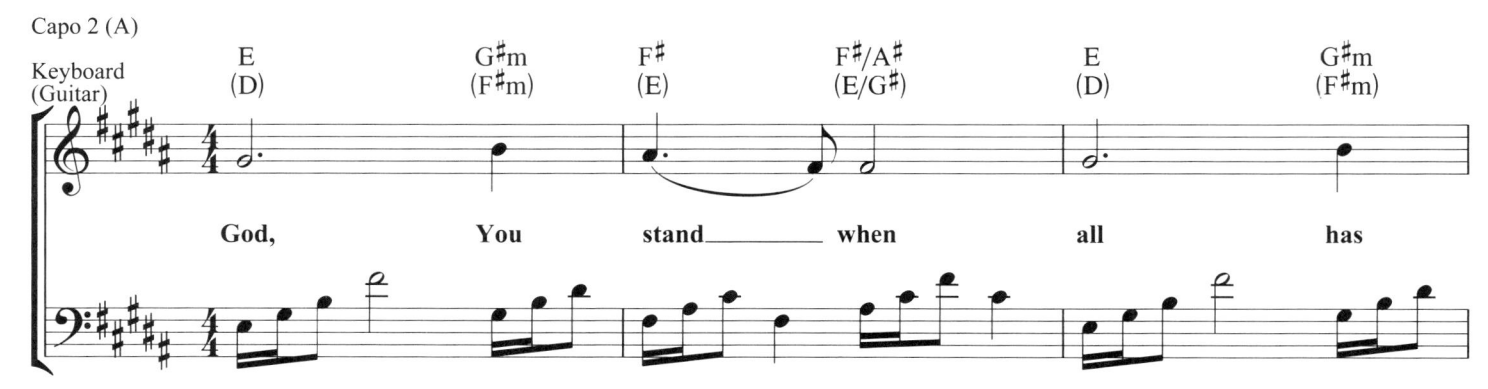

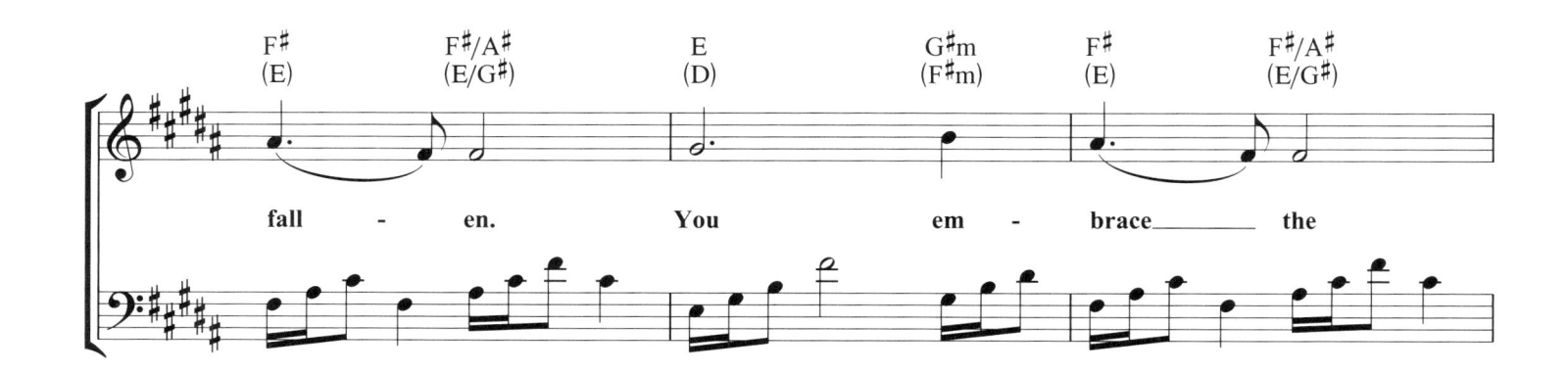

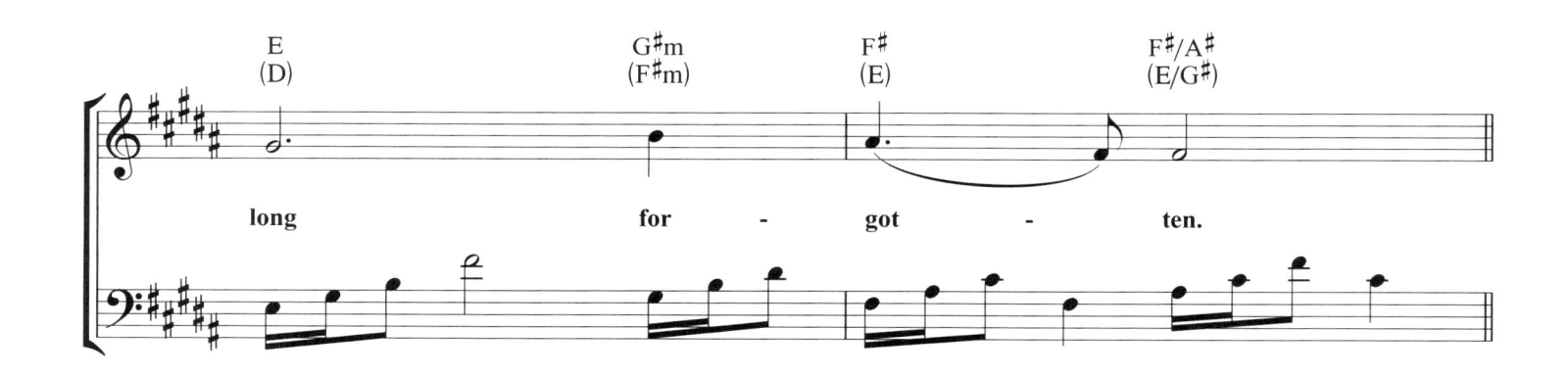

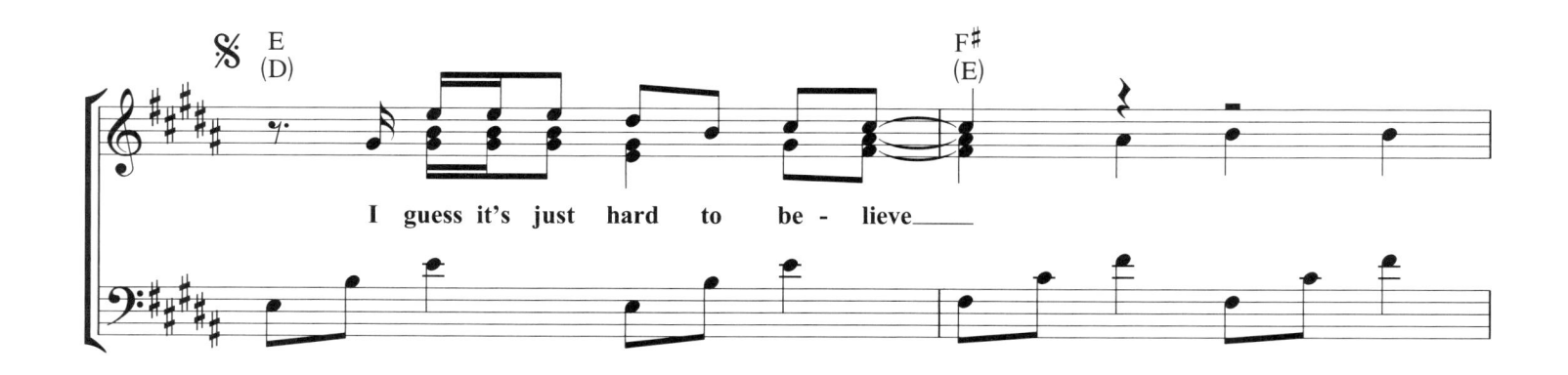

With expression and awe, ♩ = 63

Capo 2 (A)

God, You stand when all has fall-en. You em-brace the long for-got-ten.

I guess it's just hard to be-lieve

Copyright © 2006 Spinning Audio Vortex, Inc. (BMI) (adm. by EMI CMG Publishing)
All right reserved. Used by permission. CCLI Song No. 4943330

the grace You pour out on me.
(love)

I guess I'm just starting to see

how You're working in me.

This is what makes my head spin; You're for-ev-er ho-ly.

God of all cre-a-tion, pour Your life in-to me.

B (A) F♯/A♯ (E/G♯) G♯m (F♯m) F♯ (E)
This is so o - ver - whelm - ing, You're for - ev - er ho - ly.
2nd time to CODA
(E) (D) G♯m (F♯m) (E) (D) F♯ (E)
God of my sal - va - tion, clothe me in Your glo - ry, yeah.
E2 (D2) G♯m (F♯m) F♯sus (Esus) F♯ (E) D♯m7 (C♯m7) E2 (D2) G♯m (F♯m)
God, You
F♯ (E) D♯m7 (C♯m7) E2 (D2) G♯m (F♯m) F♯ (E) D♯m7 (C♯m7)
hold when all is break - ing.
E2 (D2) G♯m (F♯m) F♯ (E) D♯m7 (C♯m7)
You re - store the

55

G♯m (F♯m) F♯ (E) E (D) G♯m (F♯m)
You're for - ev - er ho - ly. God of all cre - a - tion,
E (D) F♯ (E) B (A) F♯/A♯ (E/G♯)
pour Your life in - to me. This is so o - ver - whelm - ing
G♯m (F♯m) F♯ (E) E (D) G♯m (F♯m)
You're for - ev - er ho - ly. God of my sal - va - tion,
E (D) F♯ (E) B (A) F♯/A♯ (E/G♯)
clothe me in Your glo - ry. This is what makes my head spin;
G♯m (F♯m) F♯ (E) E (D) G♯m (F♯m)
You're for - ev - er ho - ly. God of all cre - a - tion,

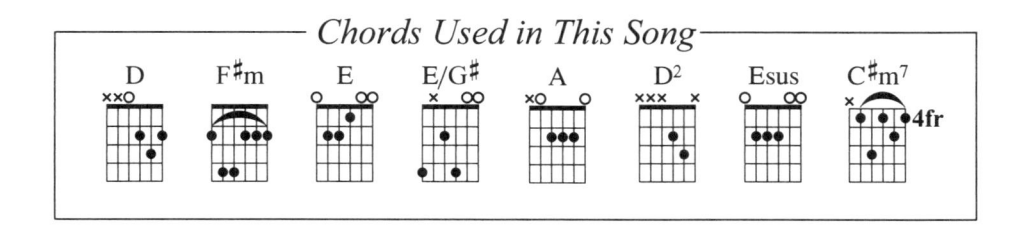

pour Your life in-to me. And this is so o-ver-whelm-ing, You're for-ev-er ho-ly. God of my sal-va-tion, clothe me in Your glo-ry, clothe me in Your glo-ry.

Chords Used in This Song: D, F#m, E, E/G#, A, D², Esus, C#m⁷

Give Me Jesus

Words and Music by
JEREMY CAMP

Moderately, ♩ = 84

1. In the morn-ing, when I rise, in the morn-ing, when I rise, in the morn-ing, when I rise, give me Je-sus. Give me Je-sus, give me Je-sus, you can have

Copyright © 2006 Thirsty Moon River Publishing / Stolen Pride Music (ASCAP) (adm. by EMI CMG Publishing)
All rights reserved. Used by permission. CCLI Song No. 4874344

Am7
F2
all this world, just give me Je -
C
to CODA 1
sus.
2. When I am a - lone,
3. When I come to die,
Am7
F2
C
Am7
when I am a - lone, oh, when I am a - lone,
when I come to die, oh, when I come to die,
1st time, D.S. al CODA 1
2nd time, to CODA 2
F2
C
give me Je - sus. Give me
give me Je - sus. Give me

CODA 1
Am7
F2
Je - sus,
C
Am7
give me Je - sus.
F2
C
D.S.S. al CODA 2
CODA 2
Em7
Je - sus,
Am7
F2
C
give me Je - sus, you can have
Am7
1.
F2
all this world, just give me Je -

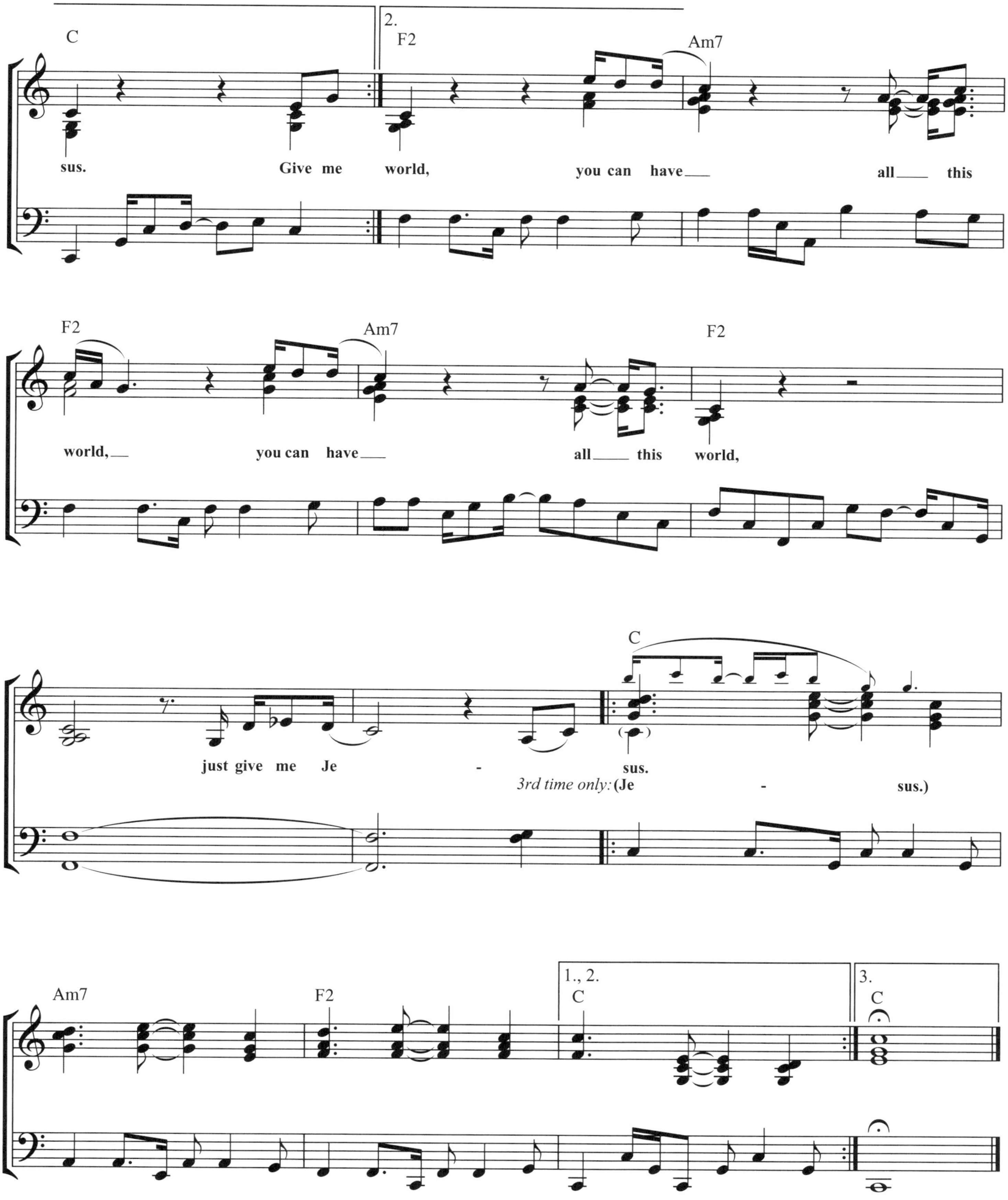

Chords Used in This Song

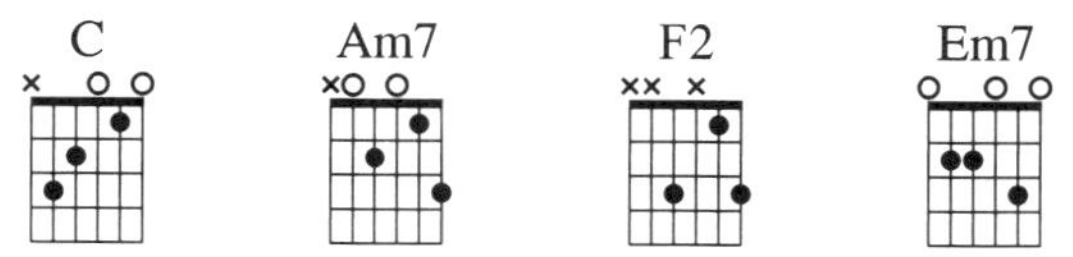

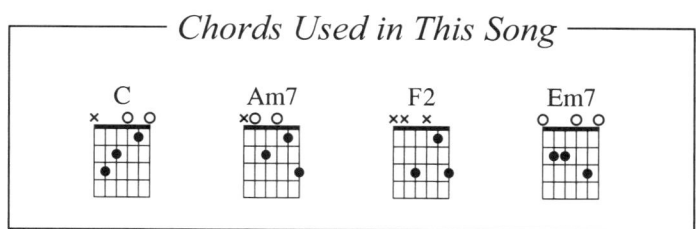

Created to Worship

Words and Music by
VICKY BEECHING

♩ = 116

1. You formed us from the dust, You breathed Your breath in us. We are the work of Your hands.
2. If we don't worship You, we'll search for substitutes to fill the void in our souls.

Now we breathe back to You love songs of gratitude,
Worshiping other things destroys our liberty.

Copyright © 2004 Thankyou Music (PRS) (adm. worldwide by EMI CMG Publishing
excluding the UK and Europe which is adm. by kingswaysongs.com)
All rights reserved. Used by permission. CCLI Song No. 3994713

A2 B C#m7 F#m7(4)
a - dor - ing You with all we have.
But as we praise You, we are free.
A2 C#m7 B E 3
'Cause we were cre - at - ed to wor - ship Your
A2 C#m7 B E A2 C#m7
name, and we were cre - at - ed
B E 3 1. A2 C#m7 B
to bring You our praise.
2. A2 C#m7 B A2 C#m7
praise. So we will wor - ship,

and so we will praise. You are Cre-at-or for all our days. For

65

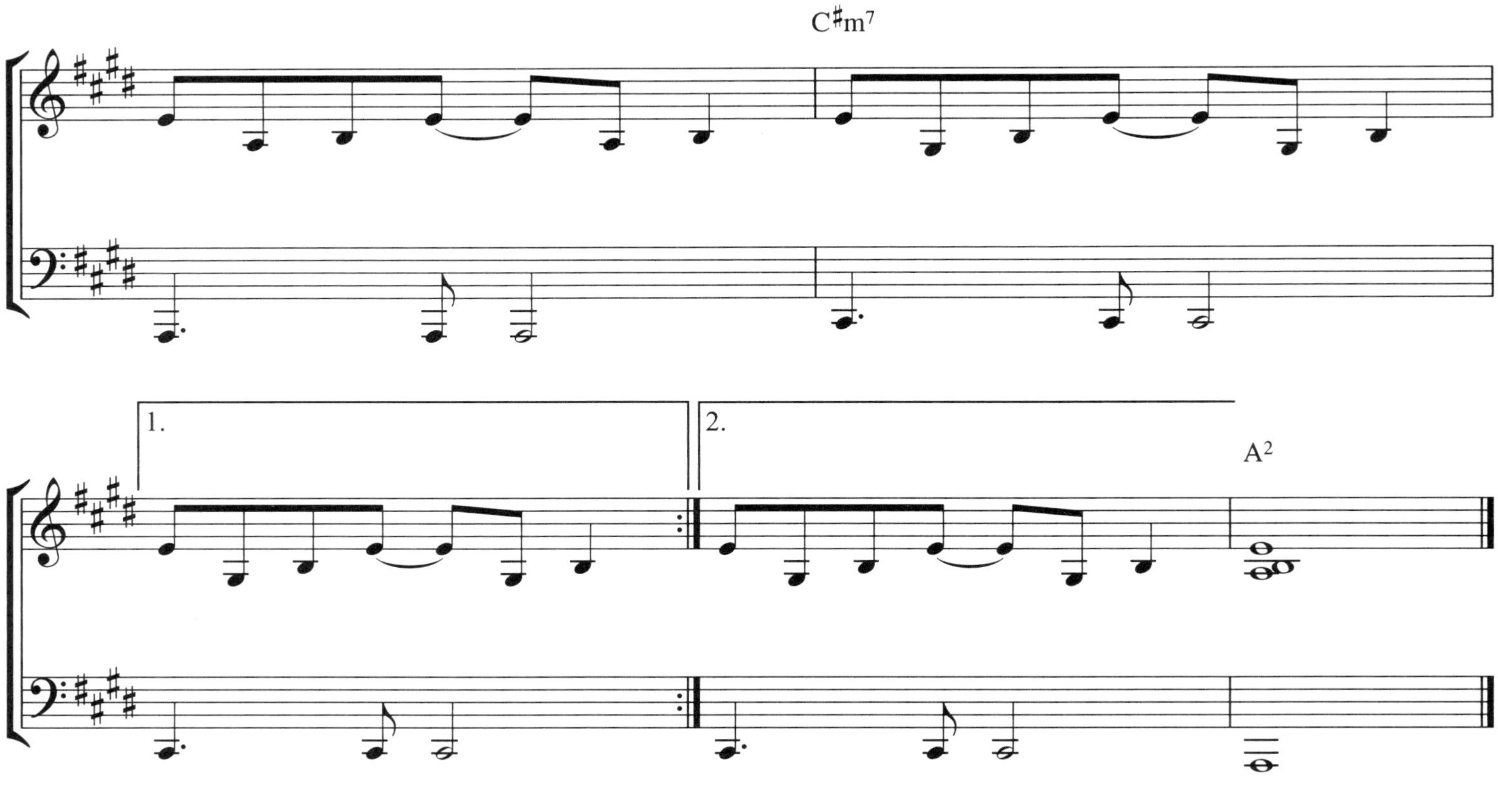

Chords Used in This Song

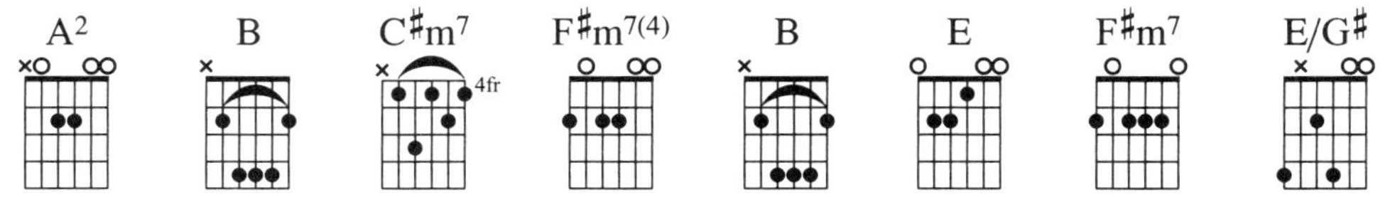

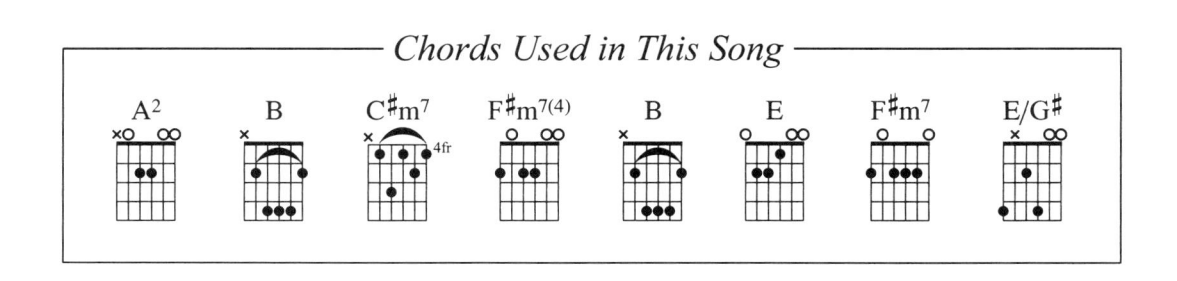

Give You Glory

**Words and Music by
JEREMY CAMP**

Moderately fast, ♩ = 132

1. We have raised a thousand voices, just to lift Your holy name, and we will raise thousands more, to sing of Your beauty in this place, oh. None can even fathom, no, not one define Your worth, as we

2. (As we) fall down before You, with our willing hearts we seek, in the greatness of Your glory, it's so hard to even speak. There is nothing we can offer, no, nothing You can repay. so we

Copyright © 2006 Thirsty Moon River Publishing / Stolen Pride Music (ASCAP) (adm. by EMI CMG Publishing)
All rights reserved. Used by permission. CCLI Song No. 4874337

G
A
mar - vel in Your pres - ence to the ends of the
give You all our prais - es, and lift our voic - es to
D
earth. We give You glo - ry, lift - ing up our hands and sing - ing
sing. Glo - ry, lift - ing up our voice and sing - ing
Bm
G
Ho - ly, You a - lone are wor - thy,
Ho - ly, You a - lone are wor - thy,
Gm
to CODA
1.
we just want to touch Your heart Lord, touch Your heart.
we just want to touch Your heart Lord, touch
2.
D.S. al CODA
(take repeats)
Your heart. 2. As we
CODA
Your heart.

Bm G A Bm G
Our hope is drenched in You, our faith has been
A Bm G A
re - newed. We trust in Your ev - 'ry word,
F G
noth - ing else can e - ven meas - ure up to You.
A D
We give You glo - ry,
Bm
lift - ing up our hands and sing - ing Ho - ly, You a - lone are

G
Gm
wor - thy, we just want to touch Your heart Lord, touch
D
Your heart. Glo - ry, lift - ing up our voice and sing - ing
Bm
G
Ho - ly, You a - lone are wor - thy,
Gm
we just want to touch Your heart Lord, touch Your heart.
D
Bm
Glo - ry, sing - ing Ho - ly, We're sing - ing
2nd time, voc. ad. lib.

Chords Used in This Song

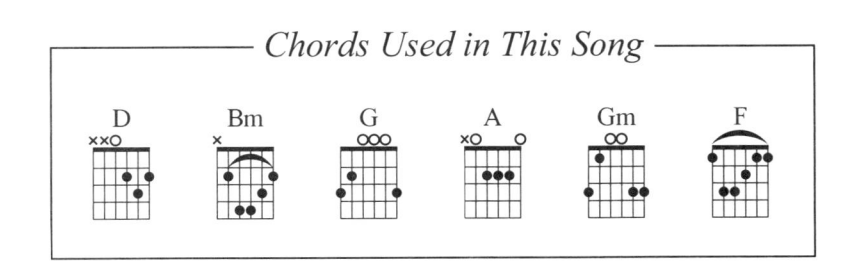

God Of Justice

Words and Music by
TIM HUGHES

Slow Rock, ♩ = 78

1. God of justice, savior to all. came to rescue the weak and the poor. Chose to serve and not be served.

Jesus, You have shown us what you
called us, require,

freely we've received, now freely we will give.
freely we've received, now freely we will give.

We must

Copyright © 2005 Thankyou Music (PRS) (adm. worldwide by EMI CMG Publishing excluding the UK and Europe which is adm. by kingswaysongs.com).
All rights reserved. Used by permission. CCLI Song No. 4447128

E
B/D♯
C♯m7
go, live to feed the hun - gry, stand be - side the bro - ken, we must go.
A2
E
B/D♯
Step - ping for - ward, keep us from just sing - ing, move us in - to
C♯m7
A2
to CODA
ac - tion, we must go.
2. To act just -
B
E
A2
B
E/G♯
- ly, ev - e - ry day.
Lov - ing mer - cy in ev - e - ry way.
A2
B
E/G♯
A2
walk - ing hum - bly, be - fore You, God.

D.S. al CODA
CODA
B E/G♯
3
You have
Bsus A2 Bsus E/G♯
Fill us up send us out, fill us up send us out,
A2
1., 2., 3.
Bsus E/G♯
4.
Bsus E/G♯
fill us up send us out Lord.
A2 B7sus E/G♯ A2
Fill us up send us out, fill us up, and send us out, fill us up send us out Lord.
B7sus E/G♯ F♯m7 C♯m
Yeah.
E B F♯m7 C♯m7

A change is made, lov-ing mer - cy. We must go, we must go. to the bro - ken and the hurt - ing we must go, we must go. We must go, live to feed the hun - gry, stand be-side the bro - ken, we must go. yeah. keep us from just sing - ing, move us in-to ac - tion, we must go. Hey yeah, (Hum

76

Great God Of Wonders

**Words and Music by
ANDY BROMLEY**

Upbeat, ♩ = 104

Great God_ of won - der, Great God_ in pow - er,_ the
Great God_ of Zi - on, Great God_ in beau - ty,_ the

heav'ns are_ de - clar - ing glo - ries_ of_ Your_ name,_
na - tions_ are gath - 'ring to wor - ship_ at_ Your_ feet,_

glo - ries of_ Your name._
to wor - ship at_ Your feet._

From the ris - ing to the set - ting_ sun,_ Your name_

Copyright © 2004 Thankyou Music (PRS) (adm. worldwide by EMI CMG Publishing
excluding the UK and Europe, which is adm. by kingswaysongs.com)
All rights reserved. Used by permission. CCLI Song No. 4443115

A
will be praised.
F♯m7
God a - bove all gods,
E/G♯
King a - bove all kings,
A
Lord of heav - en and earth.
B
We give to You
E
praise,
A
praise,
B
praise.
C♯m
Give You

praise, praise,

praise.

You are the great God a-

bove all gods, You are the great King a-

80

D.S. al CODA
(take 1st ending)
B
praise.
We give You
CODA
E
A
B
A/C♯
Free, slowly
B
On - ly Lord,
wor - thy all our praise Lord Je - sus.
Hal - le - lu - jah, Lord,
A
Hal - le - lu.
E

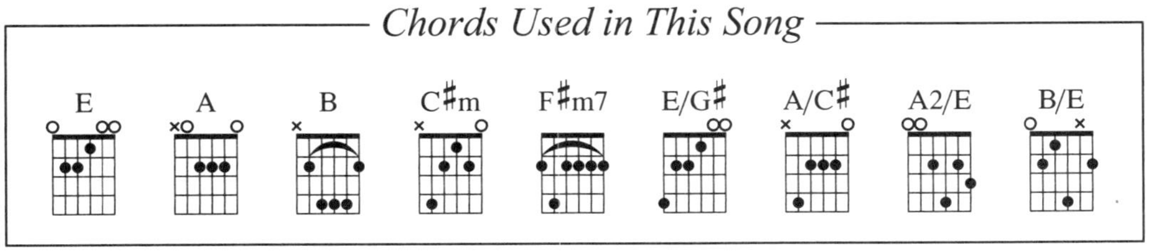
Chords Used in This Song
E
A
B
C♯m
F♯m7
E/G♯
A/C♯
A2/E
B/E

Here and Now

Words and Music by
MATT MAHER

Moderate Rock ♩ = 114

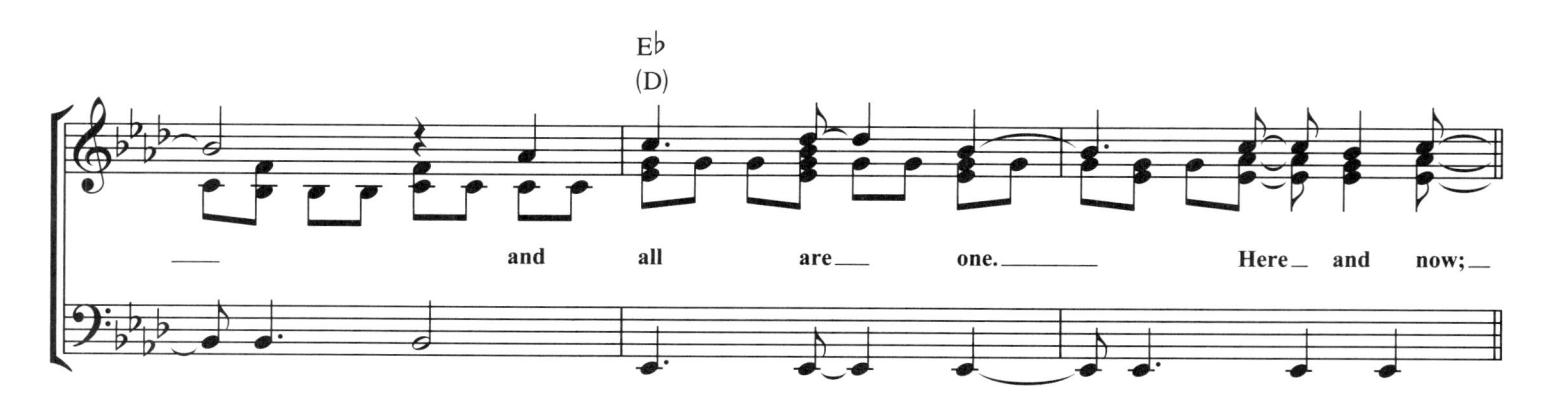

Capo 1 (G)

No more wait-ing, Your love's ex-hal-ing.
hap-pen-ing, the world is end-ing, dead and a-live, You are here and we are re-turn-ing. gin-ning,

We're com-ing home, and all are one. Here and now;

Copyright © 2005 Thankyou Music (PRS) (adm. worldwide by EMI CMG Publishing excluding the UK and Europe which is adm. by kingswaysongs.com) / spiritandsong.com Publishing (BMI) (adm. by EMI CMG Publishing) All rights reserved. Used by permission. CCLI # 4666930.

the proud made low-ly. Here and now; the Lamb made might-y. Here and now; the slave to free-dom. Here and now; the com-ing king-dom. Here and now.

The cross is

-dom. Here and now. -dom. Here and now.

Tears of gladness, in the sadness, we're falling and victorious. Bless'd and broken, the floodgates open, the sun is rising to shine.

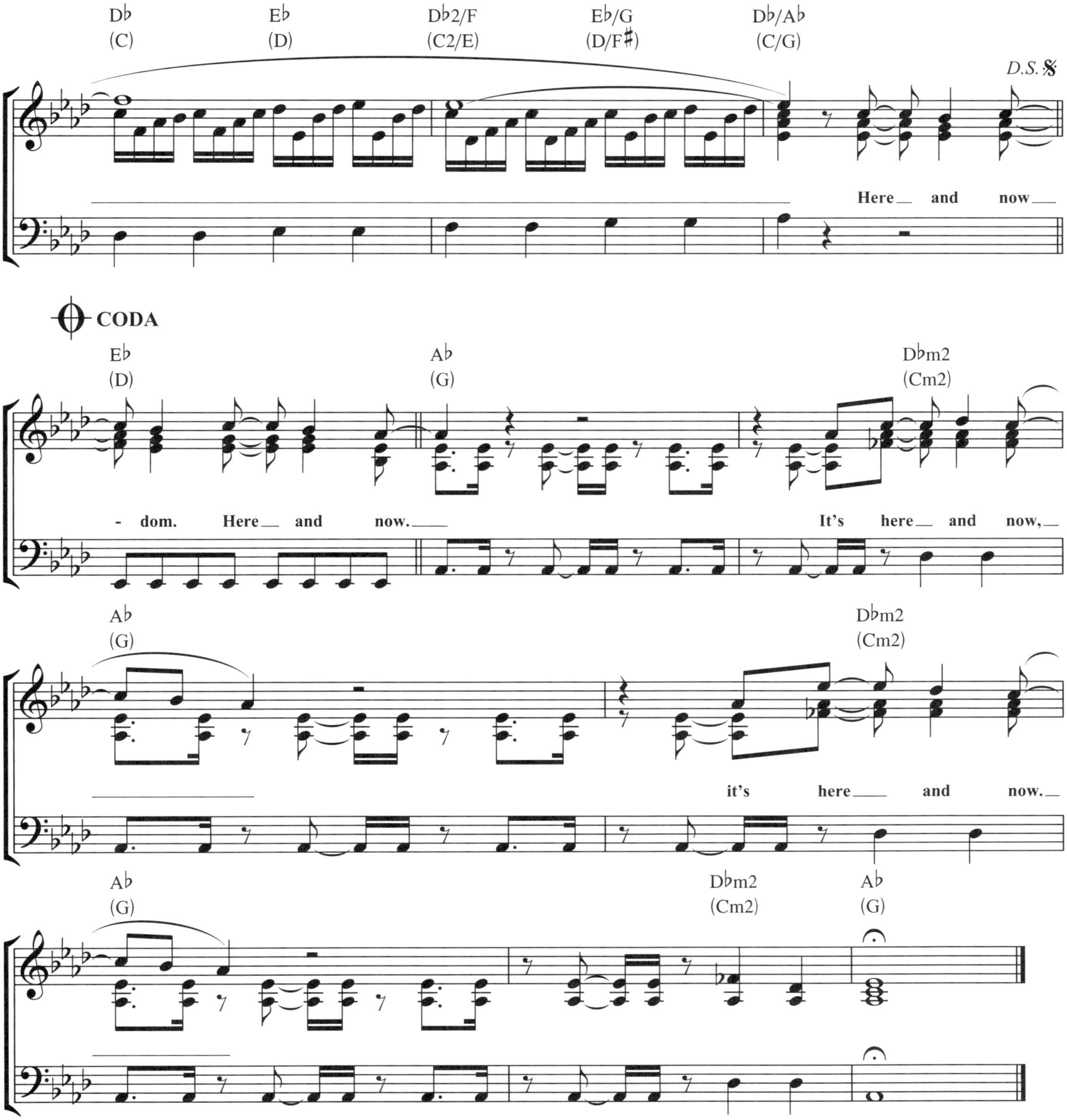

Chords Used in This Song

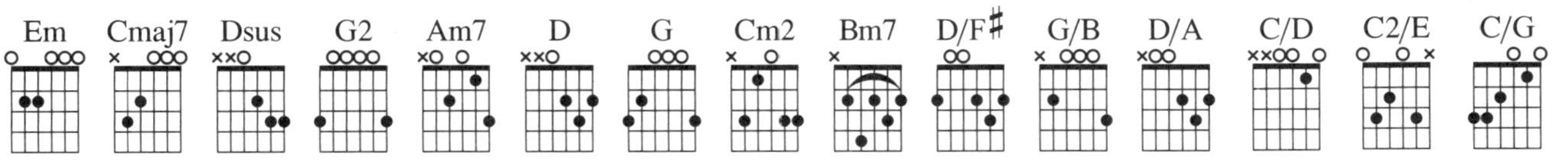

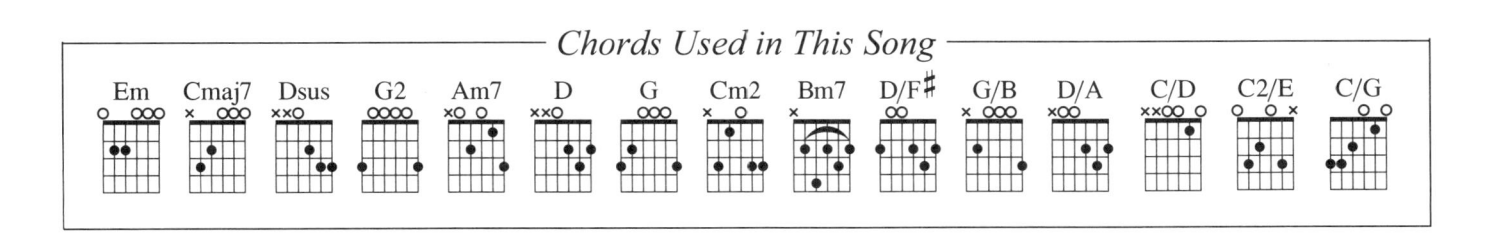

The Highest And The Greatest

Words and Music by
NICK HERBERT and
TIM HUGHES

Moderately, ♩. = 60

Capo 3 (G)

1. Wake ev-'ry heart and ev-'ry tongue, to sing the new e-ter-nal song, and crown Him King of Glo-ry now, con-fess Him Lord of all.
2. A day will come when all will sing, and glo-ri-fy our match-less King, Your name un-ri-valed stands a-lone, You are the Lord of all.

You are the high-

Copyright © 2007 Thankyou Music (PRS) (adm. worldwide by EMI CMG Publishing excluding the UK and Europe which is adm. by kingswaysongs.com)
All rights reserved. Used by permission. CCLI Song No. 4769758

2nd time, lead voc. ad. lib.
B♭ (G) F (D) Cm7 (Am7) B♭ (G)
- est, You are the great - est, You are the Lord of
F (D) B♭ (G) F (D)
all. An - gels will wor - ship, na - tions will bow down, to the
to CODA
1. 2.
Cm7 (Am7) B♭ (G) E♭ (C) E♭ (C)
Lord of all. A all,
Cm7 (Am7) B♭/D (G/B)
oh. Let ev - 'ry heart, let ev - 'ry tongue,
E♭ (C) Cm7 (Am7)
sing of Your name, sing of Your name. Let ev - 'ry heart,

88

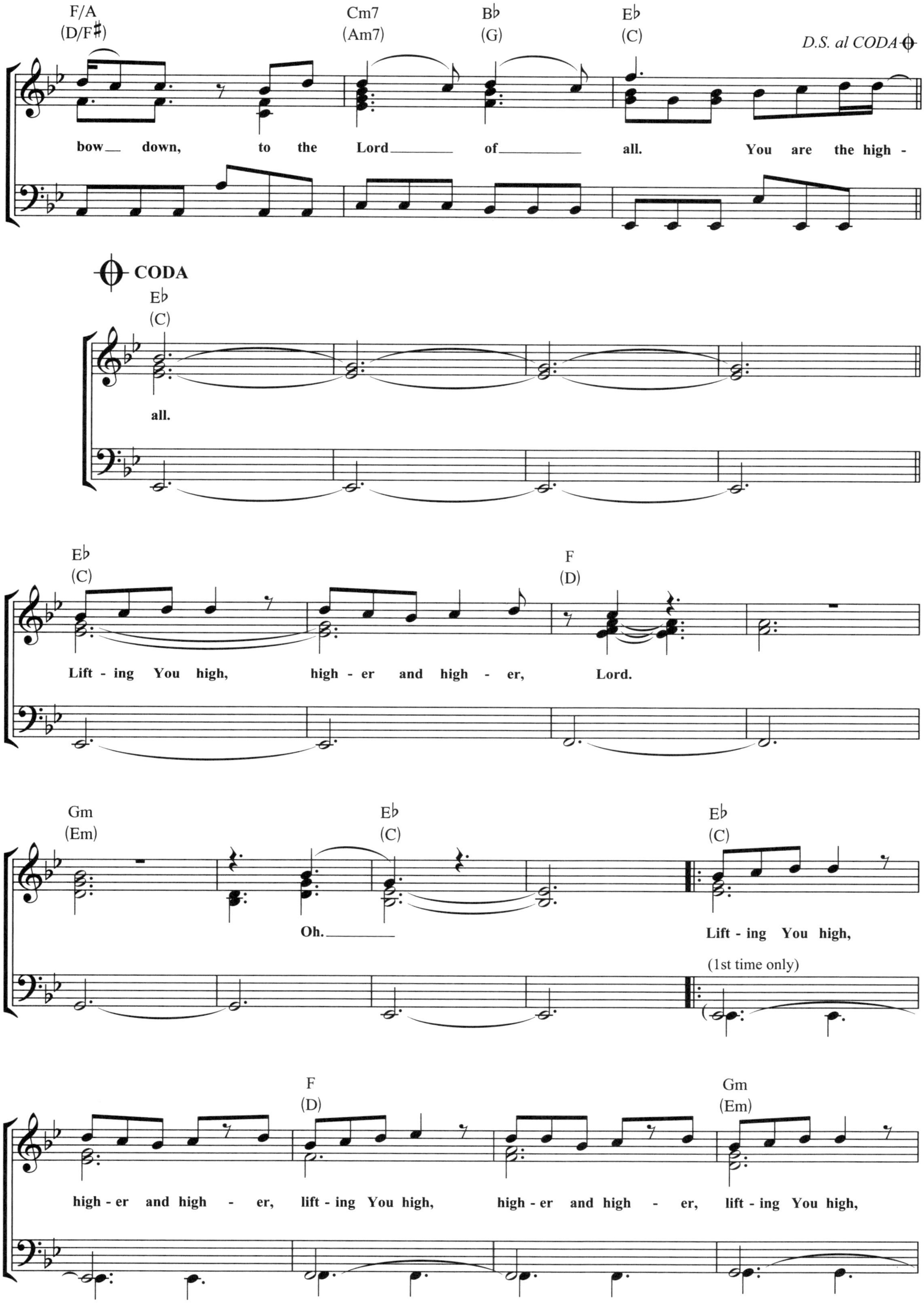
F/A (D/F♯)
Cm7 (Am7)
B♭ (G)
E♭ (C)
D.S. al CODA
bow down, to the Lord of all. You are the high -
CODA
E♭ (C)
all.
E♭ (C)
F (D)
Lift - ing You high, high - er and high - er, Lord.
Gm (Em)
E♭ (C)
E♭ (C)
Oh.
Lift - ing You high,
(1st time only)
F (D)
Gm (Em)
high - er and high - er, lift - ing You high, high - er and high - er, lift - ing You high,

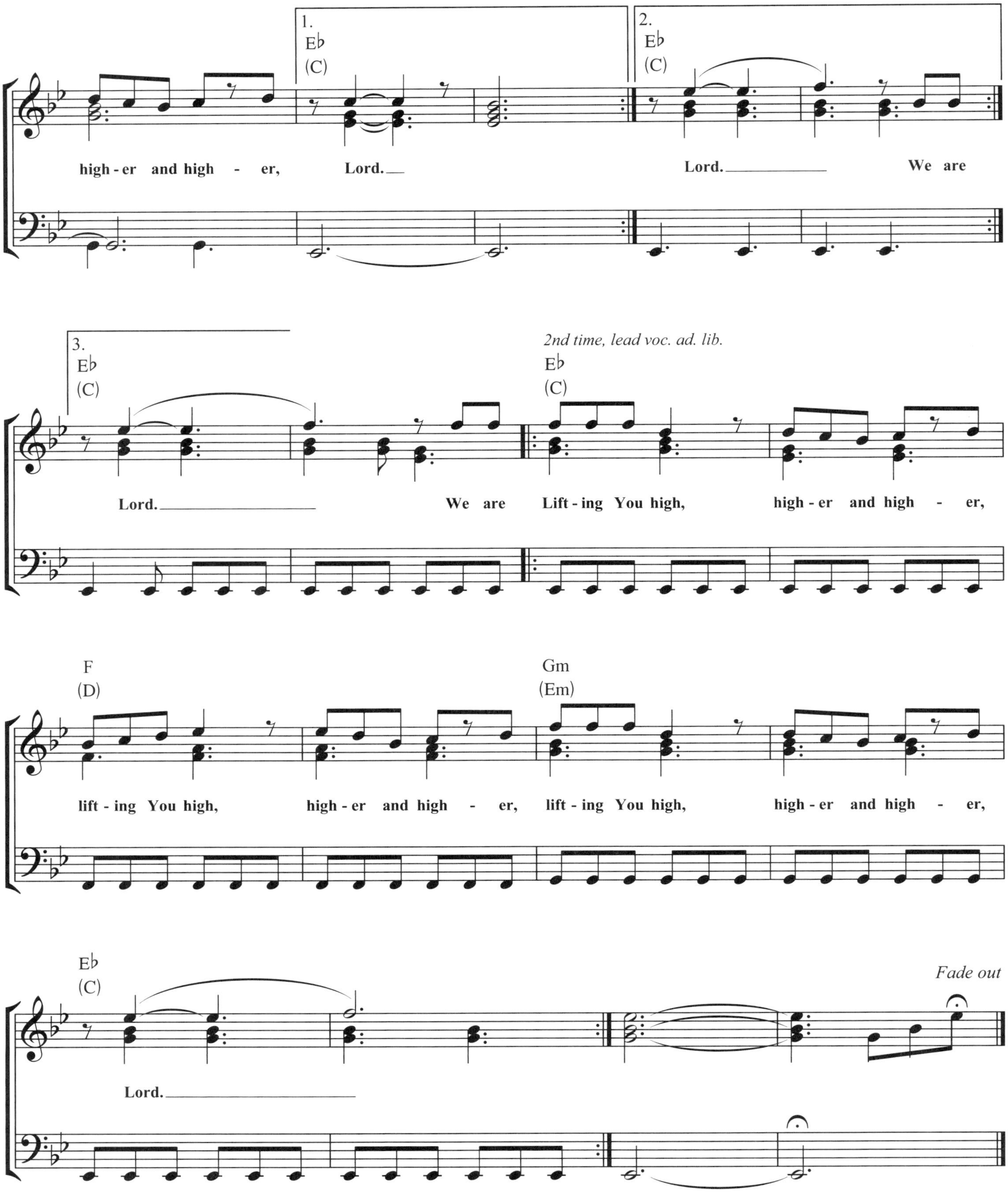

Chords Used in This Song

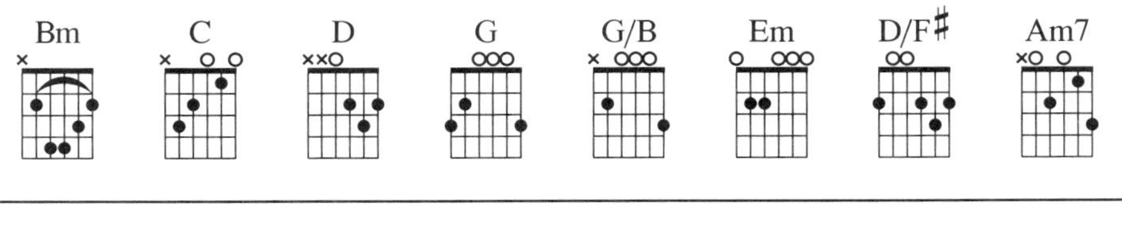

How Can I Keep From Singing

**Words and Music by
CHRIS TOMLIN, MATT REDMAN
and ED CASH**

Moderately ♩. = 74

1. There is an end-less song, ech-oes in my soul, I hear the mu-sic ring. And though the storms may come, I am hold-ing on, to the rock I cling.

2. (I will) lift my eyes in the dark-est night, for I know my Sav-ior lives. And I will walk with You know-ing You see me through, and sing the songs You give.

Copyright © 2006 worshiptogether.com Songs / sixsteps Music (ASCAP) (adm. by EMI CMG Publishing) / Alletrop Music (BMI)/
Thankyou Music (PRS) (adm. worldwide by EMI CMG Publishing, excluding the UK and Europe, which is adm. by kingswaysongs.com)
All rights reserved. Used by permission. CCLI Song No. 4822372

A
E
How can I keep from sing - ing Your praise? How can I
D A/C♯ D E
ev - er say e - nough, how a - maz - ing is Your love?
A E
How can I keep from shout - ing Your name? I know I am
To CODA
D A/C♯ D E
loved by the King, and it makes my heart want to
1.
A
sing. I will

93

2.

| A | Bm7 | A/C# |

sing. I can sing in the trou-bled times,

| D | E | Bm7 | A/C# |

sing when I win. I can sing when I lose my step and I

| D | E | Bm7 | A/C# |

fall down a-gain. I can sing 'cause You pick me up,

| D | E | Bm7 | A/C# |

sing 'cause You're there. I can sing 'cause You hear me Lord, when I

| D | E | Bm7 | A/C# |

call to You in pray-er. I can sing with my last breath,

D E Bm7 A/C♯
sing for I know that I'll sing with the an - gels, and the
D E
saints a - round the throne.
A
D.S. al CODA
How can I keep from sing - ing Your
CODA
D E
makes my heart, I am
D A/C♯ D E
loved by the King, and it makes my heart, I am
D A/C♯ D E
loved by the King, and it makes my heart want to

sing. Yeah, I can sing.

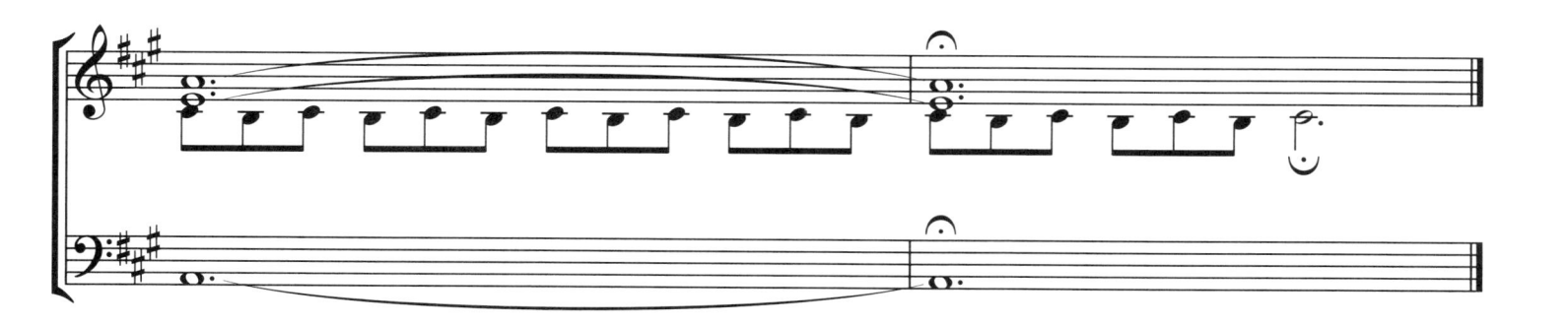

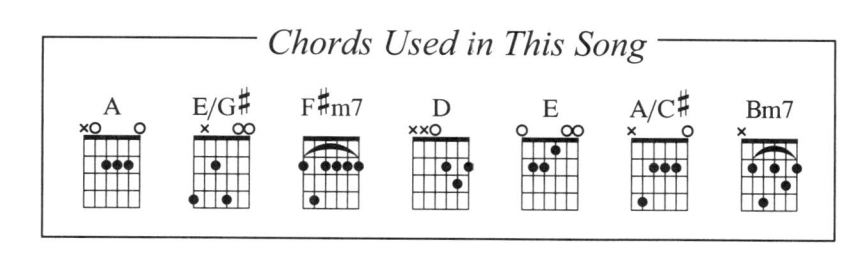

Chords Used in This Song

A E/G# F#m7 D E A/C# Bm7

I Stand For You

Words and Music by
JOHN ELLIS

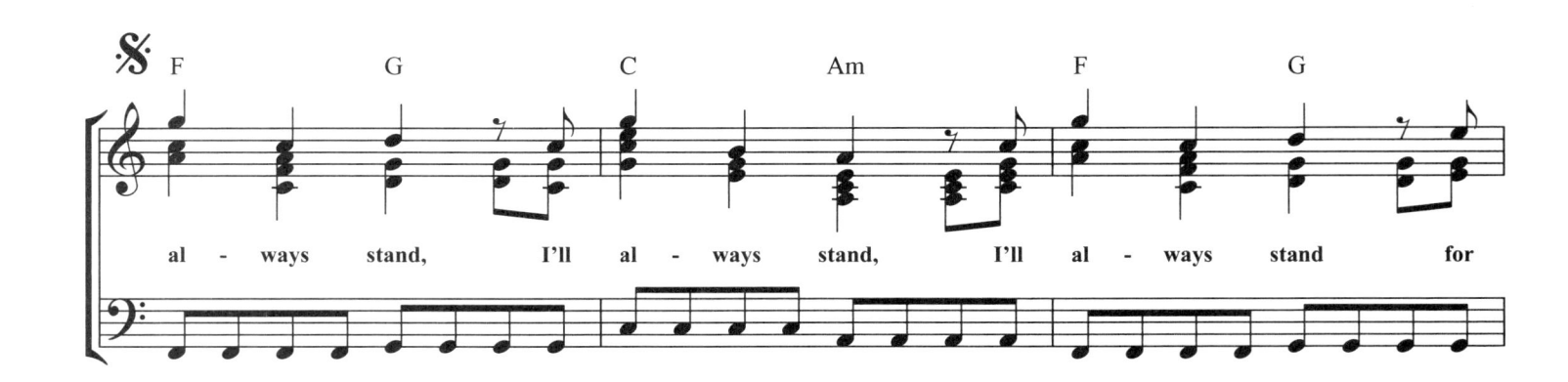

Moderate Rock ♩ = 88

1. Je-sus, I stand for You, no mat-ter what
2. I've stood my ground, when un-be-lief

you lead me through. They will chase me out and
was all a-round. I have felt the sting re-

close me down, but Je-sus, I'll stand for You.
jec-tion brings, but Je-sus, I'll still stand for You. I'll

al-ways stand, I'll al-ways stand, I'll al-ways stand for

Copyright ©2004 Birdwing Music / Near Bliss Music / Mouthfulofsongs (ASCAP) (adm. by EMI CMG Publishing)
All rights reserved. Used by permission. CCLI Song No. 4255224

C F G C D
You. In all this world, You're all that's true, I'll
Last time to CODA
1.
F G C F
al - ways stand for You. For You, yeah.
2.
Am G F C
Je - sus, for You. A time will
F Dm7 G C/E
come when ev - 'ry - one will turn their
F Dm7 G C
eyes on the ris - en Son. But un -

til that day, this world will turn a-way, and so I'll take Your hand, I'll al-ways stand for You. For You, yeah. I will al-ways, I will al-ways, al-ways.

99

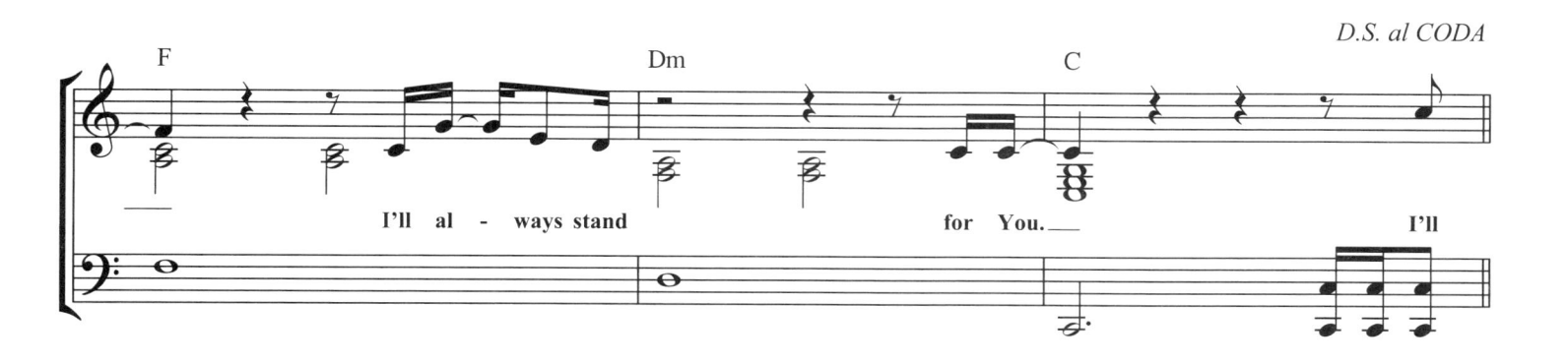

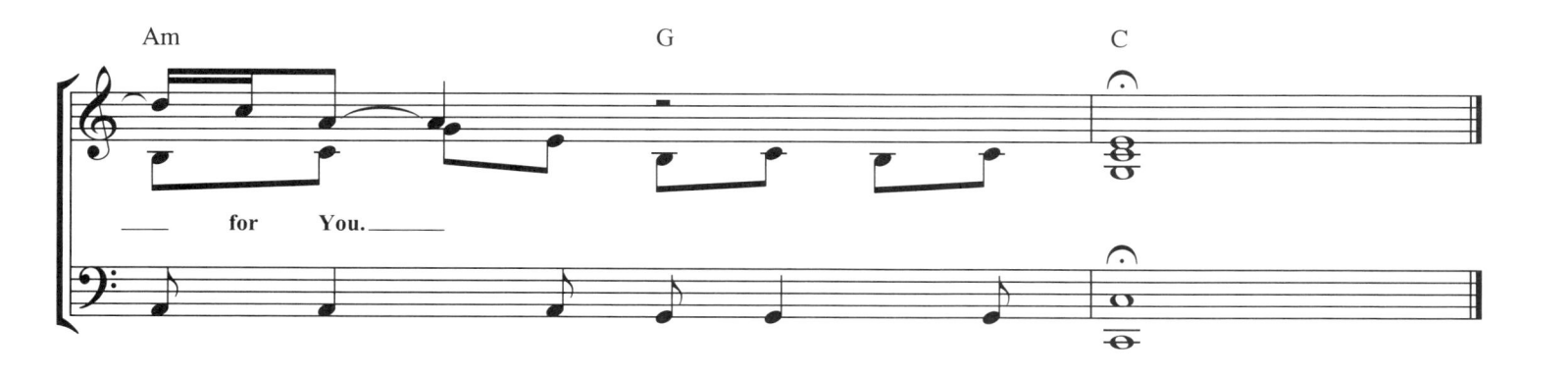

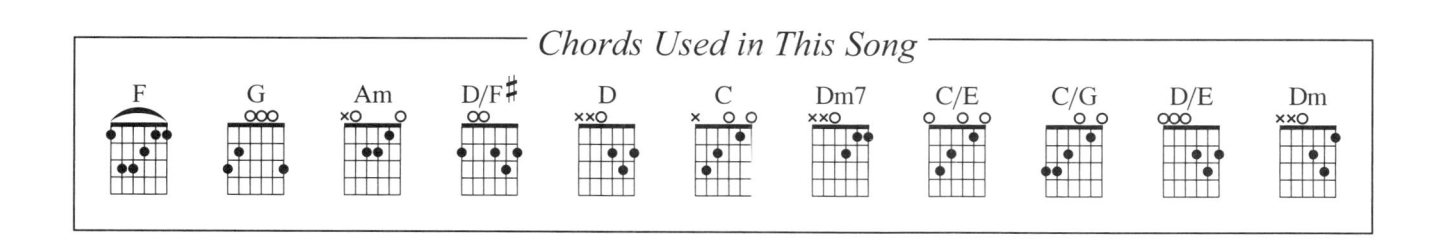

I Will Remember You

Words and Music by
BRENTON BROWN

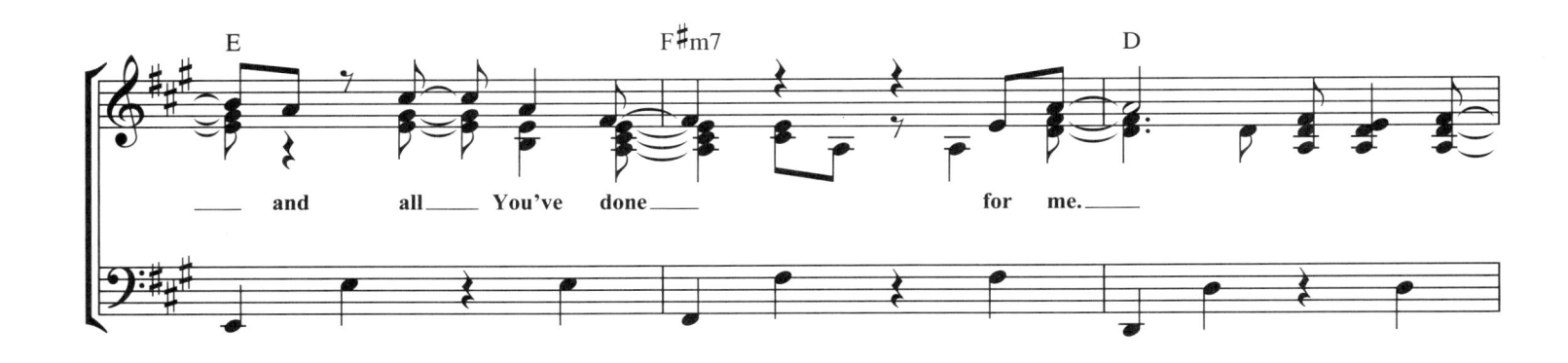

Upbeat rock, ♩ = 144

I will re-mem-ber You, always re-mem-ber You, I will re-mem-ber You and all You've done for me.

1. I will not forget
2. I will not forget

Copyright ©2006 Thankyou Music (PRS) (adm. worldwide by EMI CMG Publishing excluding the UK and Europe, which is adm. by kingswaysongs.com)
All rights reserved. Used by permission. CCLI Song No. 4707387

F♯m7 D A
all Your ben - e - fits, e - ven when
all Your ben - e - fits, how You've cho -
E F♯m7 D
the storm sur - rounds my soul.
- sen and a - dopt - ed me.
A E F♯m7
How You com - fort me, heal all my
Or - phaned by my sin, Your grace has let
D A E
dis - eas - es, how You lift me up on ea -
me in, and nev - er once have You a - ban -
F♯m7 D A
- gle's wings.
- doned me.
I will re - mem - ber You,

E F♯m7 D
always re - mem - ber You, I will re - mem -
A E F♯m7
- ber You and all You've done for me.
1. D 2. D
1st time, D.S. (take repeats)
2nd time, go on
last time, to CODA
A/C♯
I will re - mem - I have tast -
D E F♯m7
- ed and I've seen how You fa - ther faith - ful - ly,
A/C♯ D E
how You shep - herd those who fear You name.

F♯m7
A/C♯
D
When the shad - ow's start to fall
E
F♯m7
A/C♯
and my heart be - gins to fail, I will lift
D
E
F♯m7
my eyes to You a - gain. And I will re - mem -
A
ber You, I will re - mem - ber You, I will re - mem -
ber You and all You've done for me. I will re - mem -

A/C♯
F♯m7
- ber You, always re - mem - ber You,
D
A
A/C♯
I will re - mem - ber You and all You've done
F♯m7
D
D.S.S. al CODA
(take repeats)
for me. I will re-mem -
CODA
A
Yeah.
E
F♯m7
D
A
E
F♯m7
D
A
All You've done for me, yeah.

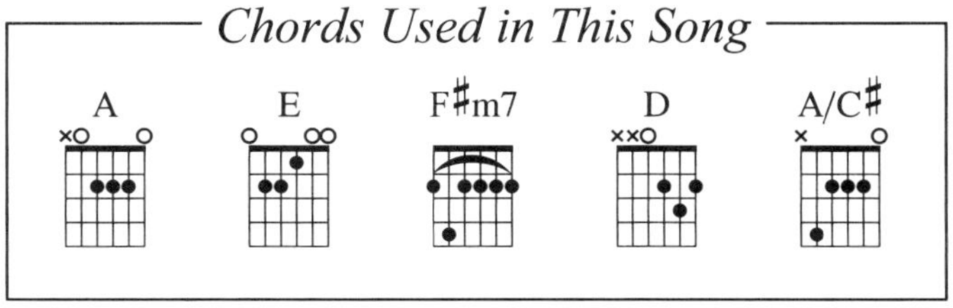
Chords Used in This Song
A
E
F♯m7
D
A/C♯

Join The Song

Words and Music by
VICKY BEECHING and
ED CASH

Moderately ♩ = 104

1. One day ev - 'ry voice will sing, ev - 'ry beg - gar, prince, and king, ev - 'ry nation, tongue and tribe, ev - 'ry o - cean in be - tween will cry, will cry.
2. Gath - ered 'round the throne a - bove, we'll be swept up in the mel - o - dy, hearts will o - ver - flow with love, we'll be sing - ing out a sym - pho - ny, we'll sing.

Copyright © 2006 Thankyou Music (PRS) (adm. worldwide by EMI CMG Publishing
excluding the UK and Europe which is adm. by kingswaysongs.com)/Alletrop Music (BMI)
All rights reserved. Used by permission. CCLI Song No. 4879961

106

Dm7
C7
F
Gm7
Dm7
C7
2.
B♭2
Come join the song
Gm7
F/A
B♭2
that fills e - ter - ni - ty,
sung through - out all his -
C7
Gm7
F/A
- to - ry, as an - gels shout and kings lay down their crowns,
B♭2
B♭dim
F/A
we bow down.
Praise God from whom all bless - ings flow,

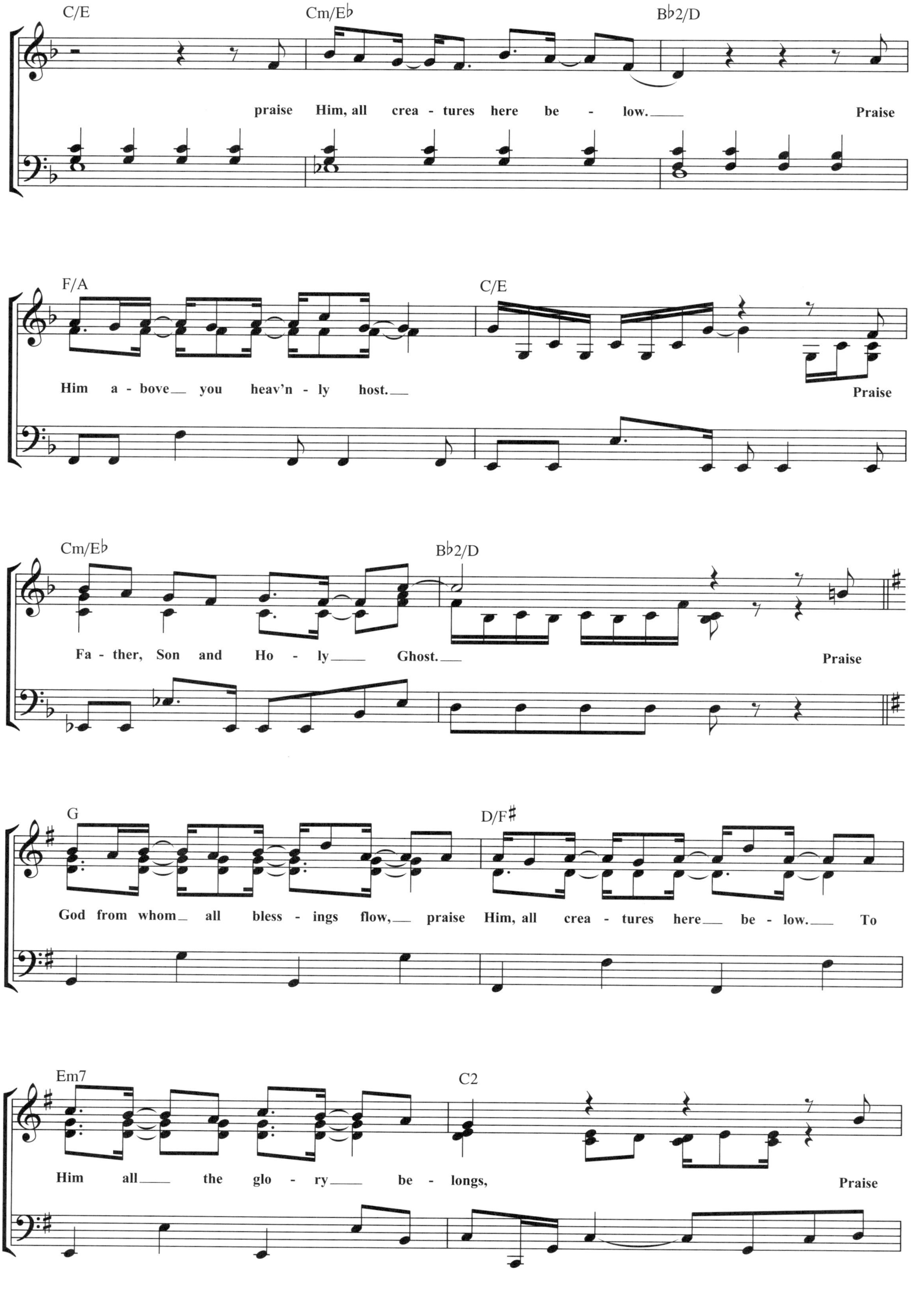
C/E
Cm/E♭
B♭2/D
praise Him, all crea - tures here be - low. Praise
F/A
C/E
Him a - bove you heav'n - ly host. Praise
Cm/E♭
B♭2/D
Fa - ther, Son and Ho - ly Ghost. Praise
G
D/F♯
God from whom all bless - ings flow, praise Him, all crea - tures here be - low. To
Em7
C2
Him all the glo - ry be - longs, Praise

109

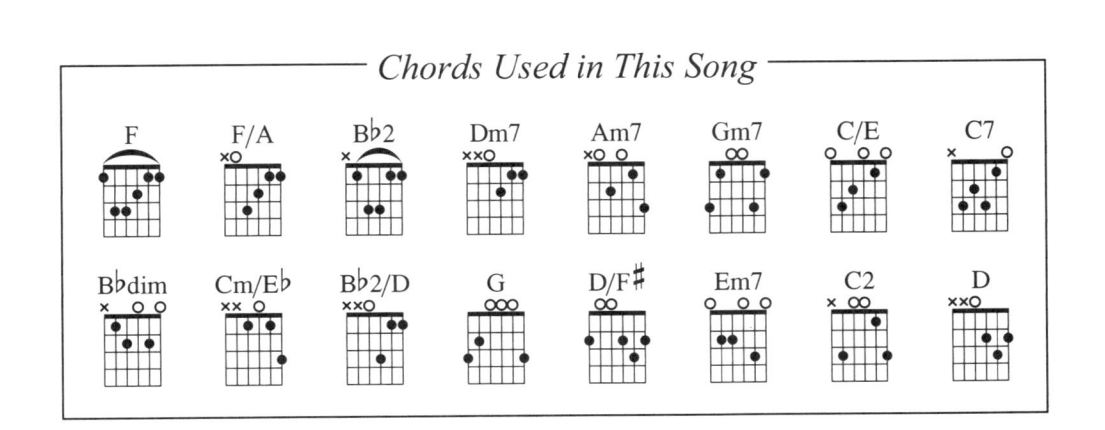

Let God Arise

Words and Music by
CHRIS TOMLIN, ED CASH
and JESSE REEVES

♩ = 144

Hear the ho - ly roar of God re - sound,
(His) en - e - mies will run for sure,

Watch the wa - ters part be - fore us now.
The church will stand, She will en - dure.

Come and see what He has done
He holds the keys of life,

for us, Tell the world of His great love,
our Lord, Death has no sting, no fi - nal word, Our God

Copyright © 2006 worshiptogether.com Songs / sixsteps Music (ASCAP) (adm. by EMI CMG Publishing) / Alletrop Music (BMI)
All rights reserved. Used by permission. CCLI Song No. 4822413

is a God who saves.

Our God is a God who saves.

Let God a-rise,

Let God a-rise. Our God reigns now and for-ev-er, He reigns now and for-ev-

1.
G A7 D
- er.
G A7 D
His en - er.
2.
God a - rise,
A D/A
Let God a - rise.
A7
Our God reigns now and for - ev - er, He reigns
D/A
now and for - ev - er.
D F♯m7
D

113

Our God reigns now and for-ev-er, He reigns now and for-ev-er. God a-rise er.

Play 4 times

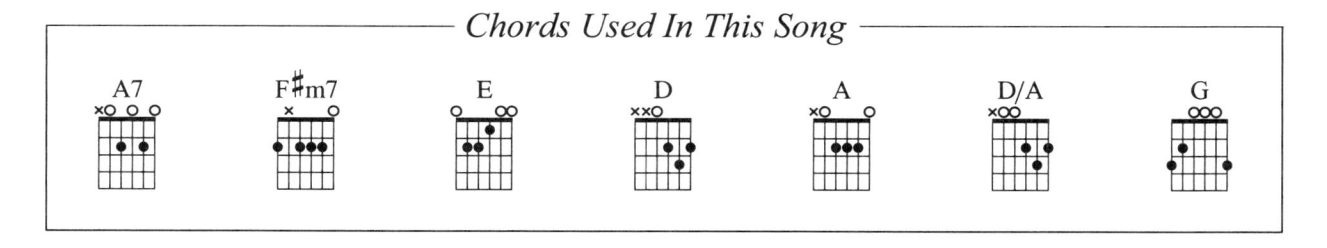

Chords Used In This Song

A7, F#m7, E, D, A, D/A, G

Love Came Down

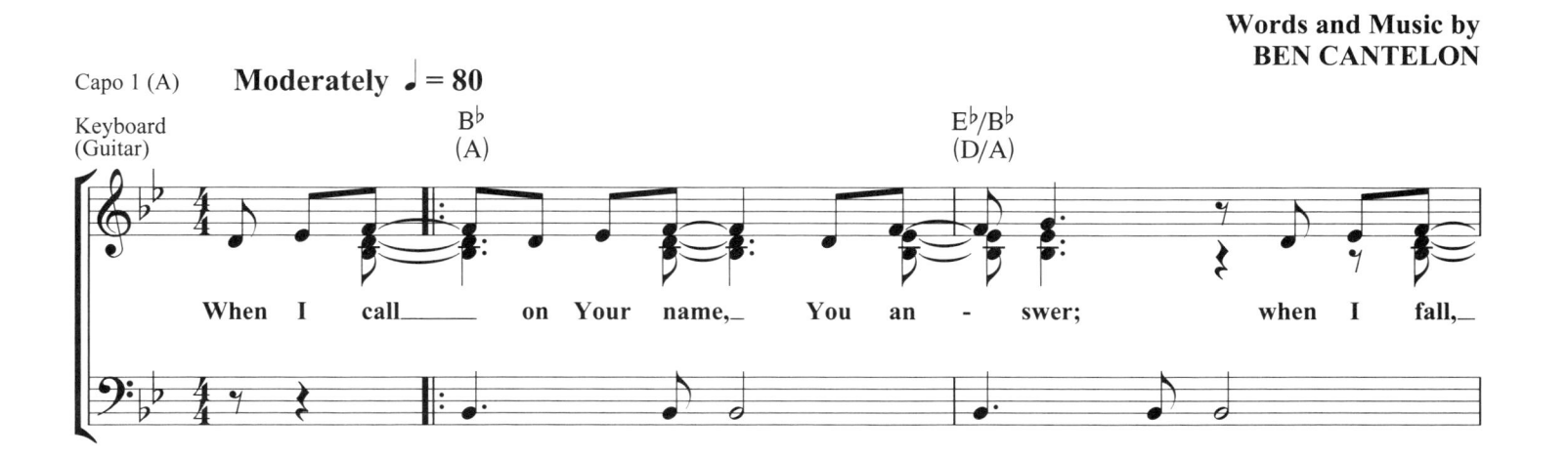

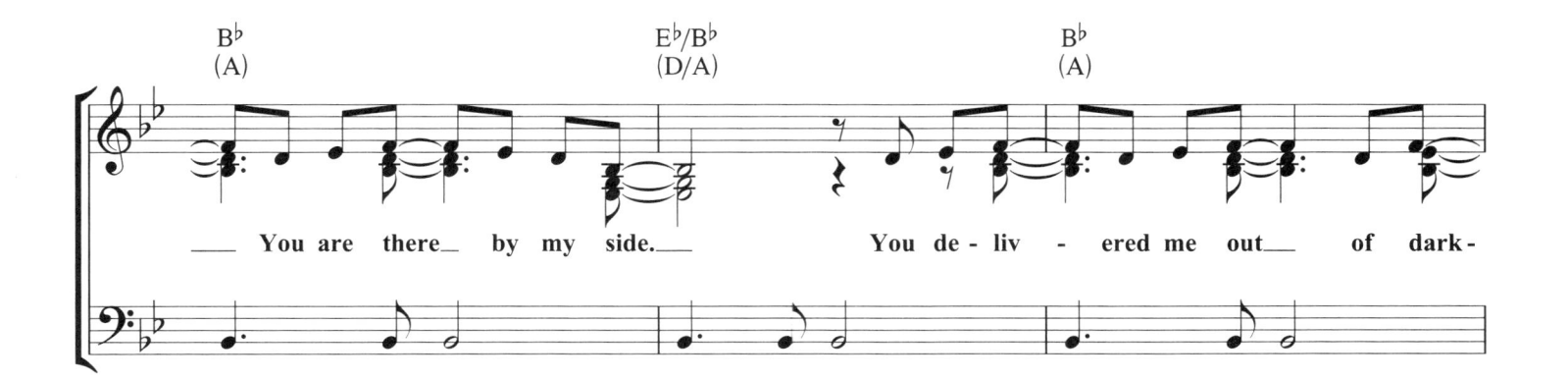

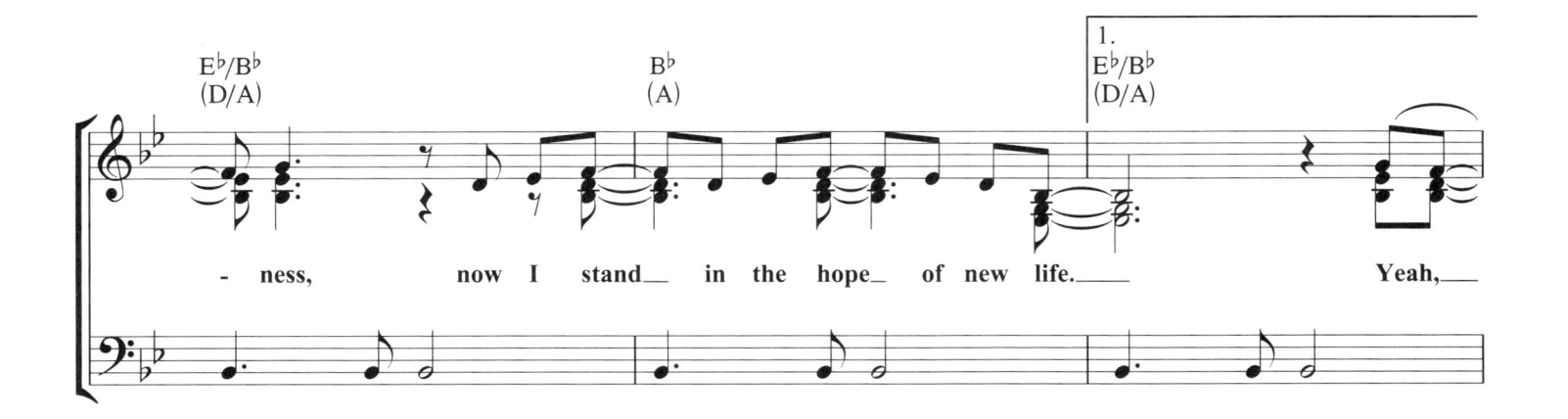

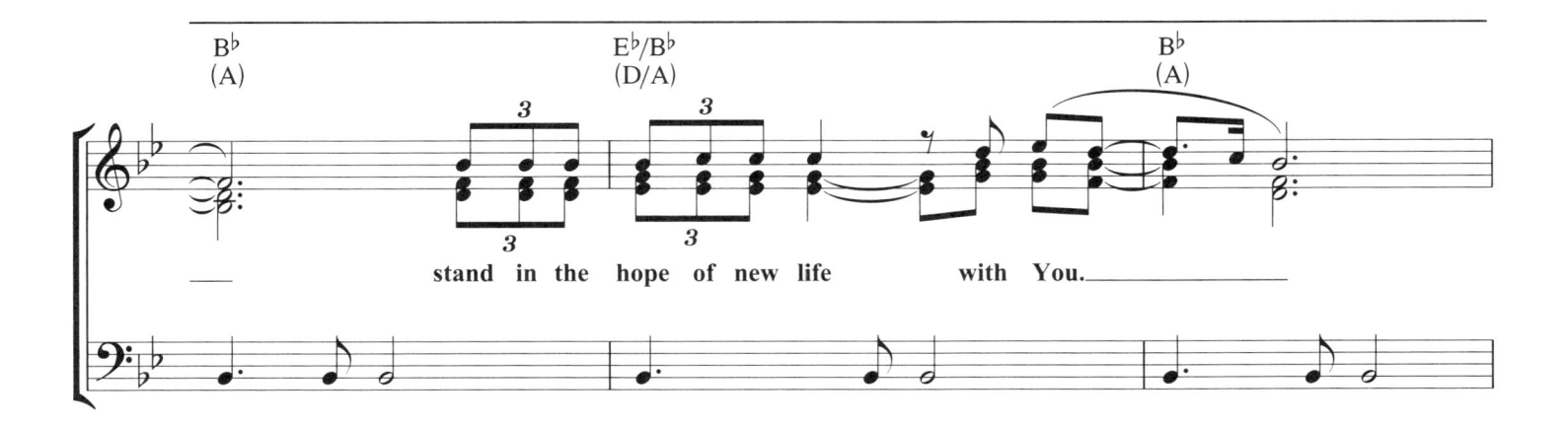

**Words and Music by
BEN CANTELON**

Capo 1 (A) **Moderately** ♩ = 80

When I call on Your name, You answer; when I fall, You are there by my side. You delivered me out of darkness, now I stand in the hope of new life. Yeah, stand in the hope of new life with You.

Copyright © 2006 Thankyou Music (PRS) (adm. by EMI CMG Publishing, excluding the UK and Europe
which is adm. by kingsway songs.com)
All right reserved. Used by permission. CCLI Song No. 4943316

2.
E♭/B♭ (D/A)
E♭/B♭ (D/A)
Cm7 (Bm7)
B♭ (A)
E♭ (D)
When I call___ By grace_ I'm free;_ You res - cued me._
Cm7 (Bm7)
B♭/D (A/C♯)
E♭ (D)
B♭ (A)
All I am__ is___ Yours._ I've found a love great-
E♭maj7 (Dmaj7)
- er than life__ it - self.___ I've found a hope strong - er and noth - ing com - pares._
Gm7 (F♯m7)
E♭ (D)
__ I once was lost, now__ I'm a - live__ in You,___ I'm a-
B♭ (A)
E♭maj7 (Dmaj7)
live in__ You.___ Thank You, Lord.___

117

118

119

B♭ (A)
F (E)
Gm7 (F♯m7)
I see You, Lord.
E♭ (D)
F/E♭ (E/D)
B♭ (A)
Cm7 (Bm7)
B♭/D (A/C♯)
E♭ (D)
By grace I'm free. You res - cued me.
Cm7 (Bm7)
B♭/D (A/C♯)
E♭ (D)
Cm7 (Bm7)
B♭/D (A/C♯)
All I am is Yours. By grace I'm free. You res -
E♭ (D)
Cm7 (Bm7)
B♭/D (A/C♯)
E♭maj7 (Dmaj7)
B♭ (A)
- cued me. All I am is Yours. I've found a love great -
E♭maj7/B♭ (Dmaj7/A)
- er than life it - self. I've found a hope strong - er and noth - ing com - pares.

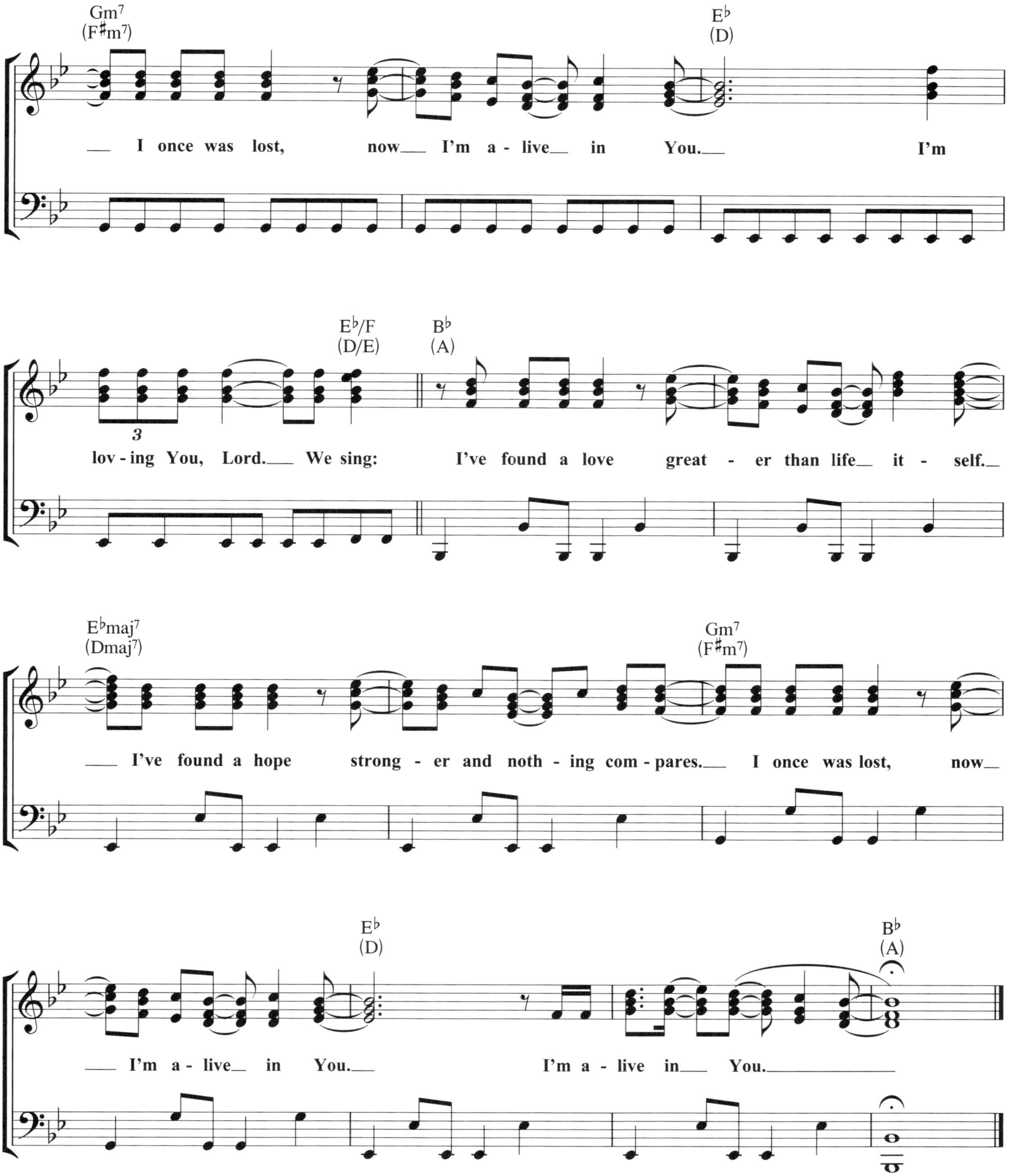

Chords Used in This Song

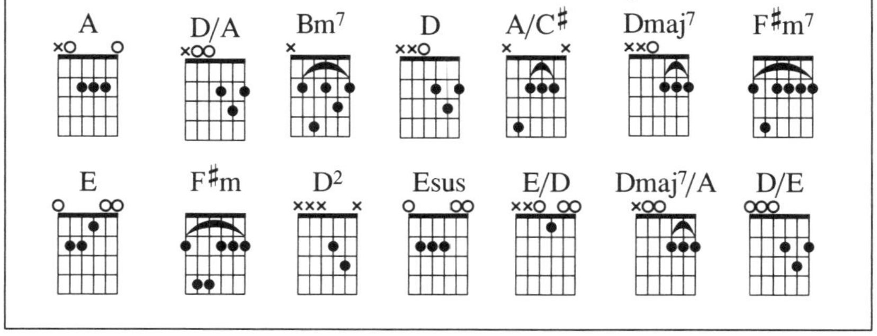

Made To Worship

**Words and Music by
CHRIS TOMLIN, STEPHAN SHARP
and ED CASH**

Moderately ♩ = 86

Be-fore the day,___ be-fore the light,___ be-fore the world___ re-volved___ a-round___ the sun.___ God on high___ stepped down in-to time,___ and wrote the sto--ry of___ His love___ for ev-ery-one.___

He has filled our hearts with won-der,

Copyright © 2006 worshiptogether.com Songs / sixsteps Music (ASCAP) (adm. by EMI CMG Publishing)
Alletrop Music (BMI) / Stenpan Music (ASCAP) All rights reserved. Used by permission. CCLI Song No. 4794118

so that we always re-mem-ber:

You and I are made to worship, you and I are called to love,

You and I are for-giv-en and free. When

you and I em-brace sur-ren-der, when you and I choose to be-lieve, then

you and I will see who we were meant to be.

C
C2/B
All we are and all we have, is
Am
F
G
all a gift from God that we re - ceive.
C
C2/B
Brought to life we o - pen up our eyes, to see the maj -
Am
F
G
- es - ty and glo - ry of the King.

see who we were meant to be. E-ven the rocks cry out, e-ven the heav-ens shout, at the sound of His Ho-ly name. So let ev-'ry voice sing out let ev-'ry knee bow down, He's wor-thy of all our praise. You and I are made to wor-ship,

| F | Dm7 |

you and I___ are called___ to love,___ You and I___ are for-giv-en and free,___

| G7 | C |

___ yeah.___ When you and I___ em-brace___ sur-ren-der, when

| F | Dm7 |

you and I___ choose to___ be-lieve,___ then you and I will see___

D.S al CODA (take 1st ending)

| G7 | **CODA** C |

___ you___ and I___ will see. Yeah,___

| F | Dm7 |

we were meant___ to be,_____ oo.___

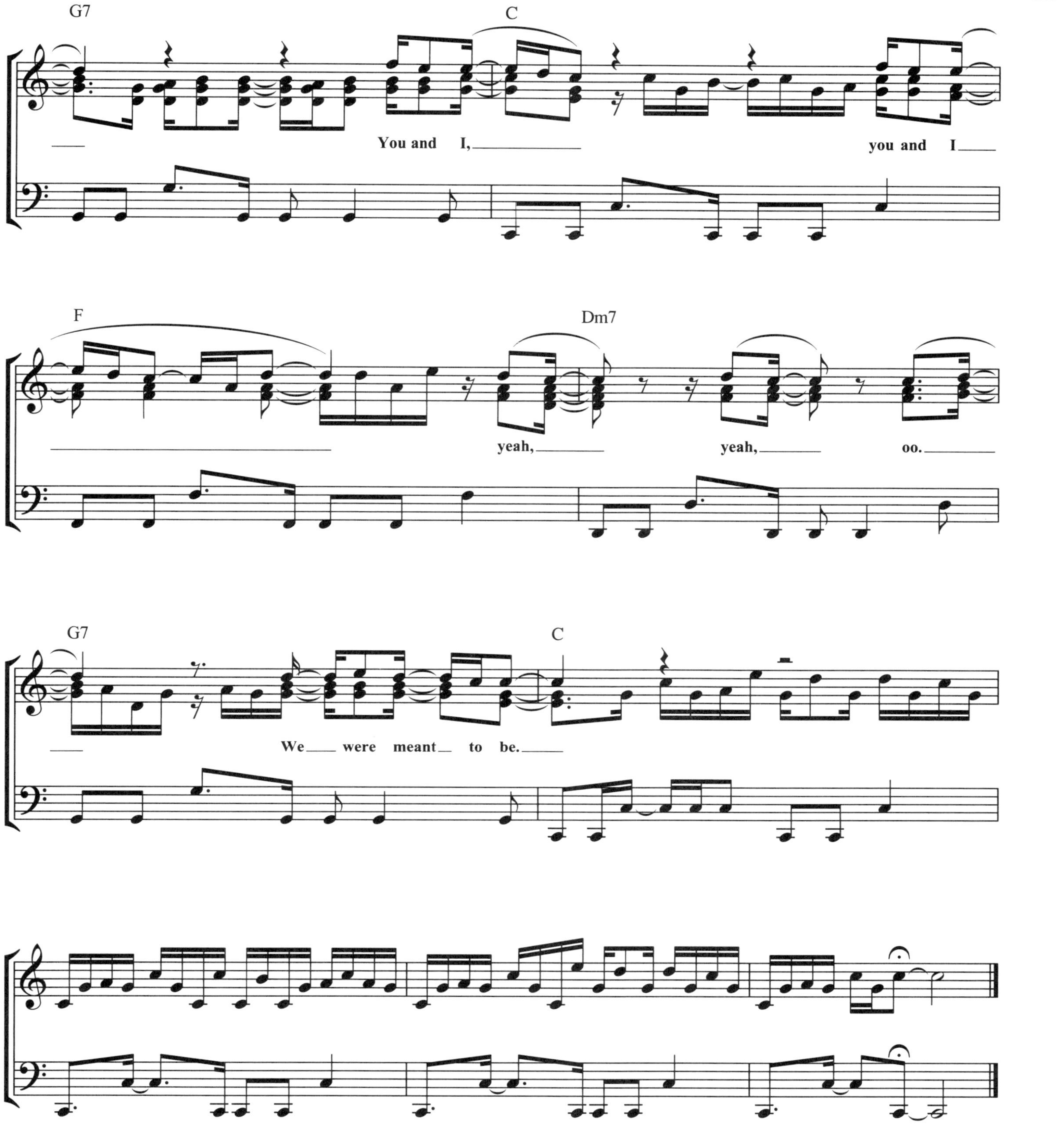

Chords Used in This Song

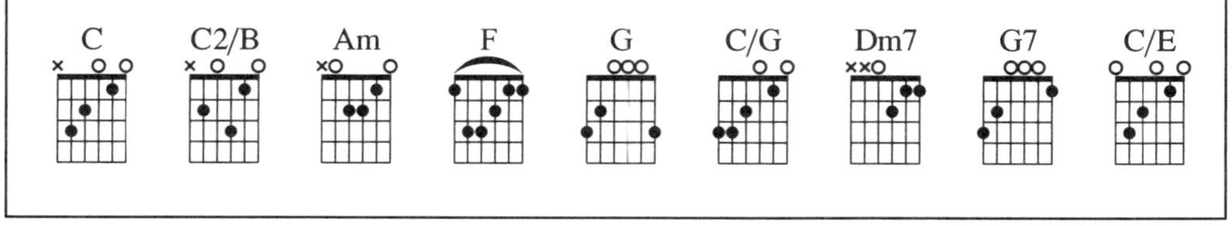

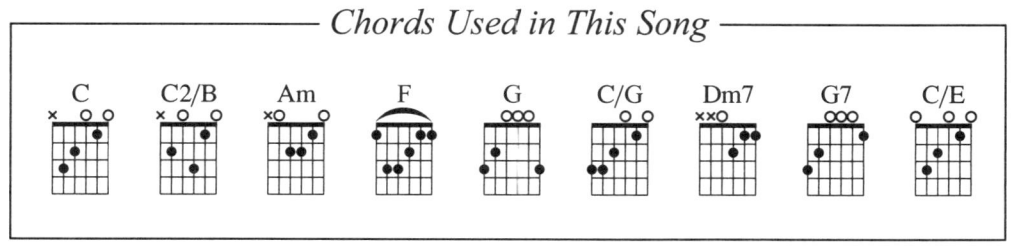

O Church Arise

Words and Music by
**STUART KENNEDY and
KEITH GETTY**

Steadily, ♩ = 72

1. O Church, a - rise, and put your ar - mor on; hear the call of Christ, our Cap - tain. For now the weak can say that they are strong in the strength that God has giv - en. With shield of
2. Our call to war, to love the cap - tive soul, But to rage a - gainst the cap - tor. And with the sword that makes the wound - ed whole we will fight and faith and val - or. When faced with
3. Come see the cross, where love and mer - cy meet. As the Son of God is strick - en. Then see His foes lie crushed be - neath His feet, for the Con - quer - or has ris - en. And as the
4. So Spir - it, come, put strength in ev - 'ry stride, give grace for ev - 'ry hur - dle. That we may run with faith to win the prize of a ser - vant good and faith - ful. As saints of

Copyright © 2005 Thankyou Music (PRS) (adm. by EMI CMG Publishing excluding UK & Europe which is adm. by kingswaysongs.com)
All right reserved. Used by permission. CCLI Song No. 4611992

faith and belt of truth, we'll stand a-
trials and on is ev - 'ry side. We know the
stone old is still rolled line the a - way. And Christ e-
way. Re - tell - ing

gainst the dev - il's lies; and ar - my bold, whose bat - tle -
out - come is se - cure. And Christ will have the prize for
merg - es from the grave. This vic - t'ry march con - tin - ues
tri - umphs of His grace. We hear their march calls and hun - ger

cry is love, reach - ing out to those in dark -
which He died, and in - her - i - tance of na -
'til the day ev - 'ry eye and heart shall see
for the day, when with Christ we stand in glo -

ness.
tions.
Him.
ry.

2. Our call to
3. Come see the
4. So Spir - it,

Chords Used in This Song

A⁷sus   D   G/B   A/C♯   D/F♯   G   Asus   A   Bm   Dsus

On The Third Day

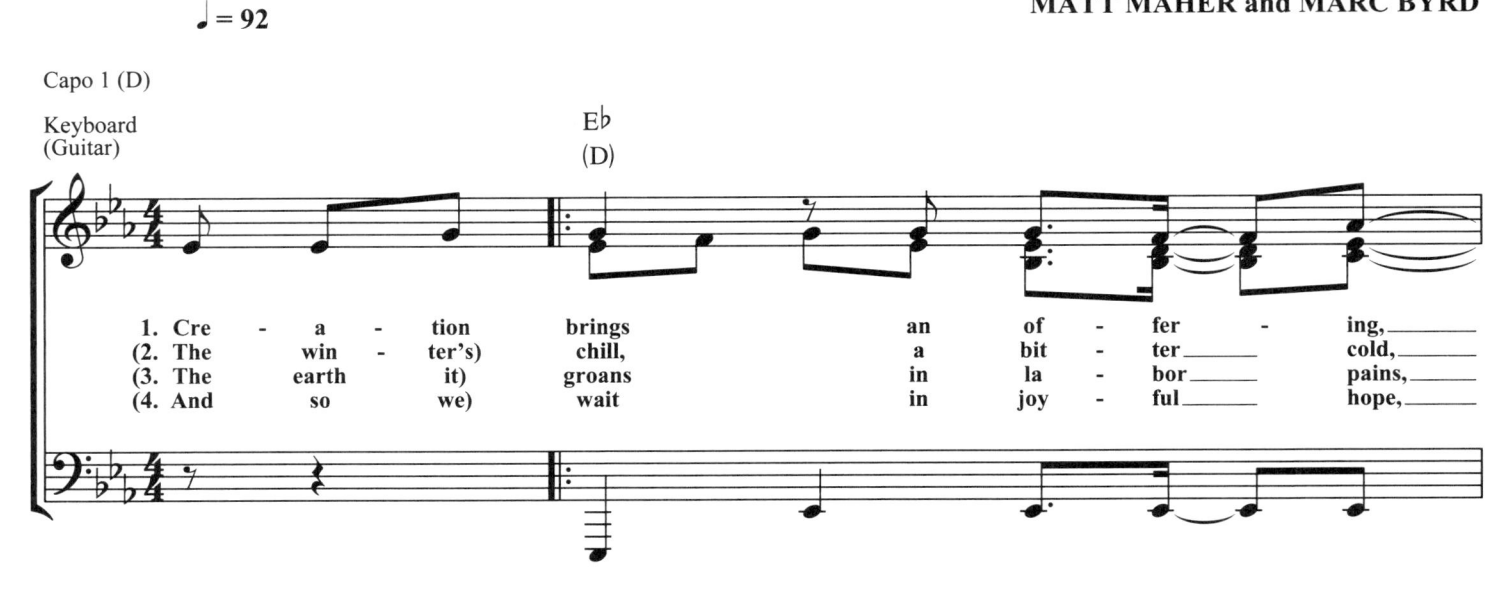

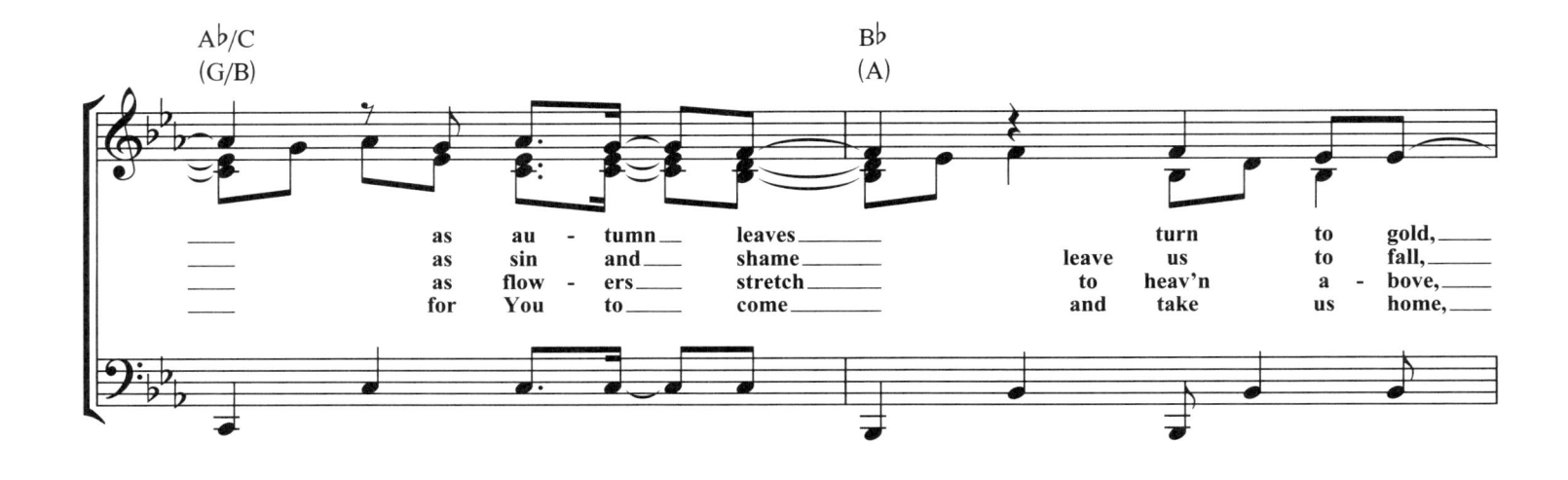

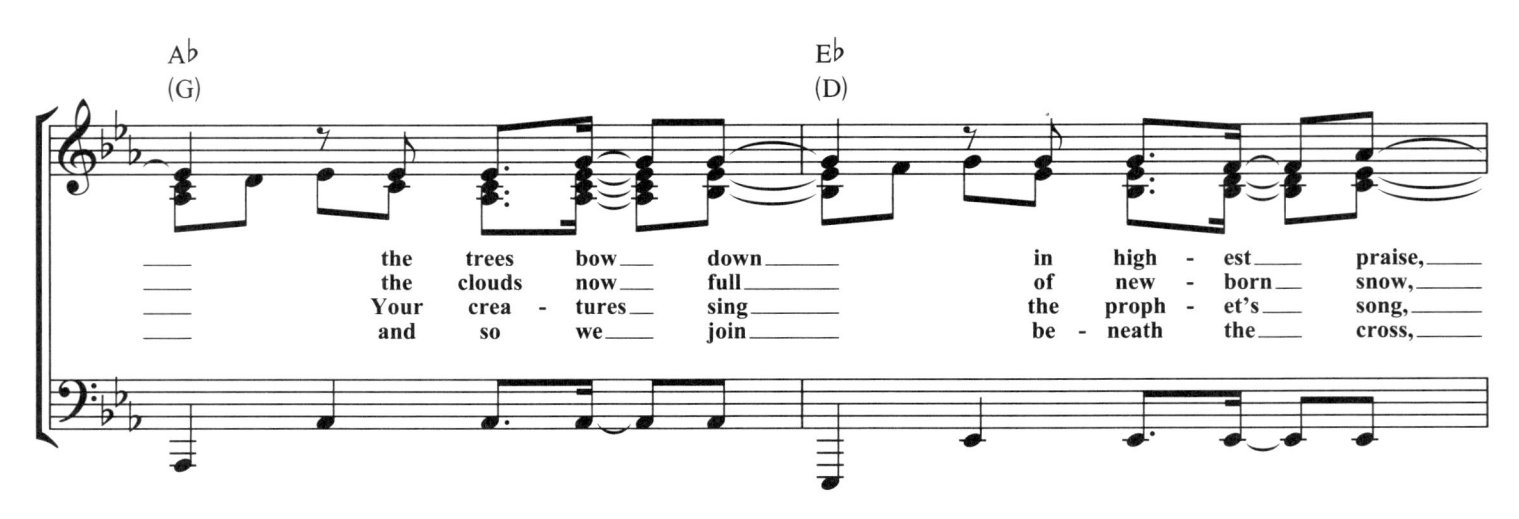

Words and Music by
MATT MAHER and MARC BYRD

♩ = 92

Capo 1 (D)

Keyboard (Guitar)

1. Cre - a - tion brings an of - fer - ing,
(2. The win - ter's) chill, a bit - ter cold,
(3. The earth it) groans in la - bor pains,
(4. And so we) wait in joy - ful hope,

as au - tumn leaves turn to gold,
as sin and shame leave us to fall,
as flow - ers stretch to heav'n a - bove,
for You to come and take us home,

the trees bow down in high - est praise,
the clouds now full of new - born snow,
Your crea - tures sing the proph - et's song,
and so we join be - neath the cross,

Copyright © 2006 Thankyou Music (PRS) (adm. worldwide by EMI CMG Publishing excluding the UK and Europe which is adm. by kingswaysongs.com) spiritandsong.com Publishing/ Meaux Mercy/Blue Raft Music (BMI) (adm. by EMI CMG Publishing) All rights reserved. Used by permission. CCLI Song No. 4724023

[Ab/C] (G/B) [Bb] (A)

now made bare before Your throne.
for grace to come and save us all,
to be a gift of self-less love.
in suf-fer-ing from whence we go.

[Ab] (G) [Eb/G] (D/F#)

The west-ern sky an am-ber blaze,
with-in the dark-est night of man,
The sun is ris-ing in the east,
The great-est act of sov-'reign grace,

[Ab] (G) [Eb/Bb] (D/A)

at the end of the day,
was found Your sav-ing hand,
and your spir-it is un-leashed,
in the u-ni-verse dis-played,

[Ab/C] (G/B) [Eb/Bb] (D/A)

For ev-'ry-thing must die

132

133

Resurrection Day

Words and Music by
MATT MAHER

Driving rock, ♩ = 126

1. It's the weight of Your glory, brings the proud to their knees, and the light of revelation, lets the blind man see. It's the power of the cross, breaks away death's embrace,

2. You declare what is holy, You declare what is good, in the sight of all the nations, You declare that You are God. It's the power in Your Blood, breaks away sin's embrace,

Copyright © 2005 Thankyou Music (PRS) (adm. worldwide by EMI CMG Publishing excluding the UK and Europe which is adm. by kingswaysongs.com)/spiritandsong.com Publishing (BMI) (adm. by EMI CMG Publishing) All rights reserved. Used by permission. CCLI Song No. 4669786

135

and we cel-e-brate our free-dom, danc-ing on an emp-ty grave.
and we cel-e-brate our free-dom, danc-ing on our bro-ken chains.

Roll a-way the stone, roll a-way the stone. We sing for joy, we shout Your name, we cel-e-brate Your res-ur-rec-tion day. We sing for joy, we shout Your name, we cel-e-brate Your res - ur - rec - tion___ day.

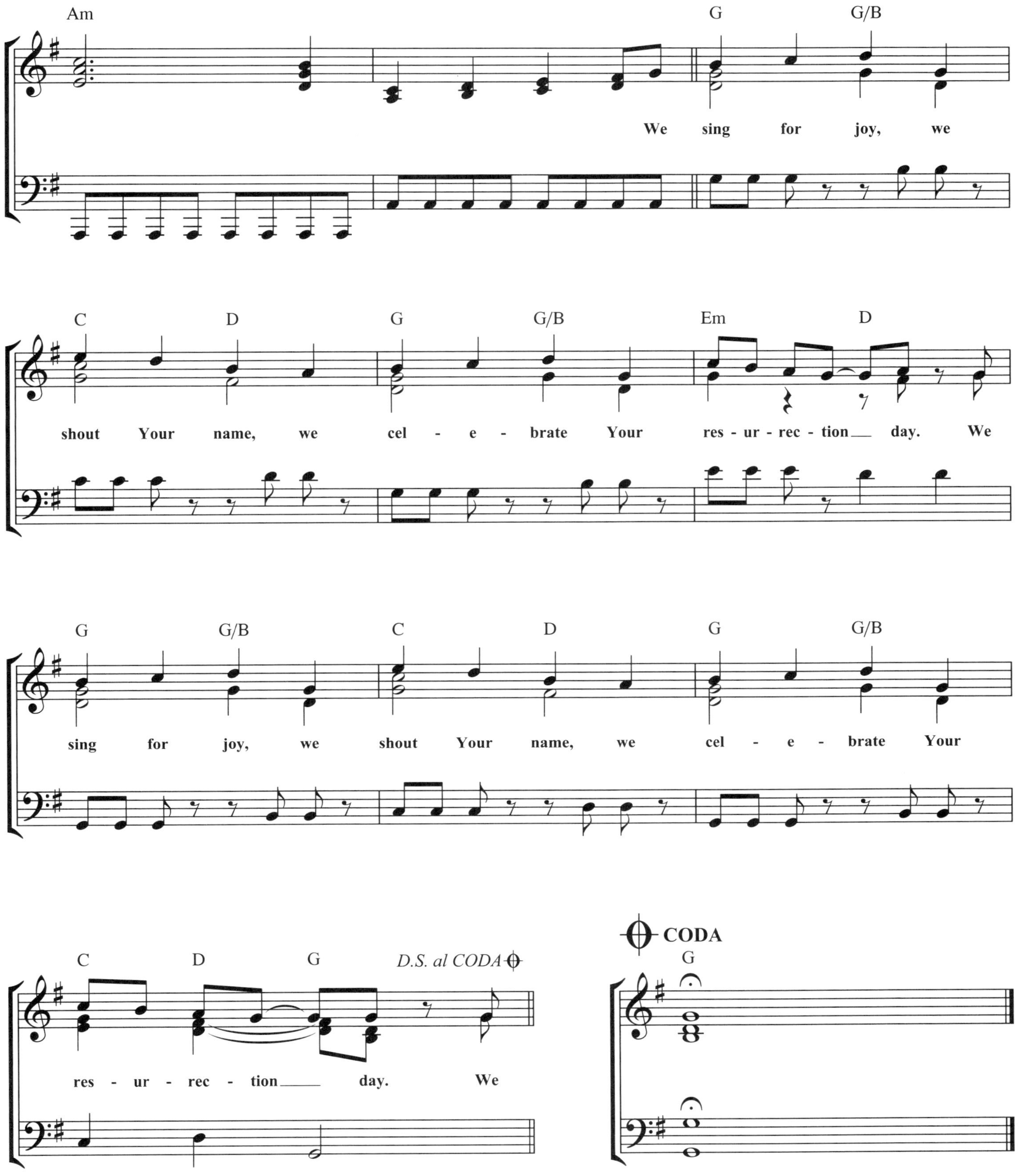

Chords Used in This Song

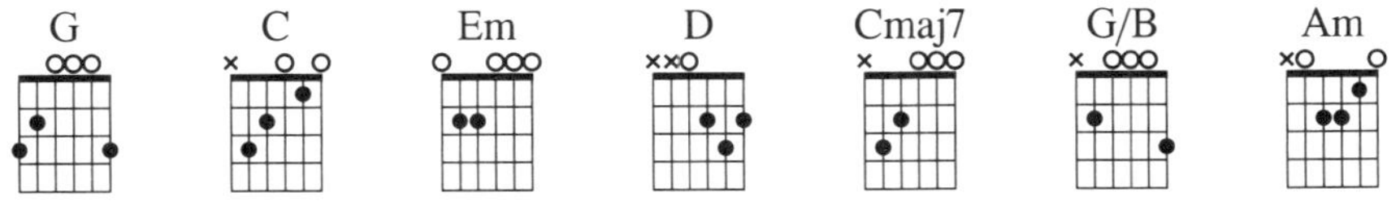

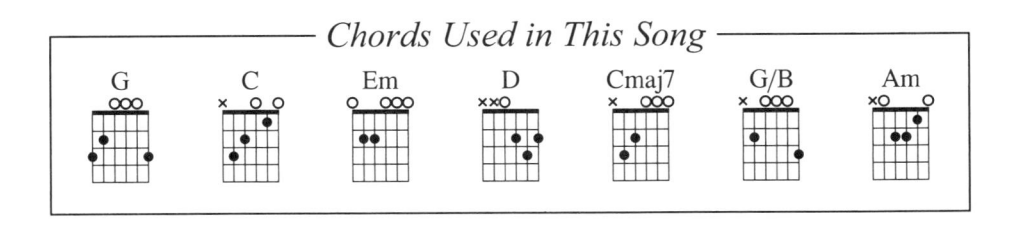

Shine

Words and Music by
MATT REDMAN

♩ = 80

Lord we have seen the rising sun, A-wak-en-ing the ear-ly dawn, And we're ris-ing up to give You praise.

(2nd time 8vb)

Lord we have seen the stars and moon see how they shine, they shine for You. And You're call-ing us to do the same,

Copyright © 2006 Thankyou Music (PRS) (adm. worldwide by EMI CMG Publishing
excluding the UK and Europe, which is adm. by kingswaysongs.com)
All rights reserved. Used by permission. CCLI Song No. 4831435

139

Lyrics:
So we rise up with a song, And we rise up with a cry, And we're giving You our lives. We will shine like stars in the universe, Holding out Your truth in the darkest place. We'll be living for Your glory,

C
1.
Je - sus we'll be liv - ing for Your glo - ry.
Lord we have seen
2., D.S.
G
We will burn so bright with Your praise,
oh, God, And de - clare Your light to this bro -
D/F♯
- ken world. We'll be liv - ing for Your glo - ry,
F
Je - sus we'll be
C
To CODA
liv - ing for Your glo - ry.
Like the sun

141

Am
ex - plod - ing in - to life. Like a su -
G/B
- per - no - va's light, Set your Ho - ly Church on fire,
C
3
G
We will shine. We will shine.
G7
D.S. al CODA
(take 2nd repeat)
We will shine

So we rise up with a song, And we rise up with a cry, And we're giving You our lives. Jesus we will shine.

Sound Of Melodies

**Words and Music by
LEELAND MOORING,
JACK MOORING and
STEVE WILSON**

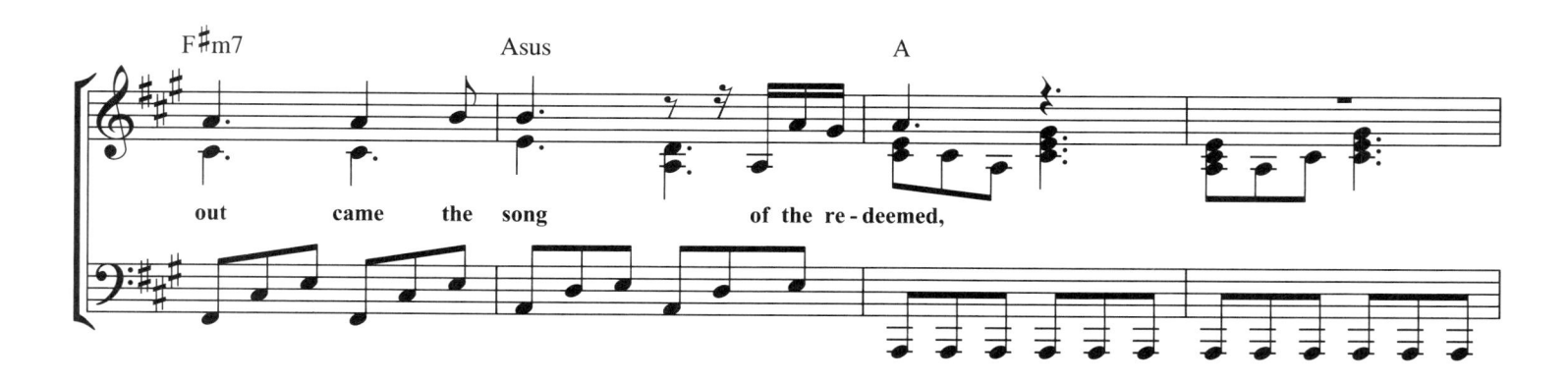

Moderately, ♩. = 70

1. We who were called to be Your peo-ple, strug-gling sin-ners and thieves. We're lift-ed up from the ash-es, and out came the song of the re-deemed,

145

to CODA
C♯m/E F♯m7sus D2 A
up to You, God? Oh,
F♯m7 Asus/D A
we have caught a rev - e - la - tion, that
F♯m7 Asus/D A
noth-ing can sep-a-rate us from. The
F♯m7 Asus/D A
love we re-ceived through sal - va - tion, it
F♯m7 Asus/D A
fills Your daugh-ters and Your sons,

F♯m7
Asus/D
A
Your daugh-ters and Your__ sons.
F♯m7
Asus/D
D.S. al CODA
Can You hear the
CODA
F♯m7sus
D2
You, God?
A
E
The sound of Your love, the sound of Your love, is what You're__
F♯m7
D2
A
__ hear - ing. The sound of Your sons, the sound of Your
E
F♯m7
D2
A
sons, You've won Your___ chil - dren. The sound of Your

love, the sound of Your love, is what You're hear-ing.

Your daugh-ters in love, Your daugh-ters in love, You've won Your

chil-dren. The sound of mel-o-dies, oh, the sound of mel-o-

dies ris-ing up to You. Ris-ing up to You, God,

ris-ing up to You,

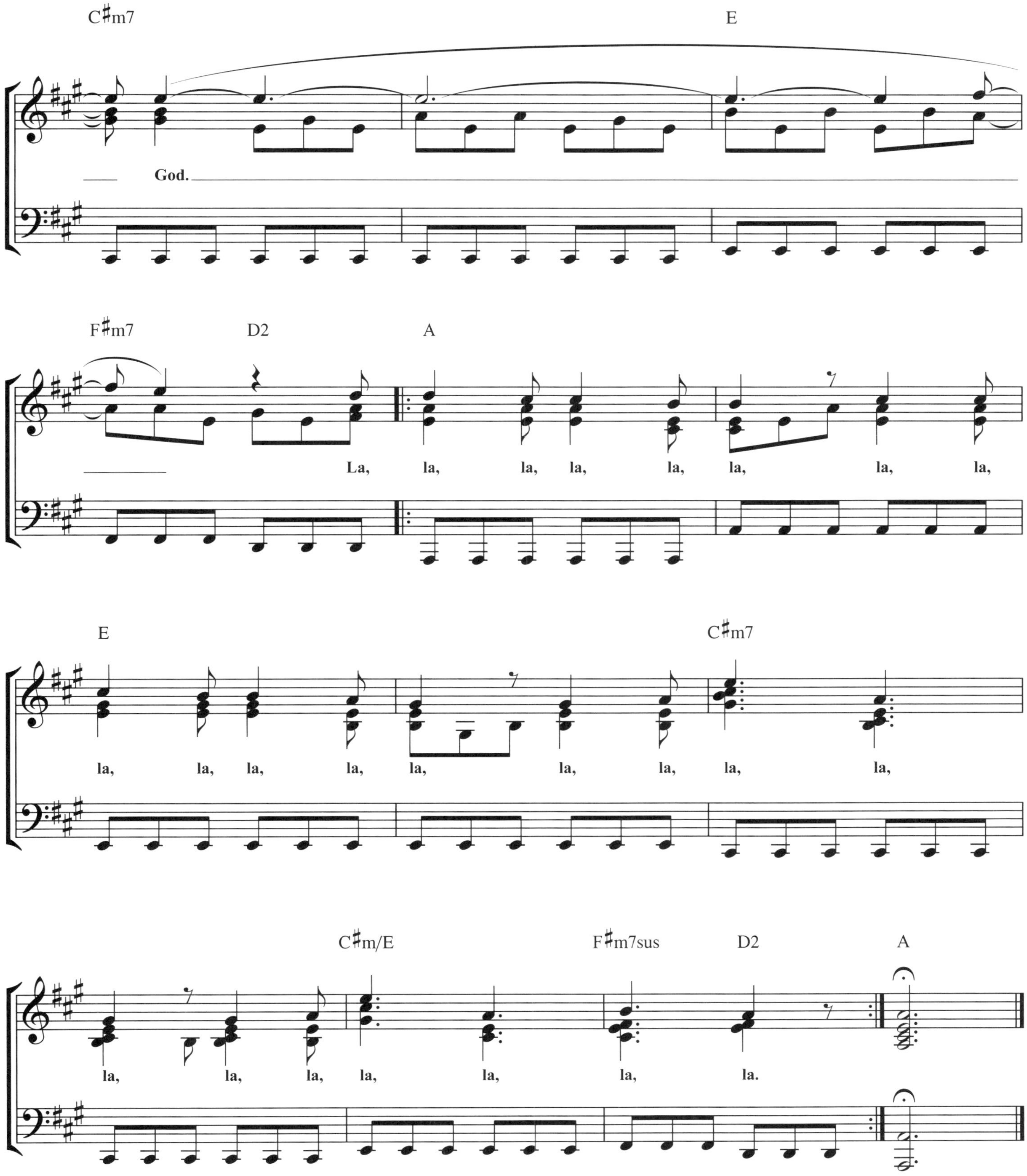

Chords Used in This Song

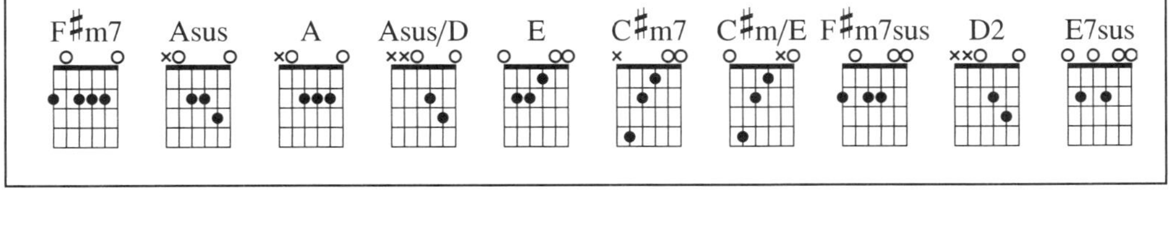

Speak, O Lord

Words and Music by
KEITH GETTY and STUART TOWNEND

Gently and prayerfully ♩ = 68

1. Speak, O Lord, as we come to You to receive the food of Your holy word. Take Your truth, plant it deep in us; shape and fashion us in Your likeness, that the light of Christ might be seen today in our acts of love and our

2. Teach us Lord, full obedience Holy reverence true humility. Test our thoughts and our attitudes In the radiance of Your purity Cause our faith to rise Cause our eyes to see Your majestic love and au-

3. Speak, O Lord, and renew our minds Help us grasp the heights of Your plans for us. Truths unchanged from the dawn of time that will echo down through eternity And by grace we'll stand on Your promises And by faith we'll walk as You

Copyright © 2005 Thankyou Music (PRS) (adm. worldwide by EMI CMG Publishing
excluding the UK & Europe which is adm by kingswaysongs.com)
All right reserved. Used by permission. CCLI Song No. 4615235

151

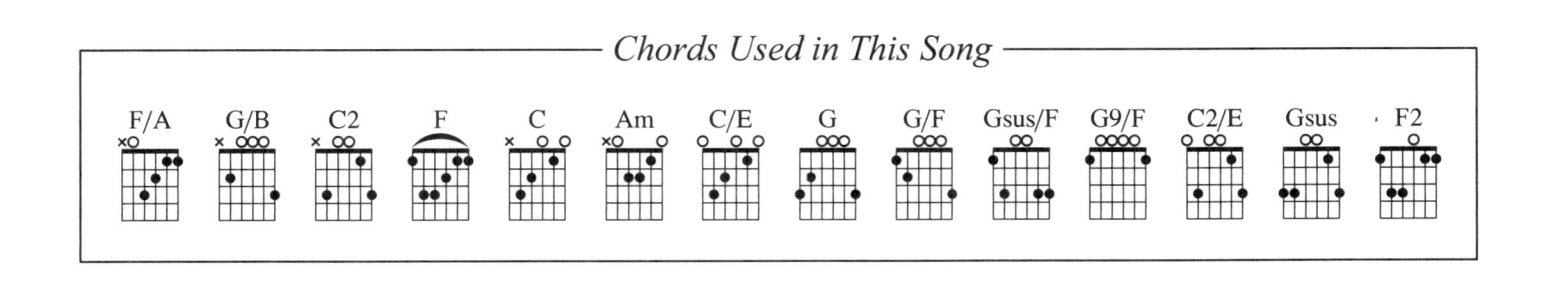

deeds of____ faith. Speak, O Lord, and ful-fill____ in us____ all your
thor - i - ty. Words of power that can ne - ver fail;___ Let their
walk with___ us. Speak, O Lord, till Your church____ is built__ and the

pur - pos - es,____ for Your glo - ry.
truth_____ pre - vail__ o - ver un - be - lief.
earth_____ is filled__ with your glo - ry.

Repeat 2 times

Chords Used in This Song

F/A G/B C2 F C Am C/E G G/F Gsus/F G9/F C2/E Gsus F2

Tears Of The Saints

**Words and Music by
LEELAND MOORING and
JACK MOORING**

Moderately ♩ = 92

Capo 4 (Em)
Keyboard
Guitar

There are many prodigal sons, on our city streets they run, searching for shelter. There are homes broken down, people's hopes have fallen to the ground, from failures. This is an e-

Copyright © 2005 Meaux Mercy (BMI) / Meaux Jeaux Music (SESAC) (adm. by EMI CMG Publishing)
All rights reserved. Used by permission. CCLI Song No. 4768694

C♯m7 (Am7)
B/D♯ (G/B)
E (C)
mer - gen - cy! There are tears from the
B (G)
F♯ (D)
saints, for the lost and un - saved, we're cry - ing for them
C♯m7 (Am7)
E (C)
come back home, we're cry - ing for them come back home.
F♯ (D)
E (C)
And all Your chil - dren will stretch out their hands, and pick up
B (G)
F♯ (D)
C♯m7 (Am7)
the crip - pled man, Fa - ther we will lead them home.

Fa - ther we will lead them home.

There are schools full of ha - tred, e - ven church - es have for - sak - en love and mer - cy. May we see this gen-er-a-tion, in its state of des-per-a-tion, for Your glo-ry. This is an e-mer-gen-cy! There are tears from the saints, for the lost and un-saved, we're cry-ing for them come back home,

156

157

B
(G)
F♯
(D)
Sin - ner,
reach out your hand!
Bsus
(Gsus)
B
(G)
F♯
(D)
Chil - dren
in Christ you stand!
G♯m
(Em)
E
(C)
C♯m7
(Am7)

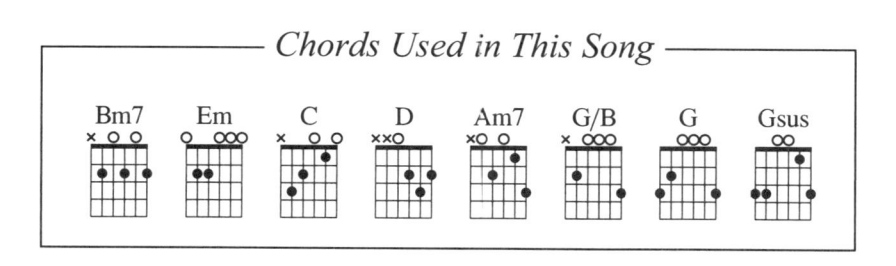

There are And all Your children will stretch out their hands and pick up the crippled man, Father we will lead them home, Father we will lead them home.

Chords Used in This Song

Bm7 Em C D Am7 G/B G Gsus

The Wonder of the Cross

Words and Music by
VICKY BEECHING

1. O precious sight, my Savior stands, dying for me with out-stretched hands. O precious sight, I love to gaze, remembering salvation's day, remembering salvation's day. Though my eyes linger on this

2. God-man crucified, the perfect sinless sacrifice. As blood ran down those nails and wood, history was split in two, yes, history was split in two. Behold the empty wooden

Copyright © 2007 Thankyou Music (PRS) (adm. worldwide by EMI CMG Publishing,
excluding the UK and Europe, which is adm. by kingswaysongs.com)
All right reserved. Used by permission. CCLI song No. 4886507

scene, may passing time and years not steal the pow'r with
tree, His body gone, alive and free. We sing with

which it impacts me, the freshness of its mystery,
everlasting joy, for sin and of death have been de-

y, the freshness of its mystery.
stroyed, yes, sin and of death have been destroyed.

May I never lose the wonder, the

wonder of the cross. May I see it like the

E♭/G (D/F♯) B♭m7 (Am7) Fm7 (Em7)
first time standing as a sinner lost, undone by
D♭ (C) A♭/C (G/B) B♭m7 (Am7)
mercy and left speechless, watching wide eyed at the cost.
Fm7 (Em7) D♭ (C) E♭/G (D/F♯) Fm7 (Em7)
3rd time to CODA
May I never lose the wonder, the
1. B♭m (Am) E♭/G (D/F♯) A♭ (G)
wonder of the cross.
2. Behold the
2. B♭m (Am) E♭/G (D/F♯) Fm7 (Em7) E♭/G (D/F♯) A♭ (G) B♭m7 (Am7) A♭/C (G/B)
wonder of the cross.

D♭ (C) E♭ (D) Fm7 (Em7) E/G (D/F♯) A♭ (G) B♭m7 (Am7) A♭/C (G/B)
D♭ (C)
D.S. al CODA
May I
CODA
B♭m (Am) E♭/G (D/F♯) A♭ (G)
won - der of the cross.
E♭/A♭ (D/G) A♭ (G)
D♭2/A♭ (C2/G) A♭ (G)

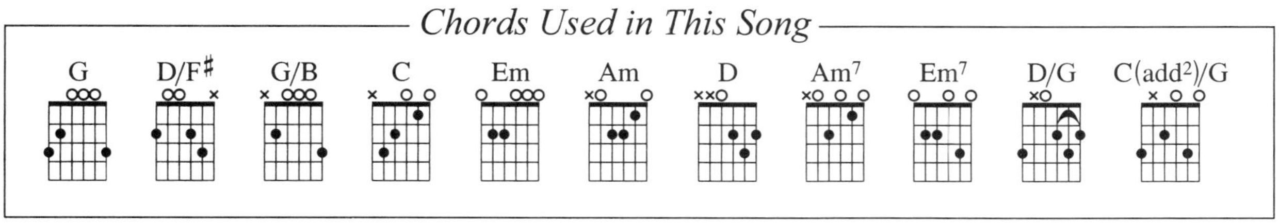
Chords Used in This Song
G D/F♯ G/B C Em Am D Am7 Em7 D/G C(add2)/G

To The Only God

Words and Music by
CHRIS TOMLIN

With feeling, ♩ = 120

Capo 1 (G)
Keyboard (Guitar)

To the on- ly God_____ who is a- ble to keep_____ us, a- ble to keep_____ us from fall- ing._____ To the on- ly God_____ be all glo- ry and ho- nor,

Copyright © 2007 Worshiptogether.com Song/sixsteps Music (ASCAP) (adm. by EMI CMG Publishing).
All rights reserved. Used with permission. CCLI Song No. 4879284

165

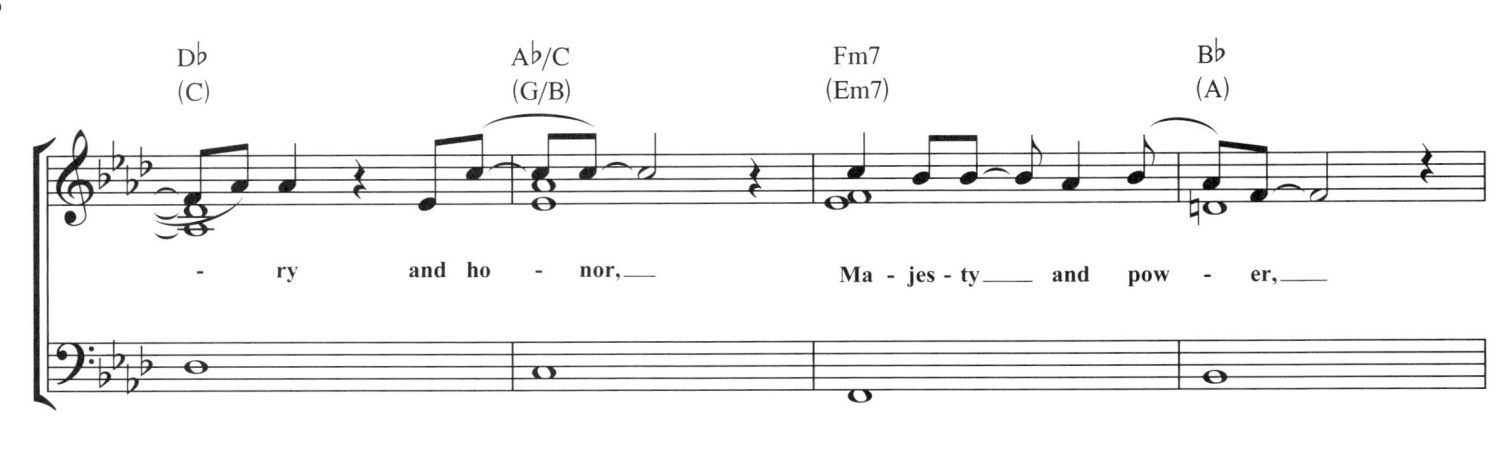

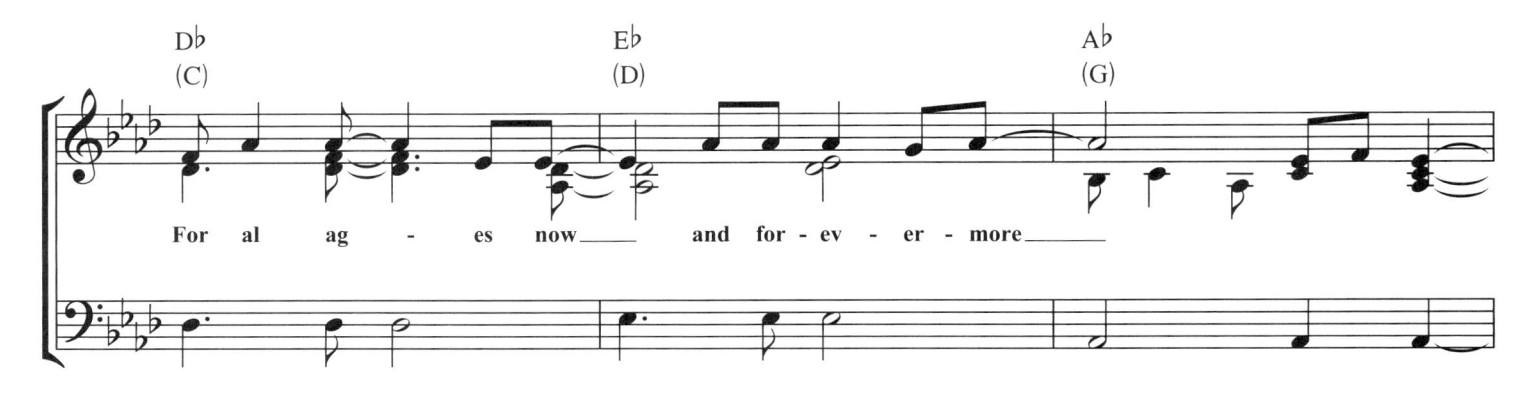

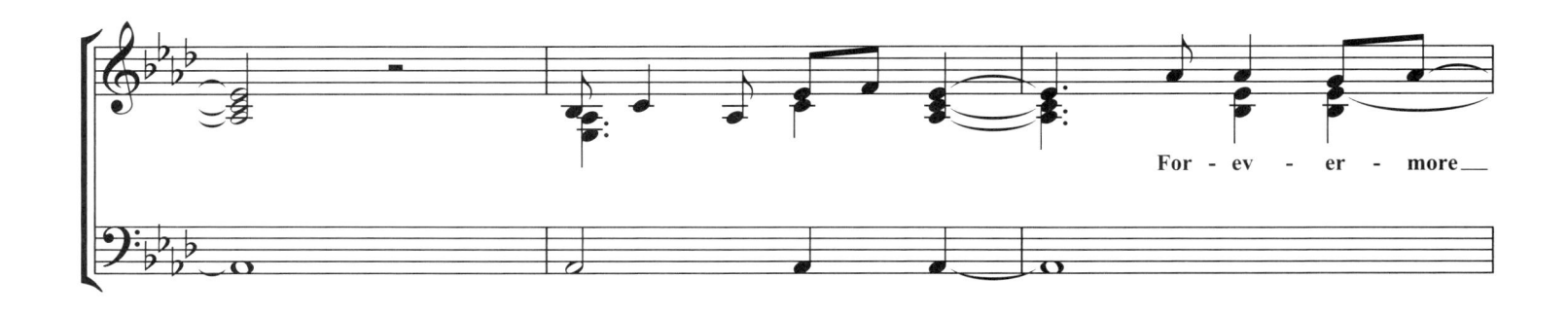

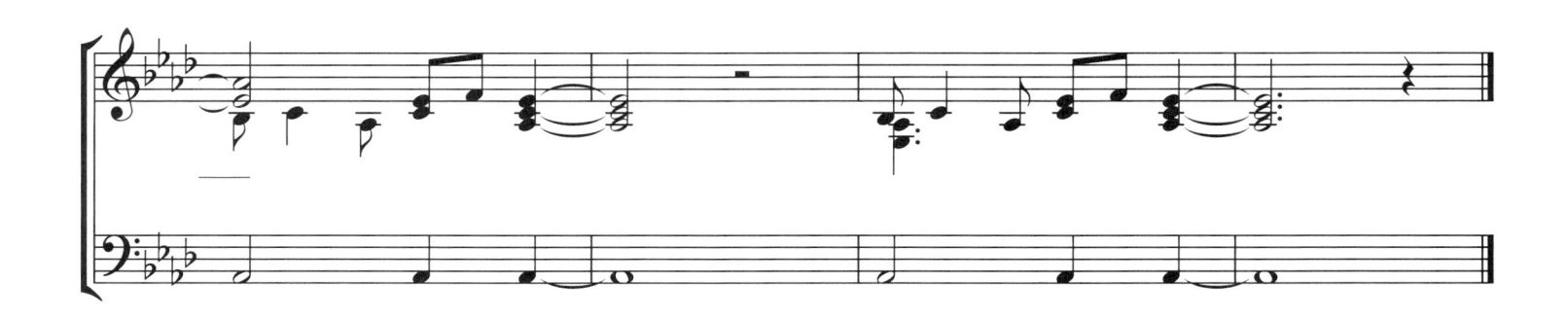

-ry and ho - nor,___ Ma - jes - ty___ and pow - er,___

For al - ag - es now___ and for - ev - er - more___

For - ev - er - more

Chords Used in This Song

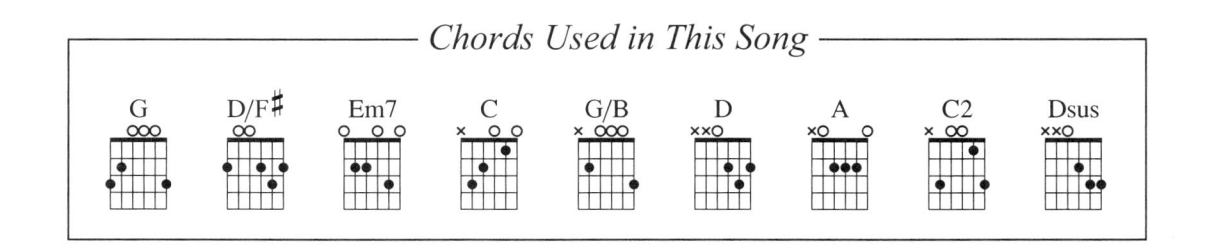

G   D/F#   Em7   C   G/B   D   A   C2   Dsus

Unwavering

Words and Music by
MATT MAHER

Moderately slow, ♩. = 46

1. Bless-ed are the poor, the king-dom is theirs. A-live in the prom-ise to be dead to the world. Bless-ed are the meek in awe of You Fa-ther, the word at Your right hand, spir-it of truth.

2. (Bless-ed are the) right-eous on bend-ed knee, found in this free-dom, com-mit-ted to You. Bless'd are those who see the heights of glo-ry, found in the val-ley, and suf-f'ring for You.

Un-wa-ver-ing

Copyright © 2006 Thankyou Music (PRS) (adm. worldwide by EMI CMG Publishing
excluding the UK and Europe which is adm. by kingswaysongs.com)/spiritandsong.com Publishing (BMI)
All rights reserved. Used by permission. CCLI Song No. 4669827

A E B E
is Your voice, un - wa - ver - ing is Your hand, un - wa - ver - ing
C♯m7 B/D♯ E C♯m7 B
is the heart that bled for the sins of man. Un - wa - ver - ing
A E B C♯m7 A
is Your will, un - wa - ver - ing is Your plan, the fount of sal -
3rd time to CODA
1.
E/B B E A E B7
va - tion on which we will stand.
E A E

169

170

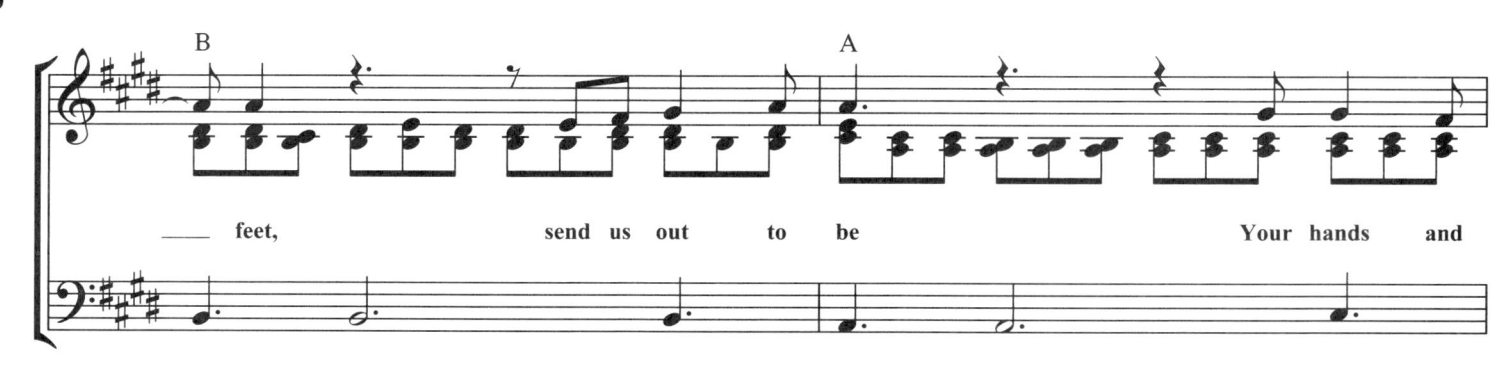

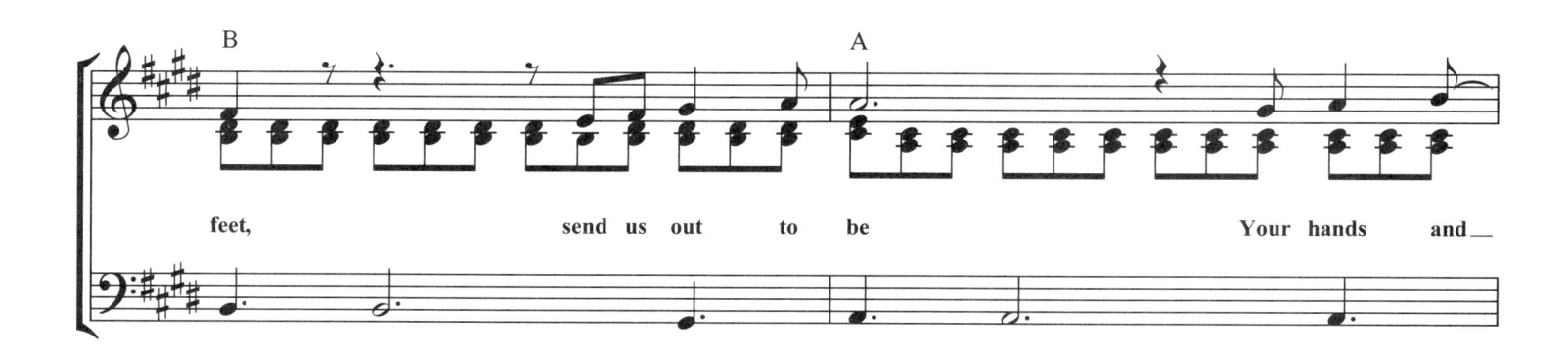

171

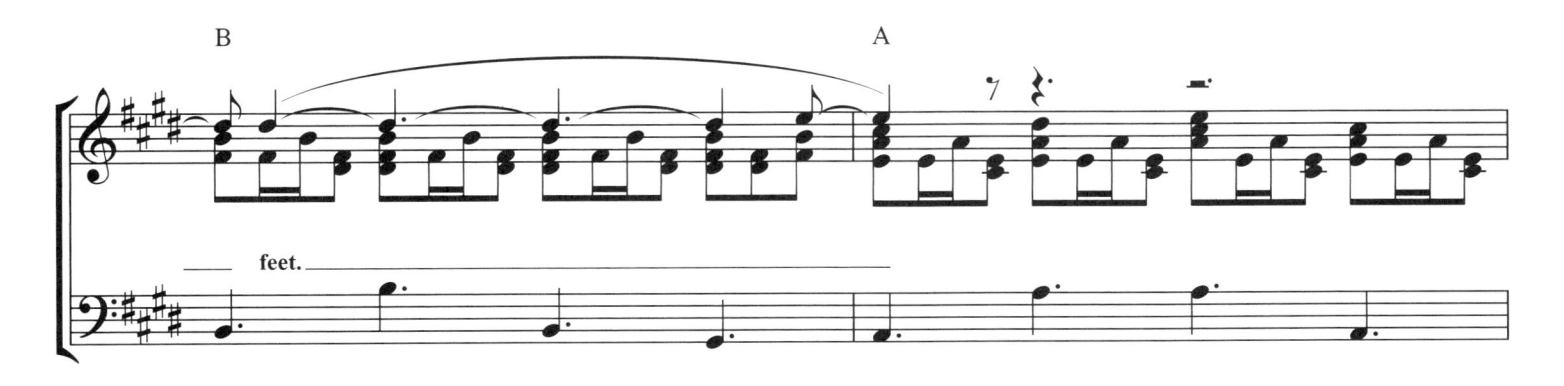

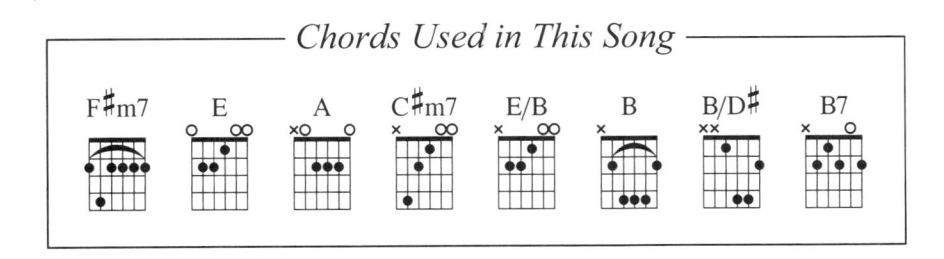

Yes And Amen

**Words and Music by
MATT REDMAN, ROBERT MARVIN
and JOSIAH BELL**

♩ = 75

Hear Your peo-ple say-ing yes, hear Your peo-ple say-ing yes to you.

Yes to an-y-thing You ask, Yes to an-y-thing we're called to do.

Hear Your peo-ple say a-men, Hear Your peo-ple say a-men

Copyright © 2006 Thankyou Music (PRS) (adm. worldwide by EMI CMG Publishing excluding the
UK and Europe, which is adm. by kingswaysongs.com) / Meaux Mercy (adm. by EMI CMG Publishing) / JLCB Music (BMI)
All rights reserved. Used by permission. CCLI Song No. 4835967

to You. Let Your kingdom come on earth,

Let it be just like we prayed to You. Yes and a-

men, to ev-'ry-thing that's in Your heart, Yes and a-

men, to ev-'ry-thing that You have planned. We

live to see Your will be done, And see Your perfect kingdom come on earth,

G Bm7 Em D
on the earth.
All the prom - is - es are yes,
Ev - 'ry good and per - fect gift,
Em D7/F♯ G D/F♯
1. G Bm
All the prom - is - es are yes in You.
Ev - 'ry bless - ing that we have was You.
2. G
Yes and a - men to ev - 'ry - thing that's in
men, we're tak - ing up our cross
Your heart Yes and a - men,
for You. Give us the strength
G/F♯
to ev - 'ry - thing that You
to take these dreams and fol -
have planned.
low through.
A/C♯
We live to see Your will be done And

175

176

G — men, to ev-'ry-thing that's in Your heart___ Yes and a-
men, we're tak-ing up___ our cross for You.___ Give us the

G/F# — men, to ev-'ry-thing___ that You have planned.___ We
strength to take these dreams___ and fol-low through.___

A/C# live to see___ Your will be done, **C** And see Your per-fect king-dom come on earth,___

G ___ on the earth,___ **1. Bm** Yes and a- **2. Bm**

G **D** **G** **C** **G**

177

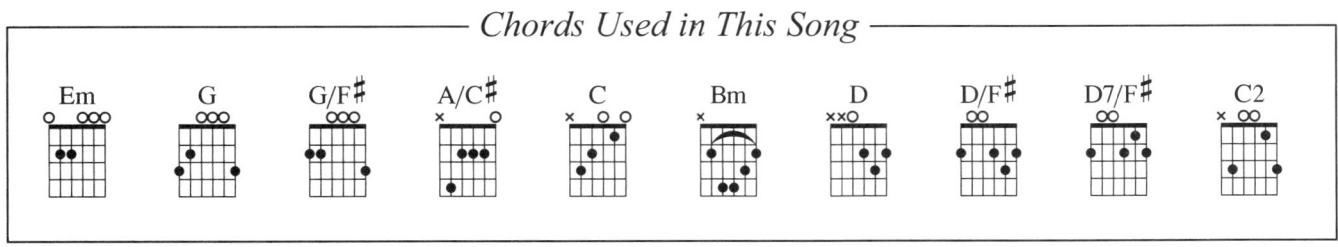

You Are God

Words and Music by
CHARLIE HALL

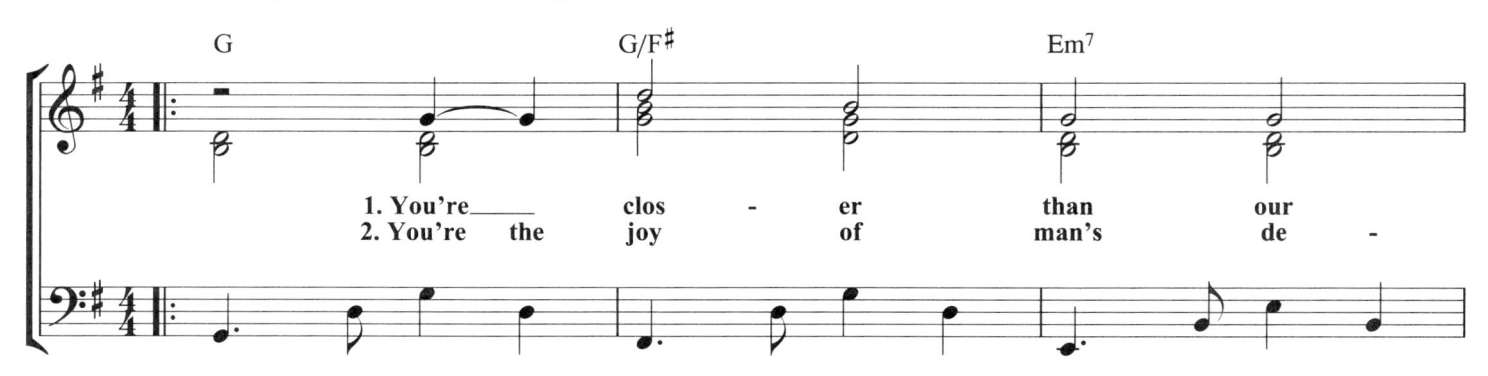

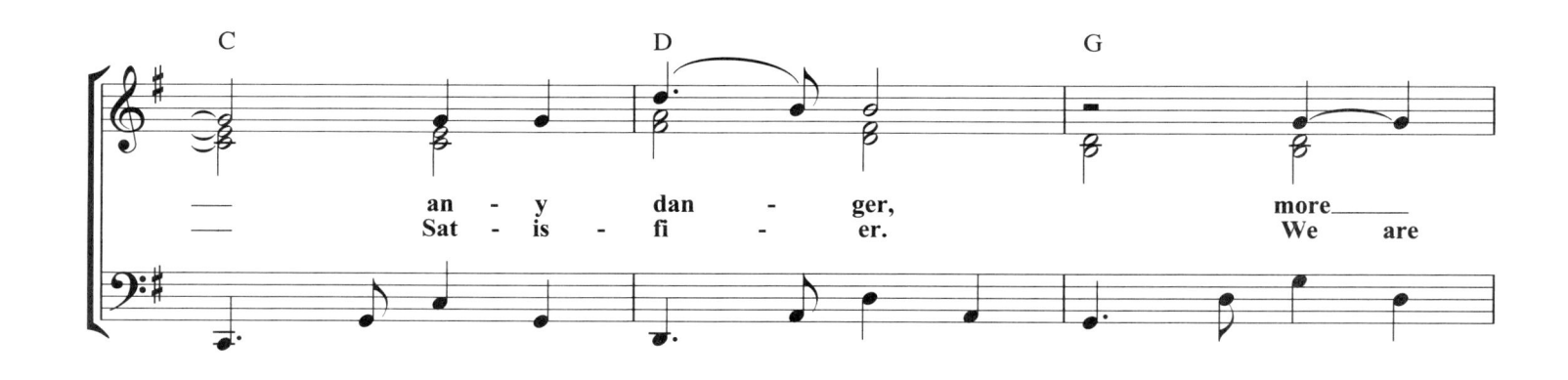

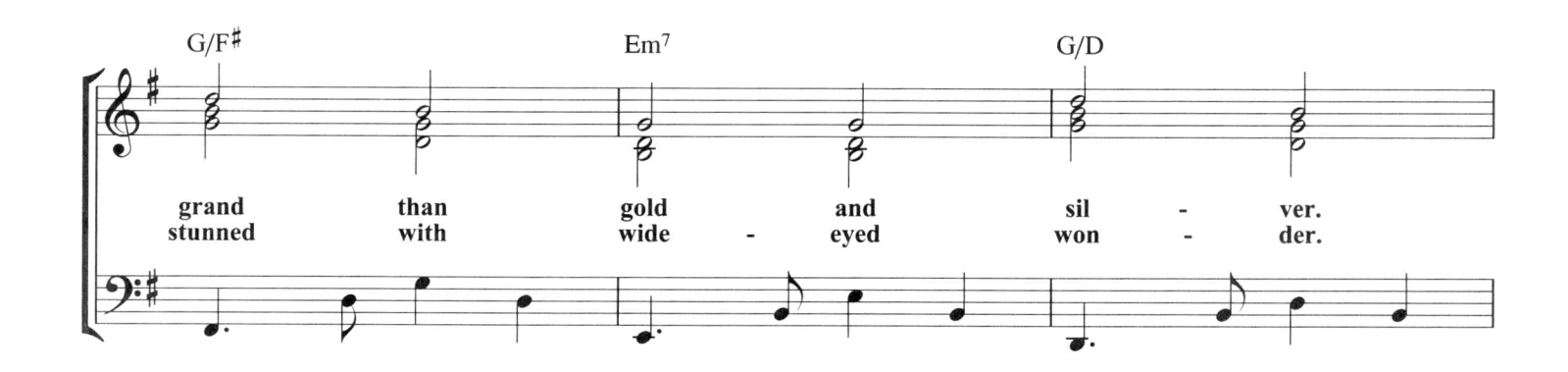

With joy ♩ = 140 (shuffle eighths)

1. You're closer than our troubles, more present than any danger, more grand than gold and silver.
2. You're the joy of man's desire; You are Father, Satisfier. We are stunned with wide-eyed wonder.

Copyright © 2007 worshiptogether.com Songs/sixsteps Music (ASCAP) (adm. by EMI CMG Publishing)
All right reserved. Used by permission. CCLI Song No. 4925303

C G/B C
You are God, You are
You are God, You are,
D G G/F♯
God.
God.
Em7 G/D C2 G/B
C2 1. D 2. D
G D/F♯ Em7
Fill our hearts with love and faith. You fight for us,

180

181

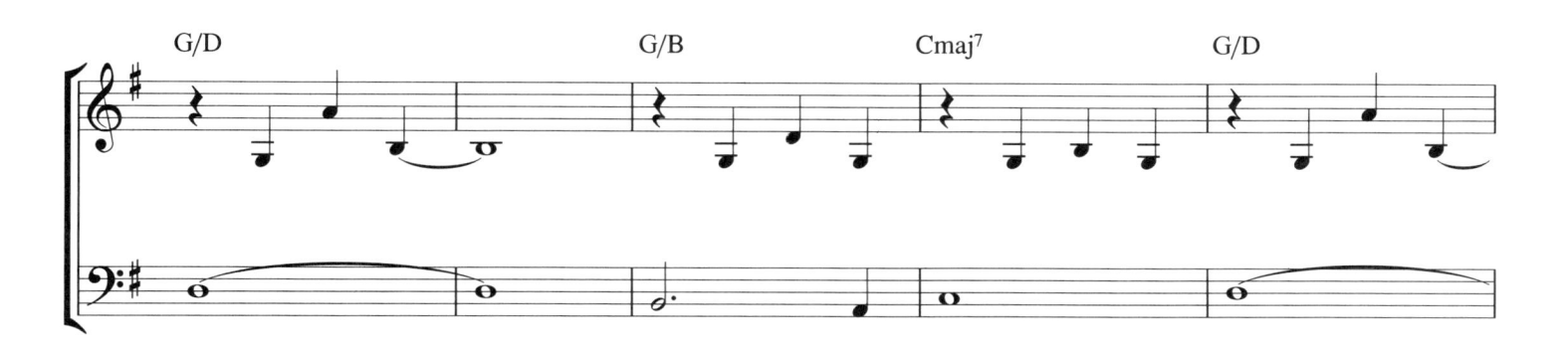

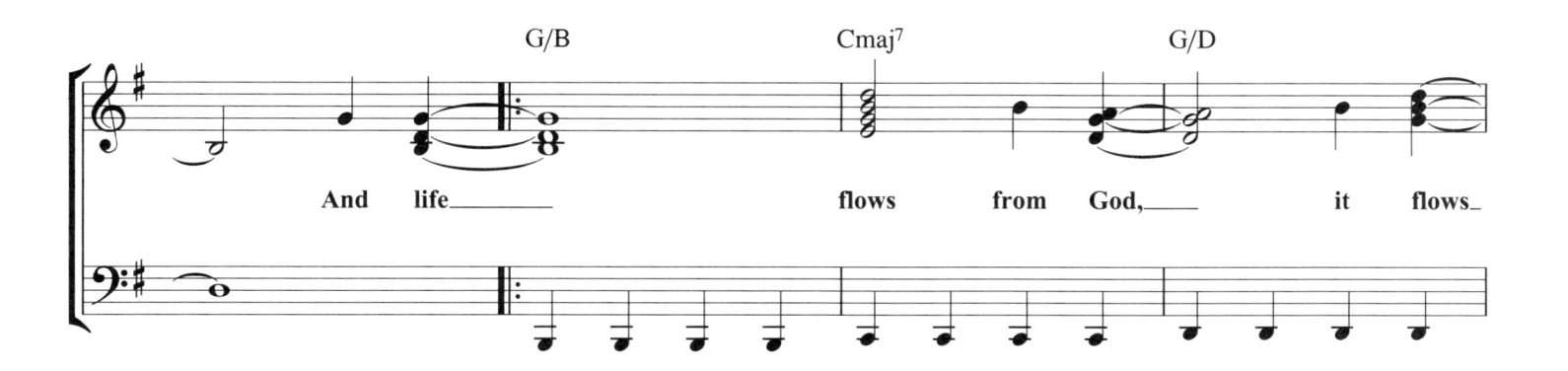

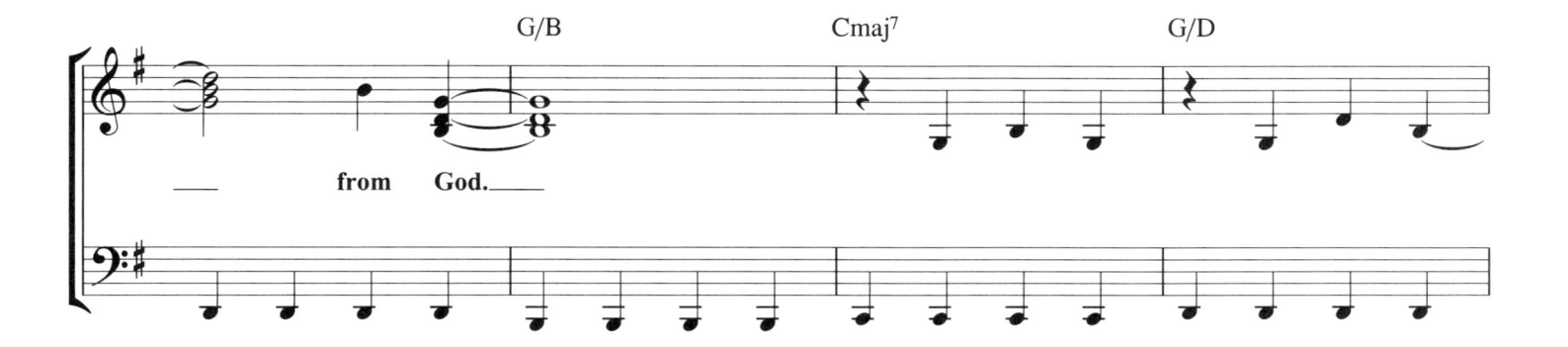

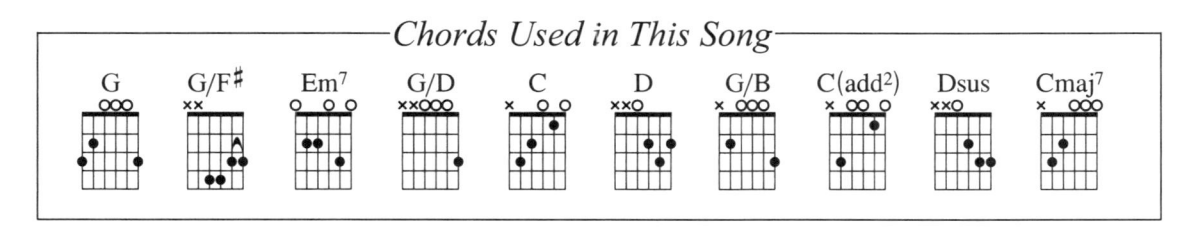

We Remember

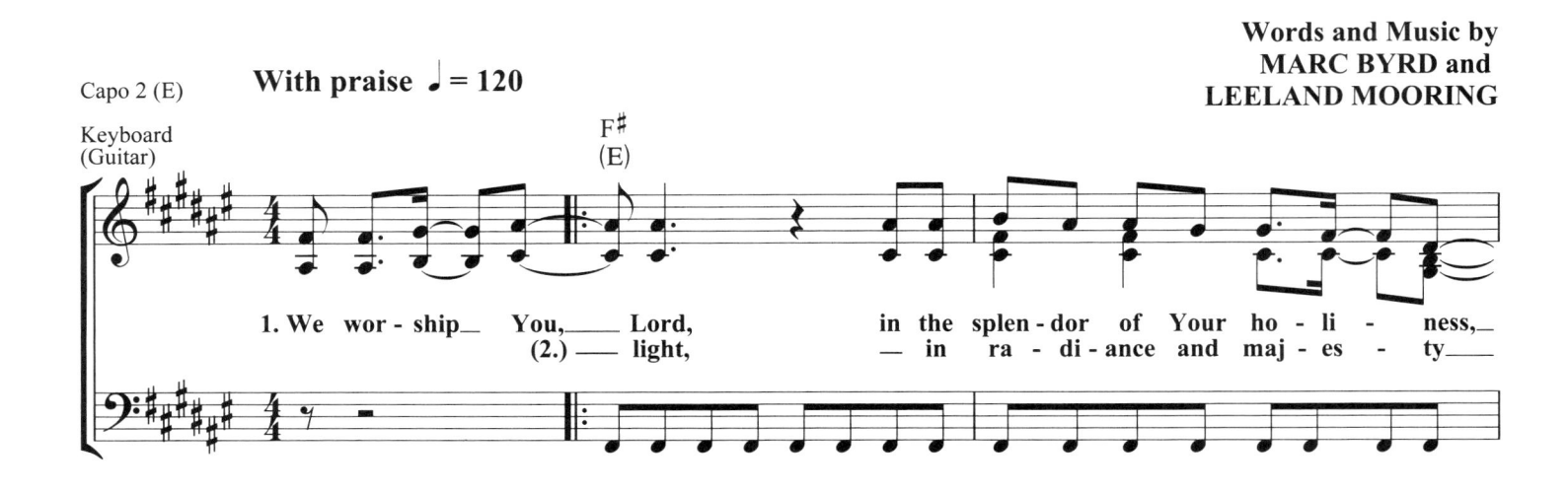

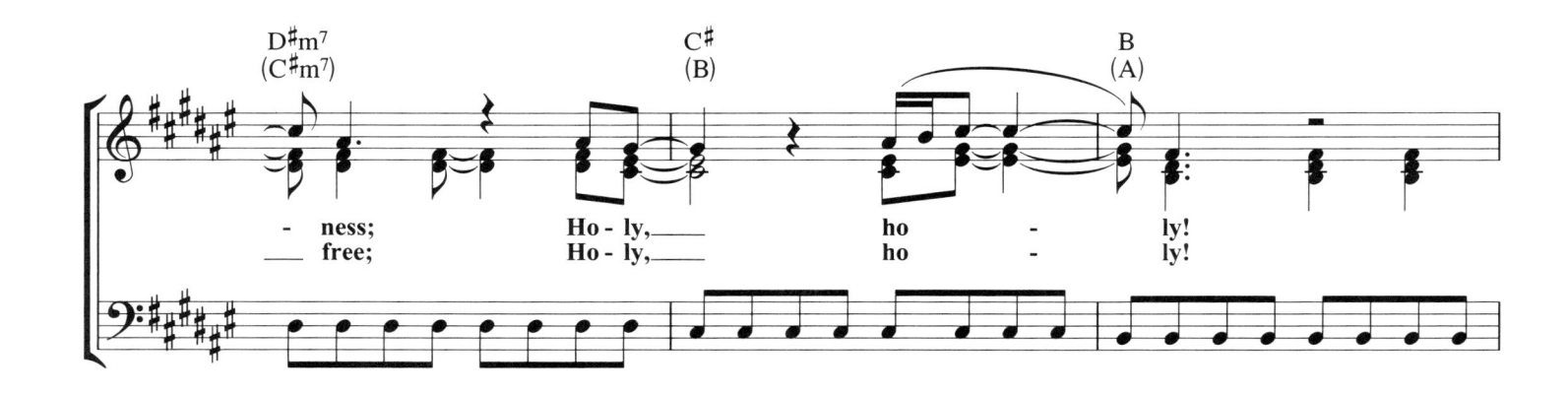

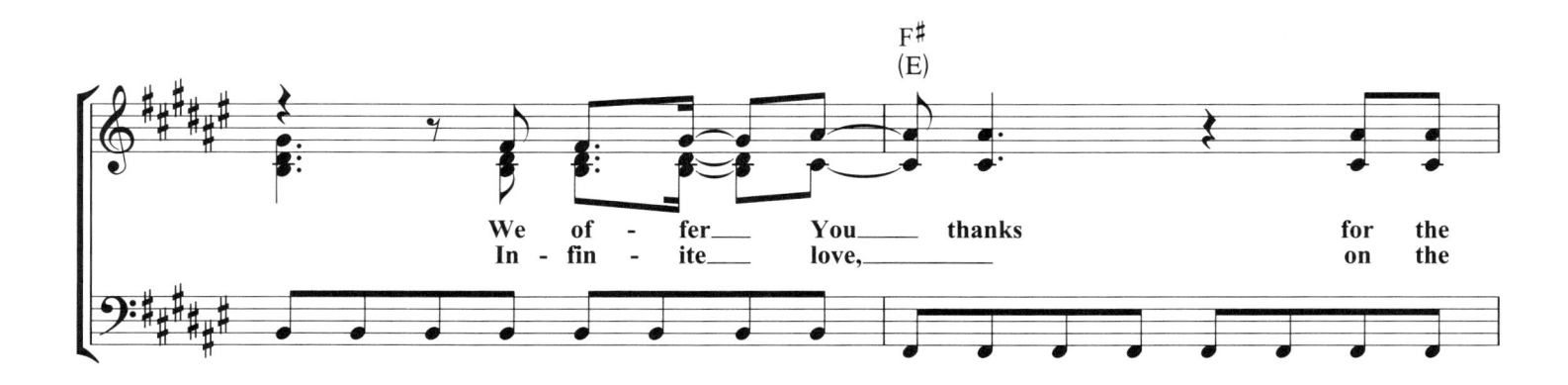

Words and Music by
MARC BYRD and
LEELAND MOORING

Capo 2 (E)
With praise ♩ = 120

Keyboard (Guitar)

1. We worship You, Lord, in the splendor of Your holiness,
(2.) light, in radiance and majesty

in the beauty of Your righteousness;
sent Your Son to set the captive free;

Holy, holy, holy!
Holy, holy, holy!

We offer You thanks for the
Infinite love, on the

Copyright © 2006 Meaux Mercy/Blue Raft Music (BMI) (adm. by EMI CMG Publishing)
All right reserved. Used by permission. CCLI #4255918

endless love You have dis - played, for the
cross You saved us from our sin, the con - quered

sac - ri - fice You free - ly gave; Wor - thy,
death and will re - turn a - gain; Wor - thy,

wor - thy! You are ho -
wor - thy!

- ly, pre - cious Lamb of God.

For - ev - er You will reign, for - ev -

C♯ (B)
- er You will reign. King of glo - ry,
D♯m7 (C♯m7)
B (A)
F♯/A♯ (E/G♯)
B (A)
ris - en Son of God. For - ev -
C♯ (B)
F♯/A♯ (E/G♯)
B (A)
3rd time to CODA
- er You will reign, fo - ev - er You will reign.
1.
F♯2 (E2)
B2(no3) (A2(no3))
2. Fa - ther of
2.
We re -

G♯m (F♯m)
F♯/A♯ (E/G♯)
B (A)
mem - ber, we re - mem - ber the cross.
C♯ (B)
B/D♯ (A/C♯)
C♯/E♯ (B/D♯)
We re - mem - ber, we re -
B/D♯ (A/C♯)
C♯/E♯ (B/D♯)
G♯m (F♯m)
mem - ber the cost. We re - mem - ber, Lord,
F♯/A♯ (E/G♯)
B (A)
C♯ (B)
we re - mem - ber the cross. We re -
B/D♯ (A/C♯)
C♯/E♯ (B/D♯)
B/D♯ (A/C♯)
mem - ber, we re - mem - ber the cost.

C#/E#
(B/D#)
D.S. al CODA
CODA
G#m
(F#m)
You are ho-
We re- mem - ber,
F#/A#
(E/G#)
B
(A)
C#
(B)
we re - mem - ber the cross.
We re -
B/D#
(A/C#)
F#maj7
(Emaj7)
B/D#
(A/C#)
C#/E#
(B/D#)
mem - ber,
we re - mem - ber the cost.

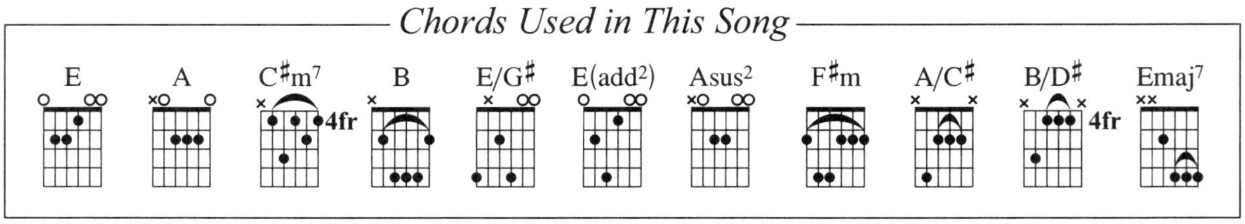
Chords Used in This Song
E
A
C#m7
4fr
B
E/G#
E(add2)
Asus2
F#m
A/C#
B/D#
4fr
Emaj7

You Are My God
(Like A Whisper)

Words and Music by
BRENTON BROWN

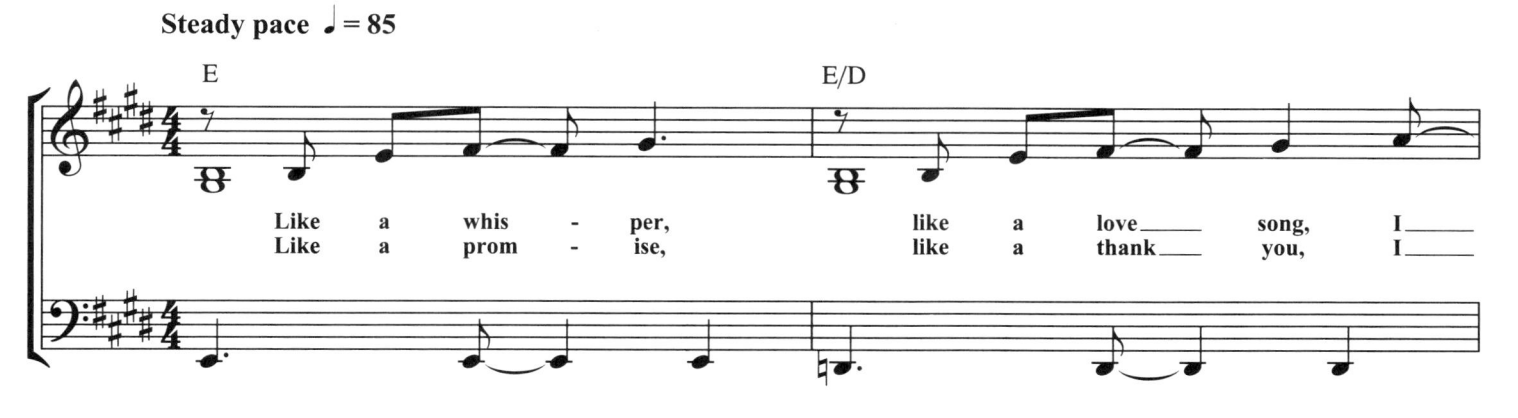

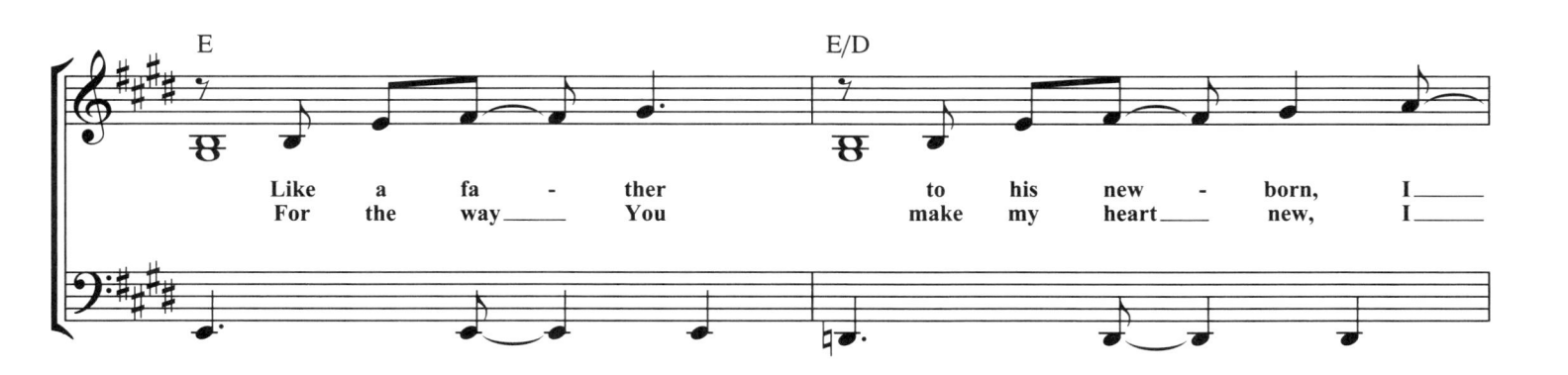

Steady pace ♩ = 85

Like a whis - per, like a love song, I can hear Your voice, I can hear Your voice. Like a fa - ther to his new - born, I can hear Your voice call - ing me: "You are My

Like a prom - ise, like a thank you, I will sing this song, I will sing this song. For the way You make my heart new, I will sing this song to You. You are my

Copyright © 2005 Thankyou Music (adm. worldwide by EMI CMG Publishing,
excluding the UK and Europe, which is administered by kingswaysongs.com)
All rights reserved. Used by permission. CCLI Song No. 4707590

child, you are My child, and I love
God, You are my God, and I love

you. You are My
You. You are my

child, you are My child, and I love
God, You are my God, and I love

1., 3. *Fine* *2.*

you." There is no
You.

A higher call, there's no greater reward than to know

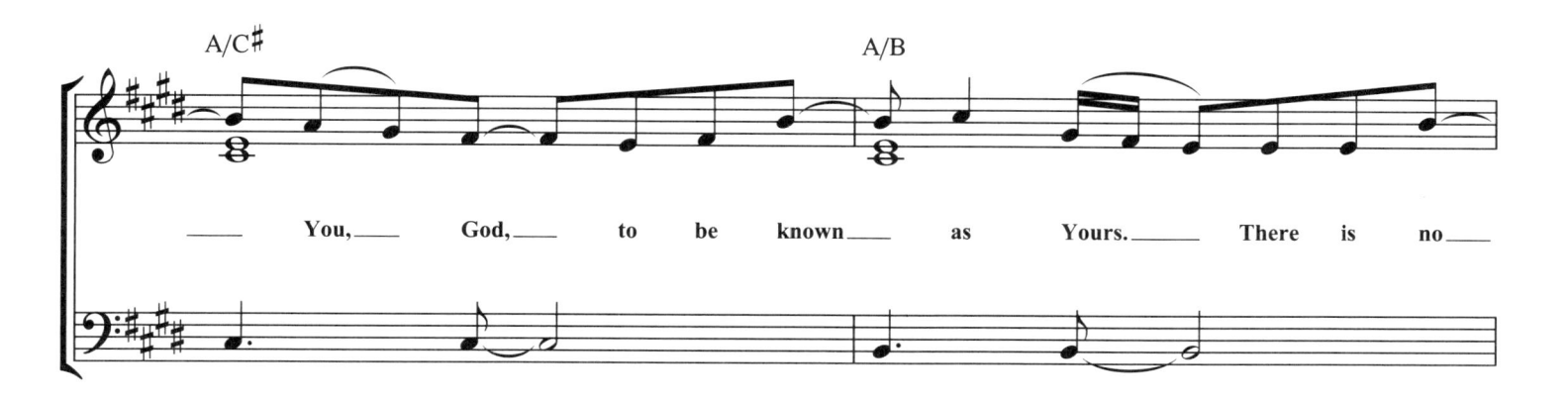

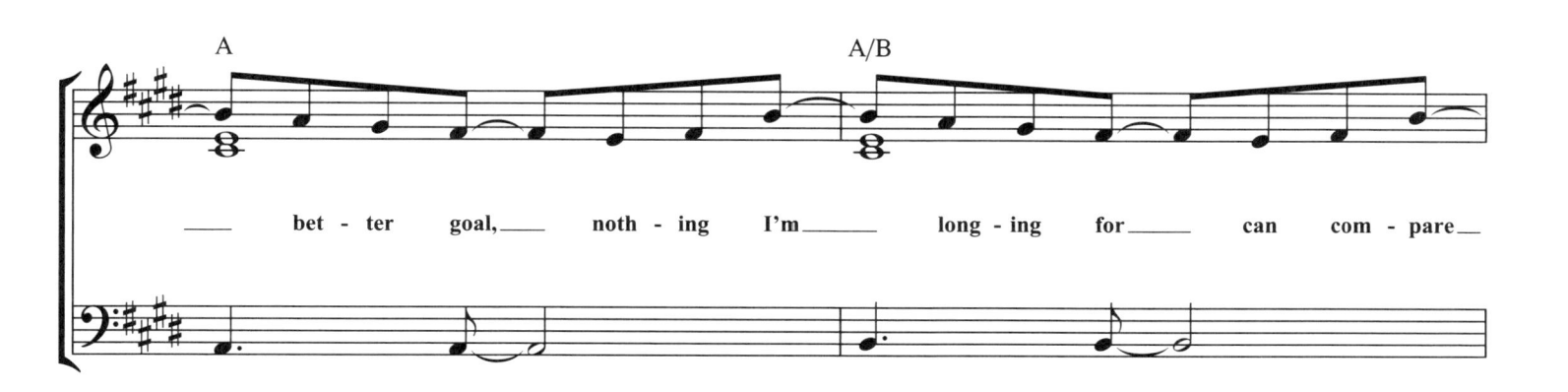

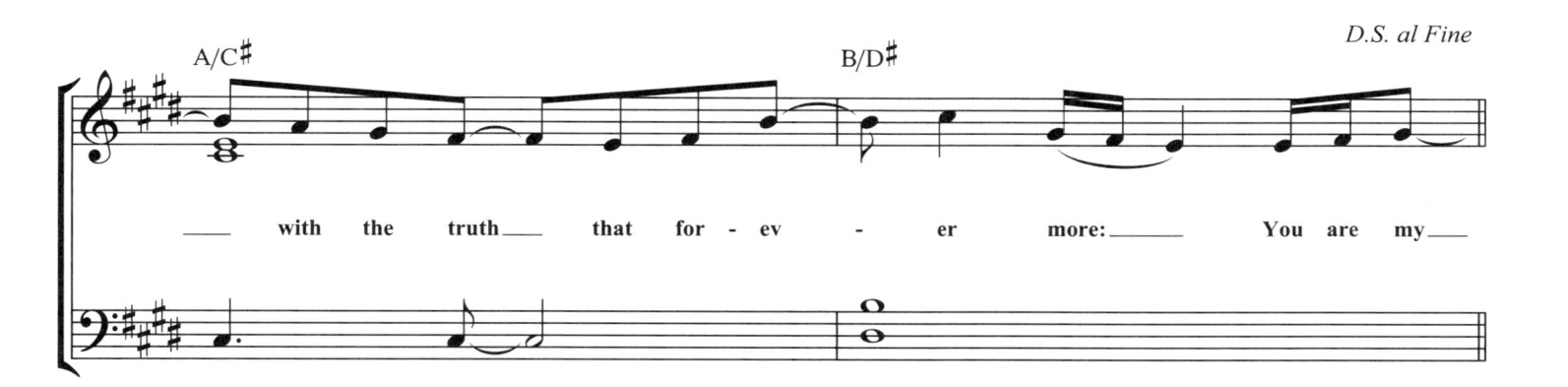

You, God, to be known as Yours. There is no better goal, nothing I'm longing for can compare with the truth that forevermore: You are my

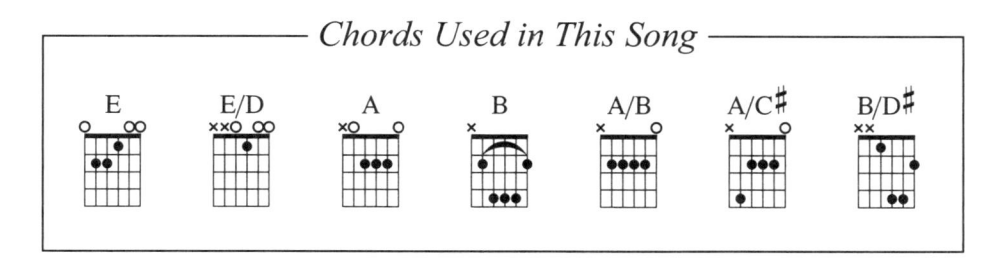

D.S. al Fine

Chords Used in This Song

E E/D A B A/B A/C# B/D#

Your Glory Endures Forever

Words and Music by
CHARLIE HALL

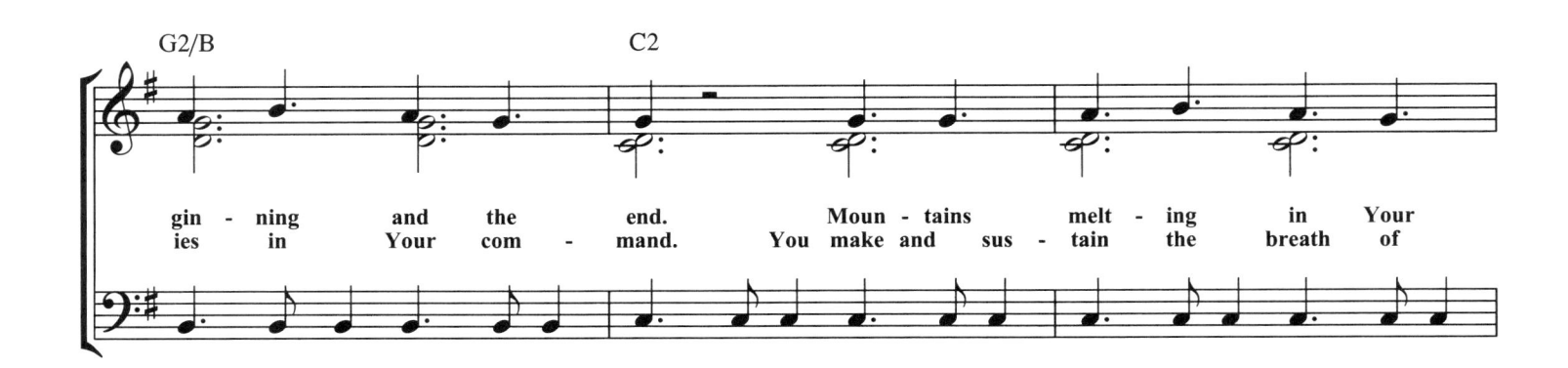

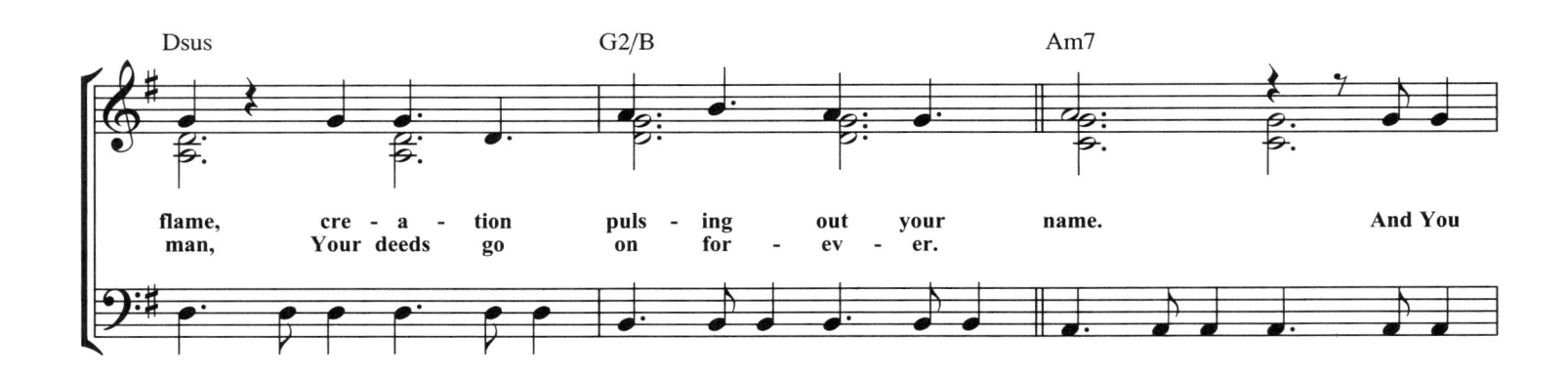

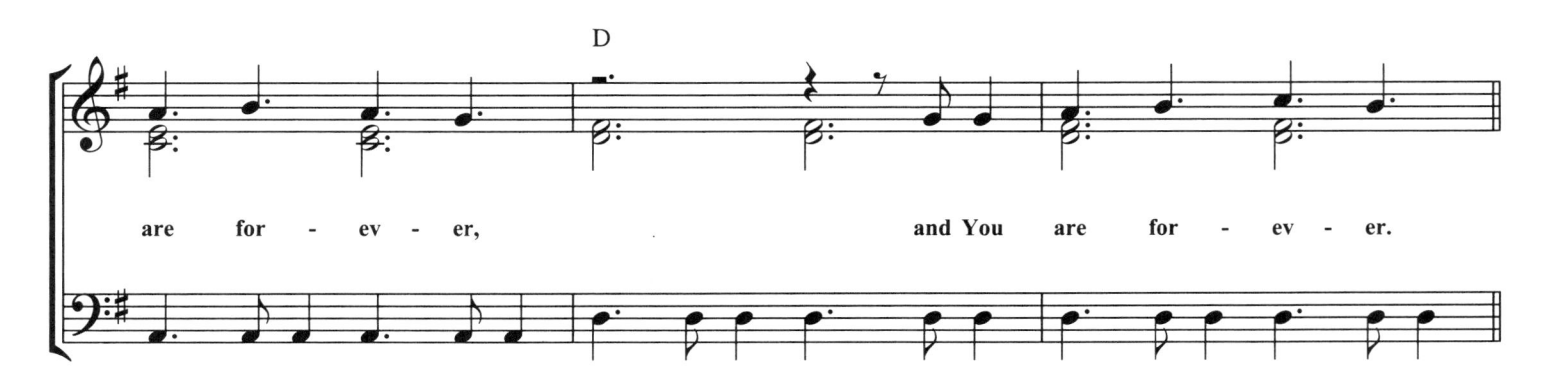

Slow Rock, in two ♩. = 54

Earth ro-ta-ting in Your hand, ga-lax-
And You ride on wings of wind, You are be-

-ies in Your com-mand. You make and sus-tain the breath of
-gin-ning and the end. Moun-tains melt-ing in Your

man, Your deeds go on for-ev-er.
flame, cre-a-tion puls-ing out your name. And You

are for-ev-er, and You are for-ev-er.

Copyright © 2005 worshiptogether.com Songs / sixsteps Music (ASCAP) (adm. by EMI CMG Publishing)
All rights reserved. Used by permission. CCLI Songs No. 4653620

191

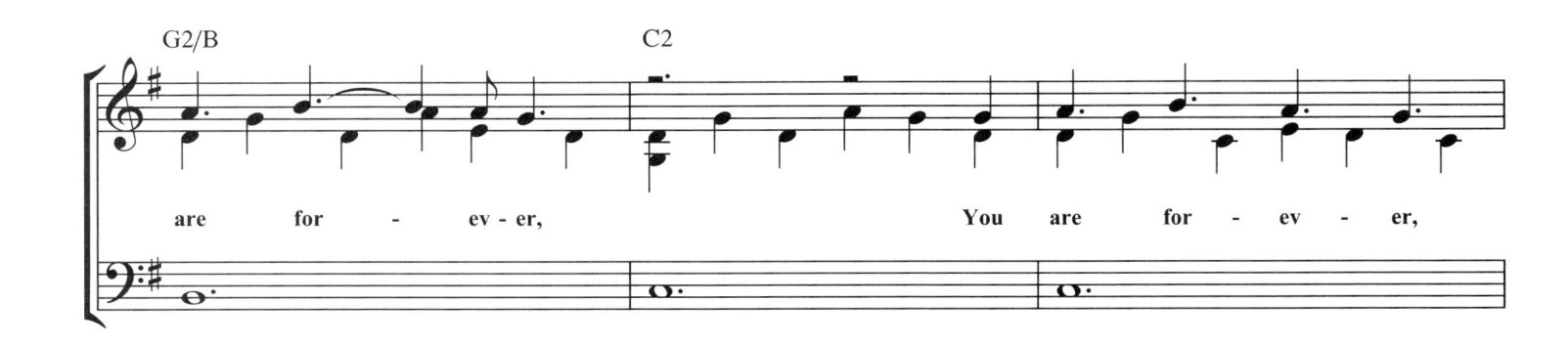

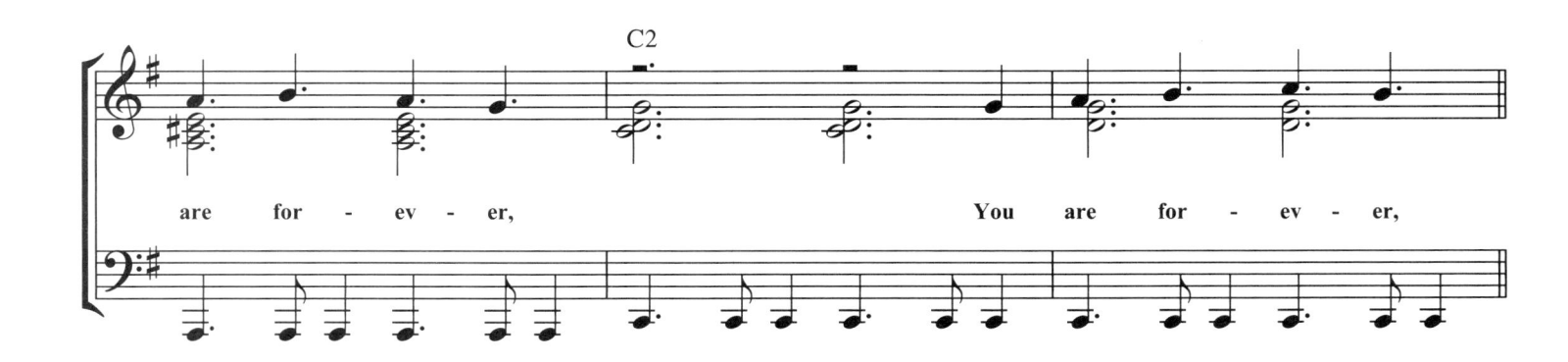

Your splen - dor, Your maj - es - ty.

You are for - ev - er, You are for - ev - er,

You are for - ev - er, You are for - ev - er,

You are for - ev - er, You are for - ev - er,

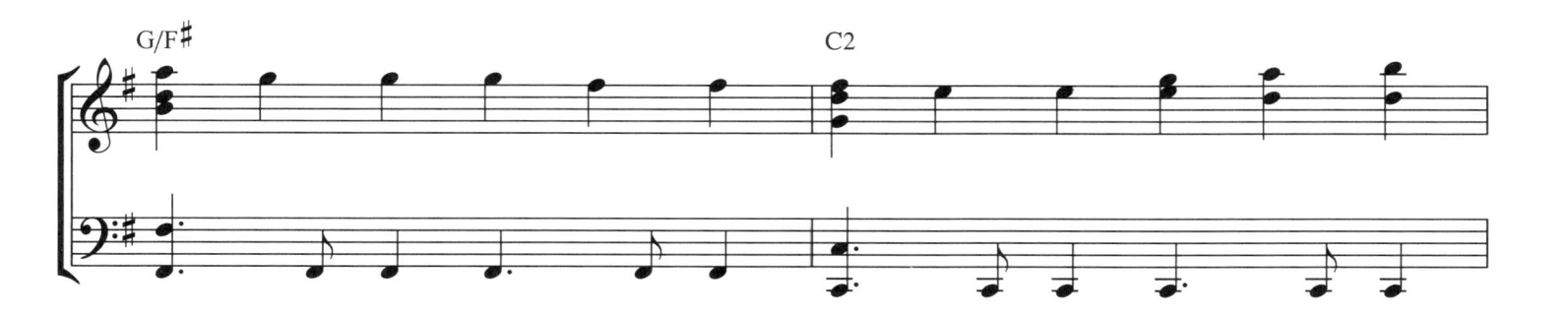

193

Your glo-ry en-dures for-ev-er,___ Your beau-ty out-shines the heav-ens.___ And we will de-clare Your won-ders, Your splen-dor, Your___ maj-es-ty.___

Em7
D
A
C2
G
Glo - ry, and ho - nor, and praise.
(Glo - ry, and ho - nor, and
G/F♯
C2
Glo - ry, and ho - nor, and praise.
praise.
Glo - ry, and ho - nor, and
Em7
D
Glo - ry, and ho - nor, and praise.
praise).

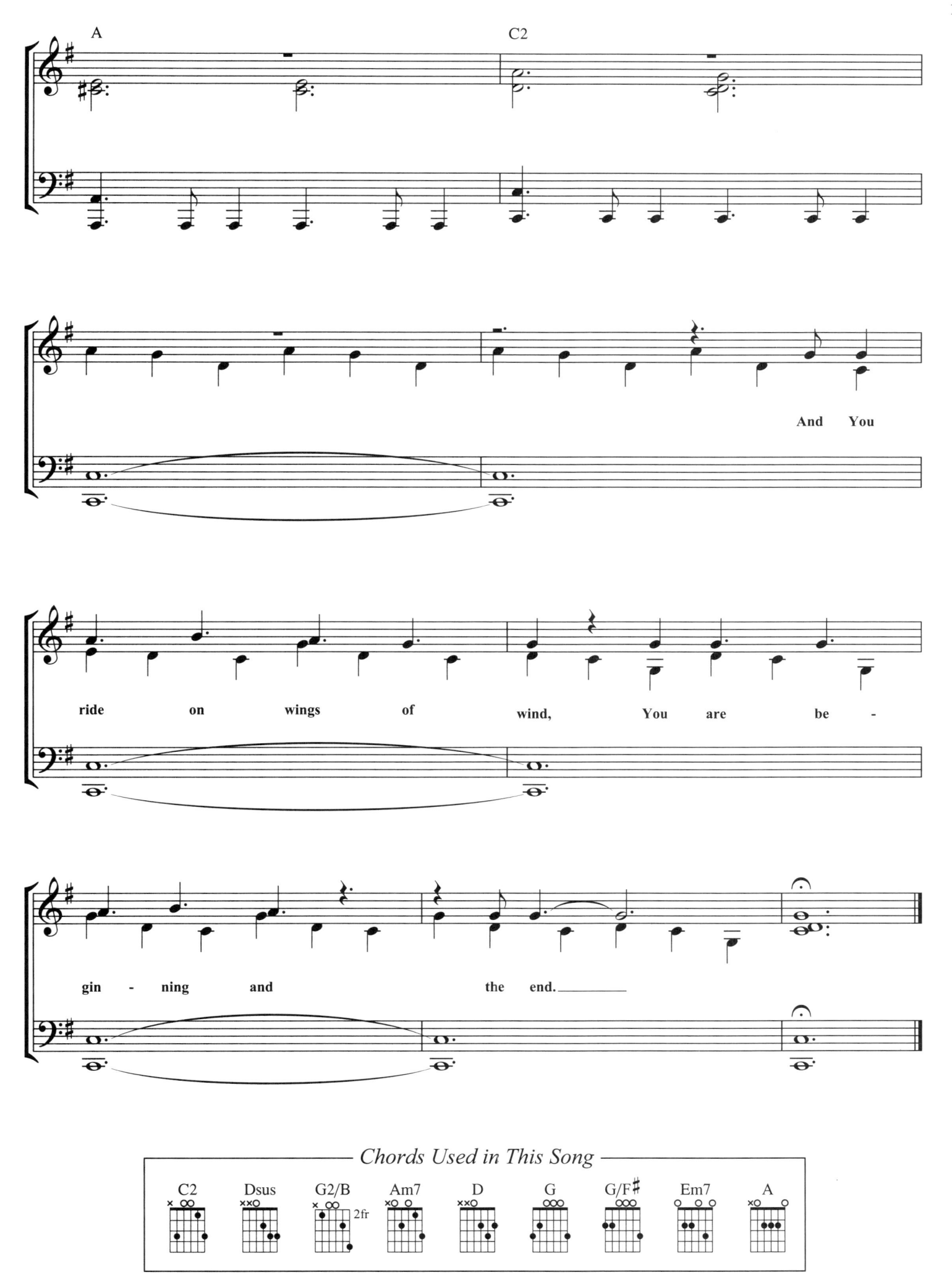

And You ride on wings of wind, You are beginning and the end.

Chords Used in This Song

C2   Dsus   G2/B   Am7   D   G   G/F#   Em7   A

A Greater Song

PAUL BALOCHE and MATT REDMAN

Capo 2 (G)

VERSE 1:

D   Bm⁷   C/E   C
Who could imagine a mel - ody,

D   Bm⁷   C
True enough to tell of Your mer - cy?

D   Bm⁷   C/E   C
Who could imagine a har - mony,

D   Bm⁷   C
Sweet enough to tell of Your love?

PRE-CHORUS:

           Em⁷
I see the heav - ens proclaiming You

D/F#
day   after day,

         G   C
And I know in my heart that there must be a way...

CHORUS 1:

           G   D/F#
To sing a great - er song,

   Em⁷   C
A great - er song to You on the earth.

           G   D/F#
To sing a great - er song,

   Em⁷   C
A great - er song to You on the earth.

VERSE 2:

D   Bm⁷   C/E   C
Who could imagine a sym - phony,

D   Bm⁷   C
Grand enough to tell of Your glo - ry?

D   Bm⁷   C/E   C
Our high - est praise but a fee - ble breath,

D   Bm⁷   C
A whisper of Your thunderous worth.

CONTINUED...

(REPEAT PRE-CHORUS)

(REPEAT CHORUS 1)

CHORUS 2:

G   D/F#
Hallelujah, we want to lift You higher.

F   C
Hallelujah, we want to lift You higher.

G   D/F#
Hallelujah, we want to lift You higher.

F   C
Hallelujah, we want to lift You higher.

Em⁷   F   Am⁷   F

Em⁷   C   Am⁷   F

(REPEAT PRE-CHORUS)

(REPEAT CHORUS 2 TWICE)

Copyright © 2006 Thankyou Music (PRS) (adm. worldwide by EMI CMG Publishing, excluding the UK and Europe, which is adm. by kingswaysongs.com)/ Integrity's Hosanna! Music (ASCAP) (c/o Integrity Media, Inc.) All rights reserved. Used by permission. CCLI Song No. 4662336

Adoration (Down In Adoration Falling)

THOMAS AQUINAS
Additional verse and chorus by MATT MAHER

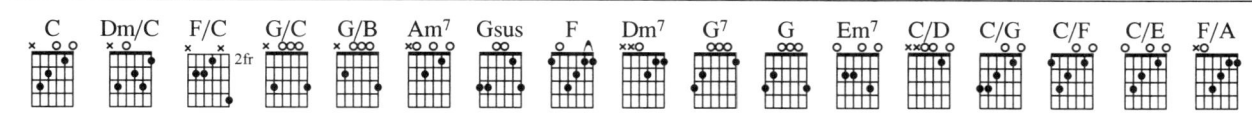

Capo 1 (C)

VERSE:

C   Dm/C
Down in ado - ration falling,

F/C   Dm/C   C
This great sacra - ment we hail;

            F/C
Over ancient forms departing,

                 G/C
Newer rites of grace pre - vail;

C   Dm/C
Faith for all de - fects supplying

F/C   Dm/C   C
Where the feeble senses fail.

PRE-CHORUS:

C
To the everlasting Father,

G/B
And the Son who reigns on high,

Am7
With the Spirit blest proceeding

Gsus
Forth from each eternally,

F
Be salvation, honor, blessing;

Dm7   G7   C
Might and endless majes - ty.

CHORUS 1:

(C)   F   G
 Jesus lamb of God, saving love for all,

               F   G
Lord of heaven and earth, Father's love for all;

   Am7   Em7   F
I bow   to   You.

CHORUS 2:

            G   F
Jesus lamb of God, saving love for all,

               G
Lord of heaven and earth,

   Am7   Em7   F   (G   C   )
I bow   to   You, (bow to You, I bow to You.) *Play first time only.*

CONTINUED...

INTERLUDE:

C   Dm7   C/D   Am7

C/G   C/F   Dm7

BRIDGE:

C   G/B
Pour upon us Lord of Mercy,

Am7   Gsus   F2
Spirit of Thy selfless love;

Am7   C/E
Make us of one true heart yearning

F   Am7   G/B
For the glory of Thy Son;

C   Dm7
Jesus, fire of justice blazing;

Am7   F   G   C
Gladdening light for - ever more.

(REPEAT CHORUS 1)

(REPEAT CHORUS 2 THREE TIMES)

ENDING:

       C   Dm7   C/E
I bow to You, bow to You, I bow to You,

       F/A   G   C
Bow to You, I bow to You.

F/C   C

Copyright © 2003 Thankyou Music (PRS) (adm. worldwide by EMI CMG Publishing, excluding the UK and Europe, which is adm. by kingswaysongs.com)
/spiritandsong.com (BMI) (adm. by EMI CMG Publishing) All rights reserved. Used by permission. CCLI Song No. 4729949

Amazing Grace (My Chains Are Gone)

Words and Music by JOHN NEWTON, JOHN P. REES and EDWIN OTHELLO EXCELL
Arrangement and additional chorus by CHRIS TOMLIN and LOUIE GIGLIO

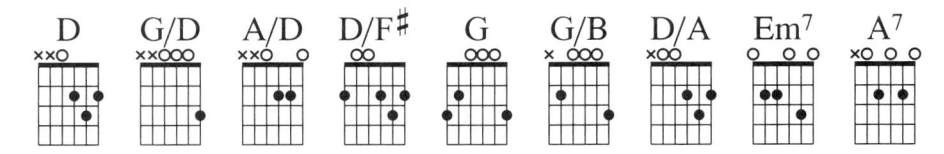

Capo 3 (D)

VERSE 1:

    D   G/D   D
Amaz - ing Grace, how   sweet the sound,

                    A/D
That saved a wretch like   me.

   D   D/F#   G   D
I once was lost, but now am found,

              A/D D
Was blind but now I see.

VERSE 2:

    D   G/D   D
'Twas Grace that taught my heart to fear,

              A/D
And Grace my fears re - lieved.

   D   D/F#   G   D
How pre - cious did that Grace appear,

        A/D   D
The hour I first believed.

CHORUS:

    D/F#   G   D/F#
My chains are gone, I've been set free,

          G/B   D/A
My God, my Savior has ransomed   me.

    D/F#   G   D/F#
And like a flood His mercy   reigns,

      Em7   A7   D
Unending love,   Amazing Grace.

CONTINUED...

VERSE 3:

    D   G/D   D
The Lord has promised good   to me,

                A/D
His word my hope secures.

   D   D/F#   G   D
He will my shield and por - tion be,

        A/D   D
As long as life endures.

(REPEAT CHORUS TWICE)

VERSE 4:

  G/D   D   G/D   D
The earth shall soon dissolve   like snow,

            A/D
The sun forbear to shine.

   D   D/F#   G   D
But God who called me here below,

       A/D   D
Will be for - ever mine,

       A/D   D
Will be for - ever mine,

      A/D   D
You are for - ever   mine.

Public Domain. Arr. Copyright © 2006 worshiptogether.com Songs/sixsteps Music (ASCAP) (adm. by EMI CMG Publishing)
All rights reserved. Used by permission. CCLI Song No. 4768151

Be Lifted High

LEELAND MOORING

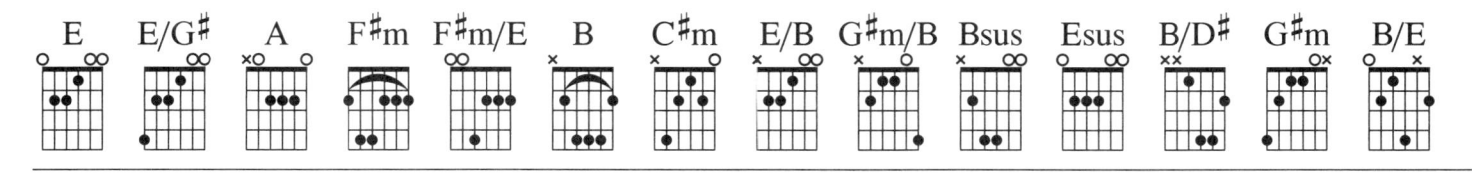

Capo 2 (E)

VERSE 1:

E   E/G#   A   E/G#
Sin and its ways   grow old,

F#m   F#m/E   B
All of my heart   turns to stone.

     C#m   E/B
And I'm left with no strength

   G#m/B   B   E/G#
to arise,

   F#m   Bsus   B   Esus   E
I need to be lift - ed high.

VERSE 2:

E   E/G#   A   E/G#
Sin and its ways   lead to pain,

F#m   F#m/E   B
Left here with hurt   and shame.

     C#m   E/B   B   E/G#
So no longer will I   leave Your side,

   F#m   Bsus   B   Esus E
Jesus, You be lift - ed high.

CHORUS:

A   E/G#   A   E/G#
You be lifted high,   You be lifted high,

F#m   F#m/E   B/D#
You be lifted high   in my life,

C#m   G#m   A
      oh   God.

   F#m   F#m/E   B/D#
And I fall to my knees   so it's You

              C#m   G#m   A
that they see,   not   I,

   F#m   Bsus   B   Esus E
Jesus, You be lift - ed high.

CONTINUED...

VERSE 3:

        E   E/G#
And even now that I'm in - side

           A   E/G#
Your hands,

          F#m   F#m/E   B
Help me not to grow pride - ful again.

         C#m   E/B   G#m/B   B   E/G#
Don't let me forsake   sac - rifice,

   F#m   Bsus   B   Esus E
Jesus, You be lift - ed high.

VERSE 4:

        E   E/G#
And if I'm blessed with the rich - es

       A   E/G#
of kings,

       F#m   F#m/E   B
How could I ever think that   it was me?

    C#m   E/B
For You brought me from dark - ness

G#m/B   B   E/G#
to light,

   F#m   Bsus   B   Esus E
Jesus, You be lift - ed high.

(REPEAT CHORUS TWICE)

   F#m   Bsus   B B/E   E   B/E   E
Jesus, You be lift - ed high.

Copyright © 2006 Meaux Mercy (BMI) (adm. by EMI CMG Publishing)
All rights reserved. Used by permission. CCLI Song No. 4831442

Be Praised

MICHAEL GUNGOR

Capo 2 (A)

VERSE 1:

A⁷   Em⁷
Prais - es to the One from whom it all began,
        A⁷
The One who formed the stars
                    Em⁷
and who gave life to man.
        Dmaj⁷
He set   the world in motion,
  F♯m⁷
creat - ed sky and ocean.
        Dmaj⁷
And here   I stand beloved and called by name.

CHORUS 1:

E   A   Em⁷
  Be praised, be praised!
  Bm⁷   Esus
Lis - ten to creation lift - ing up Your name.
E   A   Em⁷   Bm⁷
  Be praised, be praised, be praised!
Dmaj⁷   D⁶

VERSE 2:

A⁷   Em⁷
Prais - es to the One from whom it all began,
        A⁷
The One who gave Himself
        Em⁷
to save sin - ful man.
              Dmaj⁷
You scorned   the shame of Your cross.
  F♯m⁷
My sin,   my blame is now gone.
        Dmaj⁷
And here   I stand beloved and called by name.

(REPEAT CHORUS 1)

CONTINUED...

BRIDGE:

  F♯m⁷   E/G♯   F♯m/A   Dmaj⁷   Bm⁷
Oh,   oh, oh,   oh.
  F♯m⁷   E/G♯   F♯m/A   Dmaj⁷   Bm⁷
Oh,   oh, oh,   oh.

VERSE 3:

       A   Em⁷
All prais - es to the One from whom it all began,
        A
The One who conquered death
                    Em⁷
and who will come again.
            Dmaj⁷
The na - tions will behold You
       F♯m⁷
as ev - 'rything becomes new,
          Dmaj⁷
and there   I'll stand
                             E
beloved and called by name.

CHORUS 2:

          A   Em⁷
Be praised, be praised!
  Bm⁷
Lis - ten to Your people
  Esus   E
lift - ing up Your name.
          A   Em⁷   Bm⁷
Be praised, be praised, be praised!
        Dmaj⁷
(Oh!) *lyric 1st time only*

(REPEAT CHORUS 2)

D⁶   A

Copyright © 2007 worshiptogether.com Songs (ASCAP) (adm. by EMI CMG Publishing)
All right reserved. Used by permission. CCLI Song No. 4954903

Beautiful News

MATT REDMAN

Capo 5 (E)

VERSE:

E
Joy is the theme of my song,

And the beat of my heart,

                C   D
And that joy is found   in You.

   E
For You showed the pow'r of Your cross,

And Your great saving love,

            C   D
And my soul woke up   to You.

B   A
  I heard Your beautiful news,

B   A
  Grace so amazing, so true.

CHORUS:

A   E/A
  Shout it out, let the peo - ple sing,

   F
Some - thing so powerful should

G
Shake the whole wide world.

E   B/E
  Make it loud, make it lou - der still,

  C
Sav - ior, we're singing now

  D
To celebrate Your beautiful news.

(E   C D)*   (E)**
*(1st time only)   **(3rd time only)

(REPEAT VERSE)

(REPEAT CHORUS TWICE)

CONTINUED...

BRIDGE:

Am   G   E
  There's a God who came down   to save,

Am   G   E
  Showed the world His amaz - ing grace.

Am   G   E
  There's a God who came down   to save,

      C   A   A^7
And   He calls your name.

CHORUS:

E
  Shout it out, let the people sing,

   C
Some - thing so powerful should

D
shake the whole wide world.

(Shake the whole wide world,

Shake the whole wide world,

Shake the whole wide world.)

(REPEAT CHORUS)

ENDING:

E   C   D
                        To celebrate Your beautiful news,

E   C   D   E
                  beautiful news.

Copyright © 2006 Thankyou Music (PRS) (adm. worldwide by EMI CMG Publishing, excluding the UK and Europe, which is adm. by kingswaysongs.com).
All rights reserved. Used by permission. CCLI Song No. 4836007

Captivated

VICKY BEECHING

KEY OF (E)

A²   B⁷sus   C♯m   C♯m⁷   B   F♯m⁷   E/G♯   A²/C♯   E   B⁷sus/F♯   B⁷   Bsus

VERSE 1:

A²   B⁷sus   C♯m
   Your laughter it echoes   like a joyous thunder,
A²   C♯m   B⁷sus
   Your whisper it warms me like a   summer breeze.
A²   B⁷sus   C♯m⁷
   Your anger is fiercer   than the sun in its splendor,
A²   C♯m⁷   B
You're close and   yet full of mystery.
           F♯m⁷   E/G♯
And ever since the   day
         A²
that I saw Your   face,
     F♯m⁷   E/G♯   A²   B⁷sus
Try as I   may,   I cannot look away,
      A²/C♯   B⁷sus
I cannot look away...

CHORUS:

E   B⁷sus/F♯   E/G♯   A²
Capti - vated by   You,
    E   B⁷sus/F♯   E/G♯   A²
I am capti - vated by   You.
C♯m   B   A²   E/G♯
May my life be one unbroken gaze,

CHORUS ENDING 1:

F♯m⁷   B⁷   E
Fixed upon the beau - ty of   Your face.
B⁷sus/F♯   E/G♯   A²

VERSE 2:

A²   B⁷sus   C♯m
   Beholding is becoming,   so as You fill my gaze,
A²   C♯m   B⁷sus
   I become more like You   and my heart is changed.
A²   B⁷sus   C♯m⁷
   Beholding is becoming,   so as You fill my view,
A²   C♯m⁷   B
   Transform me into the   likeness of You.
        F♯m⁷   E/G♯   A²
This is what I   ask,   for all my   days,
     F♯m⁷   E/G♯   A²   B⁷sus
That I   may   never look away,
     A²/C♯   B⁷sus
never look away...

CONTINUED...

(REPEAT CHORUS)

CHORUS ENDING 2:

B⁷sus/F♯   E/G♯
Fixed upon Your beauty,
A²
Fixed upon Your beauty.

BRIDGE:

Bsus   A²   E/G♯
   No other could ever be as beautiful,
Bsus   B   A²   E/G♯
   No other   could ever steal my heart   away.
Bsus   A²   E/G♯
   No other could ever be as beautiful,
Bsus   A²   E/G♯
   No other could ever steal my heart   away.
F♯m⁷   E/G♯   A²

          C♯m⁷   B⁷sus/F♯   E/G♯   A²
I just can't look away...

(REPEAT CHORUS)

ENDING:

B⁷sus/F♯   E/G♯
Fixed upon the beauty,
A²   C♯m⁷
Fixed upon the beauty,
B⁷sus/F♯   Bsus   B
Fixed upon the beau - ty
    E   B⁷sus/F♯
of   Your face.
E/G♯   A²   E
   The beau - ty of Your face.
B⁷sus/F♯   E/G♯   A²

Copyright ©2005 Thankyou Music (PRS) (adm. worldwide by worshiptogether.com Songs excluding the UK and Europe, which is adm. by kingswaysongs.com).
All rights reserved. Used by permission. CCLI Song No. 4673703

Carried To The Table

LEELAND MOORING, MARC BYRD and STEVE HINDALONG

KEY OF (A)

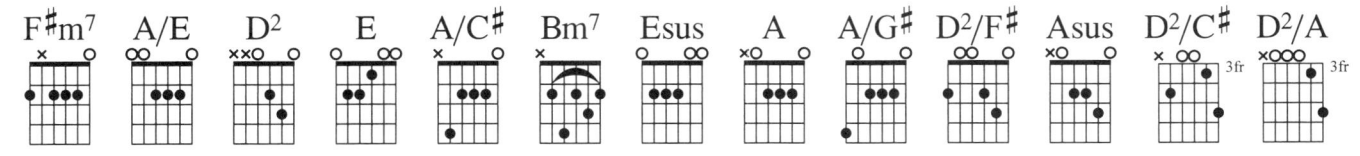

F#m7 A/E D2 E A/C# Bm7 Esus A A/G# D2/F# Asus D2/C# D2/A

VERSE 1:

F#m7   A/E
Wounded and forsaken,
     D2   E
I was shattered by the fall,
F#m7   A/E
Broken and forgotten,
     D2   A/C#
feeling lost and all alone.
Bm7
Summoned by the King
    Esus   E
into   the master's courts,
Bm7
Lifted by the Savior
   Esus   E
and cradled in His arms.

CHORUS OPENING 1:

       A/C#   D2   A/C#
I was carried to the ta - ble,

CHORUS:

Bm7   E   A   A/G#
   seated where I don't belong,
D2/F#   A/C#   D2   A/C#
   Carried to the ta - ble,
Bm7   E   A
   swept a - way by His love.
   Bm7   Asus   Esus
And I don't see my bro - kenness any - more,
E   Bm7   Asus   Esus
  When I'm seated at the ta - ble of the Lord.
 E   A/C#   D2   D2/C#
I'm carried to the ta - ble,
Bm7   E   (A   A/G#)*
   the table of the Lord.   *1st time only

VERSE 2:

F#m7   A/E
Fighting thoughts of fear,
     D2   E
wond'ring why He called my name,
   F#m7   A/E
Am I good enough to share this cup,
    D2   A/C#
this world has left me lame.

(CONTINUED...)

Bm7
Even in my weakness,
     Esus   E
the Savior called my name.
Bm7
In His Holy presence,
     Esus   E
I'm healed and una - shamed.

CHORUS OPENING 2:

        A/C#   D2   A/C#
As I'm carried to the ta - ble,

(REPEAT CHORUS)

INTERLUDE 1:

D2/F#   A/E   D2/F#   A/E

D2/F#   A/E   Bm7

CHORUS OPENING 3:

    E   A/C#   D2
I'm carried to the ta - ble

(REPEAT CHORUS)

INTERLUDE 2:

D2/A   A   D2/A   A

D2/A   A   Bm7   E

ENDING:

D2/A   A
   You carried me   my God,
D2/A   A
   You carried me.
D2/A   A
   You carried me   my God,
Bm7   E
   You carried me.

(REPEAT ENDING FIVE TIMES AND FADE)

Copyright © 2006 Meadowgreen Music Company (ASCAP)/Meaux Mercy/Blue Raft Music (BMI) (adm. by EMI CMG Publishing)
All rights reserved. Used by permission. CCLI Song No. 4681678

Closer

CHARLIE HALL, KENDALL COMBES, DUSTIN RAGLAND and BRIAN BERGMAN

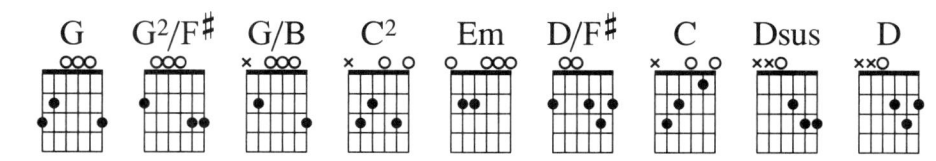

Chords: G, G²/F♯, G/B, C², Em, D/F♯, C, Dsus, D

Capo 3 (G)

VERSE:

G   G²/F♯   G/B   C²
Beautiful are the words   spoken to me,

G   G²/F♯   G/B   C²

G   G²/F♯   G/B   C²
Beautiful is the one   who is speaking.

G   G²/F♯   G/B   C²

(REPEAT VERSE)

CHORUS 1:

G   G²/F♯   G/B   C²
Come in close,

G   G²/F♯   G/B   C²
come in close   and speak,

G   G²/F♯   G/B   C²
Come in close,   come closer to me.

G   G²/F♯   G/B   C²

(REPEAT VERSE)

(REPEAT CHORUS 1)

INTERLUDE:

G   G²/F♯   G/B   C²

(CONTINUED...)

BRIDGE:

         G   G²/F♯
And the power of Your words

         G/B   C²
Are filled with grace and mercy.

         G   G²/F♯   G/B   C²
Let them fall on my ears and break my stony heart.

(REPEAT BRIDGE)

CHORUS 2:

Em   D/F♯   G   C
Come in close,   come in close and speak,

Em   Dsus   C²
Come in close,   come closer to me.

Dsus   D   *Sung 2nd time only*
 (Come closer to me.)*

(REPEAT CHORUS 2)

(REPEAT INTERLUDE)

(REPEAT BRIDGE TWICE)

(REPEAT CHORUS TWICE)

ENDING:

G

Copyright © 2005 worshiptogether.com Songs/sixsteps Music (ASCAP) (adm. by EMI CMG Publishing)
All rights reserved. Used by permission. CCLI # 4665302

Created To Worship

VICKY BEECHING

KEY OF (E)

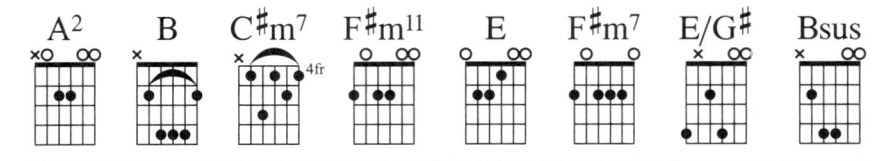

A². B. C#m⁷. F#m¹¹. E. F#m⁷. E/G#. Bsus

VERSE 1:

A². B. C#m⁷
   You formed us from   the dust,

A². B. C#m⁷
   You breathed Your breath   in us.

A². B. C#m⁷. F#m¹¹
   We are the work   of Your hands.

A². B. C#m⁷
   Now we breathe back   to You

A². B. C#m⁷
   Love songs of grat - itude,

A². B. C#m⁷. F#m¹¹
   A - doring You   with all we have.

CHORUS:

               A². C#m⁷
'Cause we were creat - ed

B. E. A². C#m⁷
   To worship Your   name,

B. E. A². C#m⁷
   And we were crea - ted

B. E. A². C#m⁷. B
   To bring You our   praise.

VERSE 2:

A². B. C#m⁷
   If we don't wor - ship You,

A². B. C#m⁷
   We'll search for sub - stitutes

A². B. C#m⁷. F#m¹¹
   To fill the void   in our souls.

A². B. C#m⁷
   Wor - shiping oth - er things

A². B. C#m⁷
   De - stroys our lib - erty.

A². B. C#m⁷. F#m¹¹
   But as we praise   You, we are free.

CONTINUED...

(REPEAT CHORUS)

BRIDGE:

               A². C#m⁷
So we will wor - ship,

B. E. A². C#m⁷
   And so we will   praise.

B. E. F#m⁷
   You are Creat - or

E/G#. A²
   For all our days.

A². C#m⁷. A². C#m⁷

ENDING:

        A². C#m⁷
For this is what we were made to do,

A². C#m⁷
This is what we were made to do.

A². C#m⁷
This is what we were made to do,

A². Bsus. B
So we lift up our praise to You.

A². C#m⁷. A². C#m⁷. A²

Copyright © 2004 Thankyou Music (PRS) (adm. worldwide by EMI CMG Publishing excluding the UK and Europe which is adm. by kingswaysongs.com).
All rights reserved. Used by permission. CCLI Song No. 3994713

Everything

TIM HUGHES

KEY OF (C)

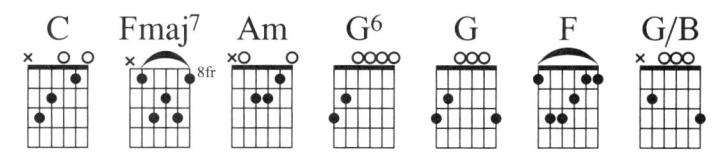

C   Fmaj7   Am   G6   G   F   G/B

VERSE 1:

       C   Fmaj7
God in my liv - ing, there in my breath - ing.

       Am   G6
God in my wak - ing, God in my sleep - ing

       C   Fmaj7
God in my rest - ing, there in my work - ing.

       Am   G6
God in my think - ing, God in my speak - ing.

CHORUS:

      Fmaj7 G   Am G
Be my ev - 'rything,   be my every - thing.

      Fmaj7 G   C
Be my ev - 'rything,   be my every - thing.

VERSE 2:

       C   Fmaj7
God in my hop - ing, there in my dream - ing.

       Am   G6
God in my watch - ing, God in my wait - ing.

       C   Fmaj7
God in my laugh - ing, there in my weep - ing.

       Am   G6
God in my hurt - ing, God in my heal - ing.

(REPEAT CHORUS)

BRIDGE:

F   G
  Christ in me, Christ in me,

Am
    Christ in me the hope of glory,

CONTINUED...

BRIDGE ENDING 1:

F   G   Am
  You   are everything.

(REPEAT BRIDGE)

BRIDGE ENDING 2:

F   G   Am   G/B
  Be my every - thing.

(REPEAT CHORUS TWICE)

(REPEAT VERSE 2)

(REPEAT BRIDGE & BRIDGE ENDING 1)

ENDING CHORUS 1:

         Fmaj7   G
You are every - thing,

         Am   G
You are every - thing.

         Fmaj7   G
You are every - thing,

         C
You are every - thing.

ENDING CHORUS 2:

        Fmaj7   G
Jesus every - thing,

        Am   G
Jesus every - thing.

        Fmaj7   G   C
Jesus every - thing, Jesus every - thing.

Copyright © 2005 Thankyou Music (PRS) (adm. worldwide by EMI CMG Publishing excluding the UK and Europe which is adm. by kingswaysongs.com).
All rights reserved. Used by permission. CCLI Song No. 4685258

Forever Holy

BEN CRIST

D F#m E E/G# A D² Esus C#m⁷

Capo 2 (A)

VERSE 1:

D	F#m	E	E/G#	D	F#m	E	E/G#

God, You stand when all has fall - en.

D	F#m	E	E/G#	D	F#m	E	E/G#

You em - brace the long for - got - ten.

PRE-CHORUS:

D   E
  I guess it's just hard to believe

D   E
  The grace You pour out on me.

D   E
  I guess I'm just starting to see

D   E
  How You're working in me.

CHORUS:

A   E/G#
This is what makes my head spin;

F#m   E
You're forever holy.

D   F#m
God of all cre - ation,

D   E
Pour Your life in - to me.

A   E/G#
This is so over - whelming,

F#m   E
You're forever holy.

D   F#m
God of my sal - vation,

D   E
Clothe me in Your glory, yeah.

(D²   F#m   Esus   E   C#m⁷) *1st time only*

CONTINUED...

VERSE 2:

D²	F#m	E	C#m⁷	D²	F#m	E	C#m⁷

God, You hold when all is break - ing.

D²	F#m	E	C#m⁷	D²	F#m	E	C#m⁷

You re - store the tired and ach - ing.

(REPEAT PRE-CHORUS & CHORUS)

BRIDGE:

D   Esus   D   Esus

                          D   Esus
Clothe me in Your glory.

                          D   Esus
Clothe me in Your glory.

(REPEAT CHORUS TWICE)

ENDING:

D   E   D
Clothe me in Your glory.

Copyright © 2006 Spinning Audio Vortex, Inc. (BMI) (adm. by EMI CMG Publishing)
All rights reserved. Used by permission. CCLI Song No. 4943330

Give Me Jesus

JEREMY CAMP

KEY OF (C)

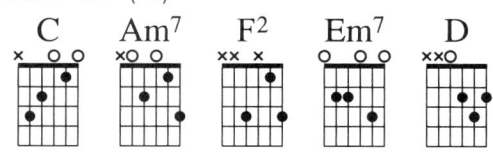

C   Am⁷   F²   Em⁷   D

VERSE 1:

        C   Am⁷
In the morn - ing when I rise,

        F²   C
In the morn - ing when I rise,

      Am⁷   F²
In the morn - ing when I rise,

     C
Give me Je - sus.

CHORUS:

    Em⁷ Am⁷
Give me Jesus,

    F² C
Give me Jesus,

       Am⁷   F²
You can have all this world,

CHORUS TAG:

       C
Just give me Je - sus.

VERSE 2:

C   Am⁷
When I am alone,

F²   C
When I am alone,

Am⁷   F²
When I am alone,

     C
Give me Je - sus.

(REPEAT CHORUS & CHORUS TAG)

CONTINUED...

INTERLUDE:

C Am⁷ F² C
      Jesus,

    Am⁷   F² C
Give me Jesus.

VERSE 3:

C   Am⁷
When I come to die,

F²   C
When I come to die,

Am⁷   F²
When I come to die,

    C
Give me Je - sus.

(REPEAT CHORUS & CHORUS TAG)

(REPEAT CHORUS)

ENDING:

      Am⁷   F²
You can have all this world,

      Am⁷   F²
You can have all this world,

      C
Just give me Je - sus.

Am⁷ F C Am⁷ F C

    Am⁷ F² C
Jesus.

Copyright © 2006 Thirsty Moon River Publishing / Stolen Pride Music (ASCAP) (adm. by EMI CMG Publishing)
All rights reserved. Used by permission. CCLI Song No. 4874344

Give You Glory

JEREMY CAMP

KEY OF (D)

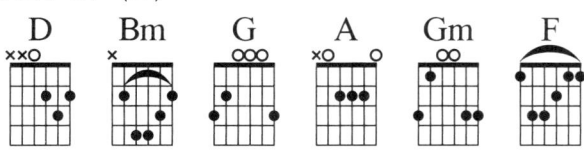

VERSE 1:

D
We have raised a thousand voices,

Bm
Just to lift Your holy name,

G
And we will raise thousands more,

A
To sing of Your beauty in this place.

D
None can even fathom,

Bm
No, not one define Your worth,

G
As we marvel in Your presence

A
To the ends of the earth.

CHORUS:

D
We give You glory,

Bm
Lifting up our hands and singing Holy,

G
You alone are worthy,

Gm
We just want to touch Your heart Lord,

Touch Your heart.

D   Bm
Glory, lifting up our voice and singing Holy,

G
You alone are worthy,

Gm
We just want to touch Your heart Lord,

Touch Your heart.

CONTINUED...

VERSE 2:

D
As we fall down before You,

Bm
With our willing hearts we seek,

G
In the greatness of Your glory,

A
It's so hard to even speak.

D
There is nothing we can offer,

Bm
No, nothing can repay,

G
So we give You all our praises,

A
And lift our voice to sing.

(REPEAT CHORUS)

BRIDGE:

Bm   G   A
Our hope is drenched in You,

Bm   G   A
Our faith has been re - newed.

Bm   G   A
We trust in Your every word,

F   G   A
Nothing else can even measure up to You.

(REPEAT CHORUS THREE TIMES)

D

Copyright © 2006 Thirsty Moon River Publishing / Stolen Pride Music (ASCAP) (adm. by EMI CMG Publishing)
All rights reserved. Used by permission. CCLI Song No. 4874337

God Of Justice

TIM HUGHES

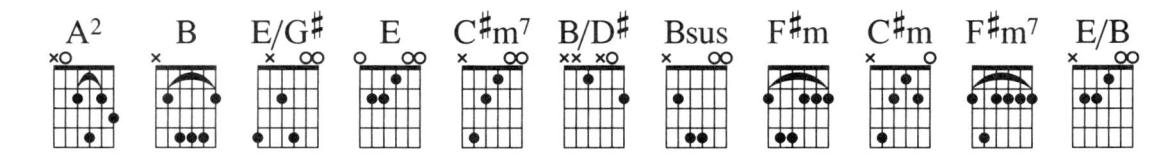

A²   B   E/G♯   E   C♯m⁷   B/D♯   Bsus   F♯m   C♯m   F♯m⁷   E/B

VERSE 1:

A²   B   E/G♯   A²
God of jus - tice, Sav - ior to   all.
            B   E/G♯   A²
Came to res - cue the weak and the poor.
           B   E   A²
Chose to serve and not be served.
B   E/G♯   C♯m⁷

PRE-CHORUS 1:

C♯m⁷   B/D♯
Jesus, You have called us,
A²   B
Freely we've received, now freely we will   give.

CHORUS:

           E(E/B)*   B/D♯ (B)*
We must   go, Live to feed the hungry, *3rd time only
          C♯m⁷   A²
Stand beside the broken,   We must go.
             E   B/D♯
Stepping forward, Keep us from just   singing,
             C♯m⁷   A²
Move us into action, we must go.

VERSE 2:

A²   B   E
To act just - ly, ev-ery day.
A²   B   E/G♯
   Loving mer - cy, in ev - ery way.
A²   B   E/G♯
   Walking hum - bly, before You, God.
A²   B   E/G♯

PRE-CHORUS 2:

        C♯m⁷   B/D♯
You have shown us what You   require,
A²   B
Freely we've received, now freely we will   give.

(REPEAT CHORUS)

CONTINUED...

BRIDGE:

(Bsus) *A²
           Fill us up and send us out, *1st time only
Bsus   E/G♯
    Fill us up and send us out,
A²   Bsus   E/G♯
    Fill us up and send us out Lord.

(REPEAT BRIDGE FOUR TIMES)

INSTRUMENTAL:

F♯m   C♯m   E   B   F♯m⁷   C♯m⁷   E   B

CHANNEL:

           F♯m⁷   C♯m⁷
A change is   made, loving mer - cy.
             E   B
We must go,   we must go
            F♯m⁷   C♯m⁷
to the bro - ken and the hurt - ing,
             F♯m⁷   B
We must go,   we must go.

(REPEAT CHORUS)

ENDING (INSTRUMENTAL):

E   B/D♯   C♯m⁷   A²

E   B/D♯   C♯m⁷   A²

E   B/D♯   C♯m⁷   A²

E/B   B   C♯m   A²

E/B   B   C♯m   A²

E   B/D♯   C♯m⁷   A²

E   B/D♯   C♯m⁷   A²   E

Copyright © 2005 Thankyou Music (PRS) (adm. worldwide by EMI CMG Publishing excluding the UK and Europe which is adm. by kingswaysongs.com).
All rights reserved. Used by permission. CCLI Song No. 4447128

Great God Of Wonders

ANDY BROMLEY

KEY OF (E)

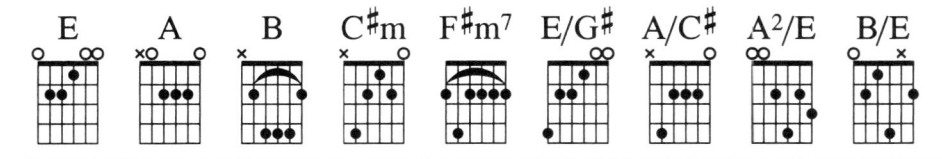

E A B C#m F#m7 E/G# A/C# A²/E B/E

VERSE:
E
Great God of wonders, Great God in power,
A
The heavens are declaring glories of Your name,
B A   E
   Glories of Your name.

Great God of Zion, Great God in beauty,
   A
The nations are gathering to worship at Your feet,
B A   E
   To worship at Your feet.

PRE-CHORUS:
B   C#m
   From the rising to the setting sun,
        A
Your name   will be praised.
F#m7
God above all gods,
E/G#
King above all kings,
A   B
Lord of heaven and earth.

CHORUS 1:
             E   A   B
We give to You praise, praise, praise.
A/C#
      Give You
E   A   B   (E) *1st time only*
  praise, praise, praise.

(REPEAT VERSES)

(REPEAT PRE-CHORUS)

(REAPET CHRUS)

CONTINUED...

BRIDGE:
               E   B
You are the   great God a - bove all gods,
               A   B
You are the   great King a - bove all kings
               E   B
You are the   great Lord of heaven and earth,
            A   B
We give You   praise.

(REPEAT BRIDGE)

CHORUS 2:
             E   A²/E   B/E
We give You praise,   praise,   praise.
             E   A²/E   B
We give You praise,   praise,   praise.

(REPEAT CHORUS 1)
E   A   B   A/C#

ENDING:
         B
Only Lord, worthy all our praise, Lord Jesus.
            A   E
Hallelujah, Lord,   Hallelu.

Copyright © 2004 Thankyou Music (PRS) (adm. worldwide by EMI CMG Publishing excluding the UK and Europe, which is adm. by kingswaysongs.com).
All rights reserved. Used by permission. CCLI Song No. 4443115

Here and Now

MATT MAHER

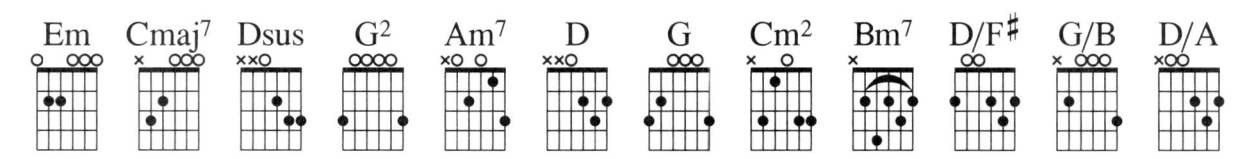

Capo 1 (G)

VERSE 1:

     Em   Cmaj7
No more waiting, Your love's ex - haling.
     Dsus   G2
You are   here and re - turning.
     Am7   D
We're coming home, and all are one.

CHORUS:

          G   Cm2
Here and now; the proud made low - ly.
          G   Cm2
Here and now; the Lamb made might - y.
          Em   Bm7
Here and now; the slave to free - dom.
          C   D
Here and now; the coming King - dom.

CHORUS ENDING 1:

         G   Cm2
Here and now.
G   Cm2
       (The cross is)

VERSE 2:

     Em   Cmaj7
The cross is happening, the world is ending,
     Dsus   G2
Dead and a - live, we are be - ginning,
     Am7   D
We're coming home, and all are one.

(REPEAT CHORUS TWICE)

CONTINUED...

CHORUS ENDING 2:

(D)
   Here and now.

BRIDGE:

G Em D/F# G   G/B C G/B   D/A
      Tears of   glad - ness, in the   sad - ness,
   Em D/F# G G/B C
We're fall - ing   and vic - torious.
Em   D/F# G G/B C G/B   D/A
Bless'd and   brok - en, the flood - gates o - pen,
   Em   D/F# G G/B C
The sun is   ris - ing to shine
D   Em   D/F#   G

(REPEAT CHORUS TWICE)

(REPEAT CHORUS ENDING 2)

ENDING:

G   Cm2   G   Cm2
  It's here   and now, it's here   and now.
G   Cm2   G

Copyright © 2005 Thankyou Music (PRS) (adm. worldwide by EMI CMG Publishing excluding the UK and Europe which is adm. by kingswaysongs.com)/ spiritandsong.com Publishing (BMI) (adm. by EMI CMG Publishing) All rights reserved. Used by permission. CCLI Song No. 4666930.

The Highest And The Greatest

NICK HERBERT and TIM HUGHES

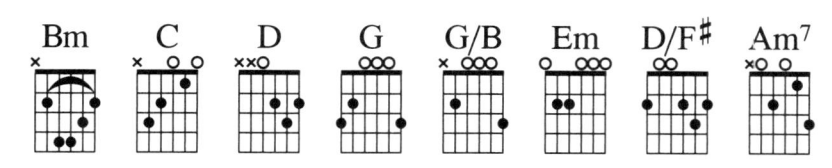

Bm　C　D　G　G/B　Em　D/F#　Am7

Capo 3 (G)

VERSE 1:

```
    Bm       C         D       G
Wake    every heart and every tongue,
    Bm       C         D       G
To    sing the new e - ternal song,
    D       C        G/B         C
And   crown Him   King of     Glory now,
    D        C        Em    D/F#
Con - fess Him   Lord of    all.
```

CHORUS:

```
            G
You are the high - est,
            D
You are the great - est,
           Am7    G   D
You are the Lord    of   all.
    G(Em)*
Angels will worship,
          D(D/F#)*            *3rd time only
Nations will bow   down,
           Am7   G   C
To the Lord       of   all.
```

VERSE 2:

```
    Bm       C        D        G
A    day will come when all will sing,
    Bm        C       D         G
And    glori - fy our matchless King,
    D         C        G/B         C
Your   name un - rivaled    stands a - lone
    D       C     Em    D/F#
You   are the  Lord of   all.
```

(REPEAT CHORUS)

CONTINUED...

BRIDGE:

```
    Am7            G/B
Let every heart, let every tongue,
    C
Sing of Your name, sing of Your name.
    Am7            G/B
Let every heart, let every tongue,
    C
Sing, sing, sing.
```

(REPEAT BRIDGE)

(REPEAT CHORUS THREE TIMES)

1st time, harmony tacet until last C chord.

CHANNEL:

```
C                          D      Em    C
Lifting You high, higher and higher,   Lord.
```

ENDING:

```
C
Lifting You high, higher and higher,
D
Lifting You high, higher and higher,
Em                              C
Lifting You high, higher and higher,  Lord.
```

(REPEAT ENDING FOUR TIMES & FADE)

Copyright © 2007 Thankyou Music (PRS) (adm. worldwide by EMI CMG Publishing excluding the UK and Europe which is adm. by kingswayongs.com).
All rights reserved. Used by permission. CCLI Song No. 4769758

How Can I Keep From Singing

CHRIS TOMLIN, MATT REDMAN and ED CASH

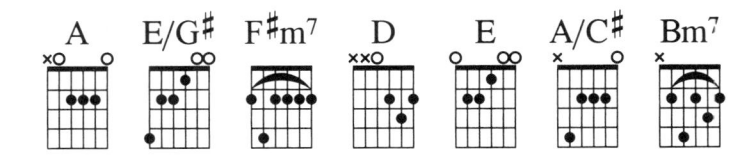

VERSE 1:

      A   E/G#
There is an endless song, echoes in my soul,
 F#m7   D
I hear the music ring.
     E   A   E/G#
And though the storms may come, I am holding on,
F#m7   E/G#   A   F#m7   D
To   the   rock   I   cling.

CHORUS:

A   E
How can I keep from singing Your   praise?
      D   A/C#
How can I ever say e - nough,
        D   E
How a - mazing is Your   love?
A   E
How can I keep from shouting Your   name?
     D   A/C#
I know I am loved by the King,

CHORUS TAG:

     D   E   A
And it makes my heart want to sing.

VERSE 2:

      A   E/G#
I will lift my eyes in the darkest night,
 F#m7   D
For I know my Savior lives.
    E   A
And I will walk with You
           E/G#
Knowing You see me through,
 F#m7   E/G#   A   F#m7   D
And sing   the   songs   You   give.

(REPEAT CHORUS & CHORUS TAG)

CONTINUED...

BRIDGE:

   Bm7   A/C#   D   E
I can sing in the troubled times, sing when I win.
   Bm7   A/C#
I can   sing when I lose my step
     D   E
and I   fall down a - gain.
   Bm7   A/C#
I can   sing 'cause You pick me up,
 D   E
Sing 'cause You're there.
   Bm7   A/C#
I can   sing 'cause You hear me Lord,
     D   E
When I   call to You in pray - er.
   Bm7   A/C#
I can   sing with my last breath,
 D   E   Bm7   A/C#
Sing for I know that I'll   sing with the angels,
     D   E
And the saints around the throne.

(REPEAT CHORUS)

ENDING:

     D   E
And it makes my heart,
     D   A/C#
I am loved by the King,
     D   E
And it makes my heart,
     D   A/C#
I am loved by the King,
     D   E   A
And it makes my heart want to sing.

Yeah, I can sing.

I Stand For You

JOHN ELLIS

KEY OF (C)

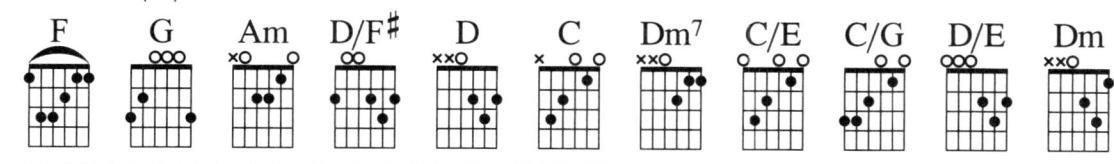

VERSE 1:

```
    F   G    Am  G
Jesus,  I stand for You,
           F    G    D/F#  D
No matter what  you lead me through.
         F   G    C    D
They will chase me out and close me down,
         F    G    C
But Jesus,  I'll stand for You.
```

CHORUS:

```
      F    G    C    Am
I'll always stand, I'll always stand,
      F    G    C
I'll always stand for You.
         F    G    C    D
In all this world, You're all that's true,
      F    G    C
I'll always stand for You.
```

CHORUS TAG:

```
F         Am   G   F
  For You, yeah.
```

VERSE 2:

```
    F   G    Am  G
Jesus,  I've stood my ground,
            F    G    D/F#  D
When unbelief   was all a - round.
           F    G    C    D
I have felt the sting re - jection brings,
         F    G    C
But Jesus,  I'll still stand for You.
```

(REPEAT CHORUS)

CONTINUED...

BRIDGE:

```
         F   Dm7        G   C/E
A time will come    when every - one
           F   Dm7      G   C
Will turn their eyes    on the risen Son
         F    C          F     C/G
But un - til that day, this world will turn a - way,
       D/F#     D/E    D
And so I take Your hand,
      F    G    C
I'll always stand for You.
```

INTERLUDE:

```
(C)       F         Am   G
(for You.)  For You, yeah.
 D/F#   D        F        G       C
   I will always, I will always, always.
         F    G         C    D
Guilty of dis - grace, But You took my place,
         F        Dm       C
So Jesus,  I'll always stand   for You.
```

(REPEAT CHORUS)

ENDING:

```
   F         Am     G   C
For You. Always stand    for you.
```

Copyright © 2004 Birdwing Music/Near Bliss Music/Mouthfulofsongs (ASCAP) (adm. by EMI CMG Publishing)
All rights reserved. Used by permission.   CCLI Song No. 4255224

I Will Remember You

BRENTON BROWN

KEY OF (A)

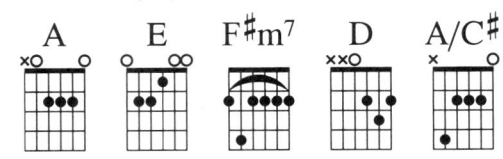

A   E   F#m7   D   A/C#

CHORUS 1:

      A   E
I will remem - ber You,

      F#m7   D
always re - member You,

      A   E
I will remem - ber You,

              F#m7   D
and all You've done   for me.

VERSE 1:

  A   E   F#m7   D
  I will not   forget   all Your ben - efits,

A   E   F#m7   D
Even when   the storm surrounds   my soul.

A   E
  How You com - fort me,

F#m7   D
   heal all   my diseases,

A   E
  How You lift   me up

   F#m7   D
on ea - gle's wings.

(REPEAT CHORUS 1 TWICE)

VERSE 2:

  A   E   F#m7   D
  I will not   forget   all Your ben - efits,

A   E   F#m7   D
  How You've cho - sen and adopt - ed me.

A   E
  Orphaned by   my sin,

F#m7   D
   Your grace has let   me in,

A   E
  And never once

       F#m7   D
have You aban - doned me.

CONTINUED...

(REPEAT CHORUS 1 TWICE)

BRIDGE:

A/C#   D   E
  I have tast - ed and I've seen

      F#m7
how You fa - ther faithfully,

A/C#   D
  How You shep - herd those

      E   F#m7
who fear   Your name.

A/C#   D   E
  When the shad - ow's start to fall

       F#m7
and my heart   begins to fail,

A/C#   D   E   F#m7
  I will lift   my eyes to You   again.

CHORUS 2:

                   A
And I will remem - ber You, always remember You,

I will remember You and all You've done for me.

                  A/C#
I will remember You,

     F#m7   D
always re - member You,

            A   A/C#
I will remem - ber You

              F#m7   D
and all You've done   for me.

(REPEAT CHORUS 1 TWICE)

ENDING:

A   E   F#m7   D
Yeah.

A   E   F#m7   D   A
  All You've done   for me,   yeah.

Copyright © 2006 Thankyou Music (PRS) (adm. worldwide by EMI CMG Publishing excluding the UK and Europe, which is adm. by kingswaysongs.com).
All rights reserved. Used by permission. CCLI Song No. 4707387

Join The Song

VICKY BEECHING and ED CASH

KEY OF (F)

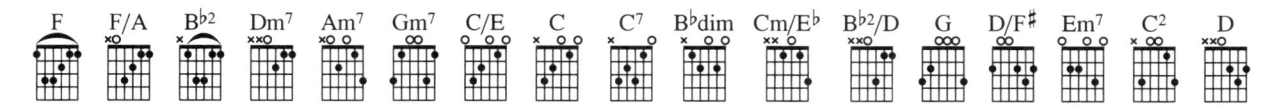

F   F/A   B♭2   Dm7   Am7   Gm7   C/E   C   C7   B♭dim   Cm/E♭   B♭2/D   G   D/F♯   Em7   C2   D

CONTINUED...

VERSE 1:

F   F/A   B♭2
One day every voice will sing,
Dm7   Am7   B♭2
Every beggar, prince and king,
F   F/A   B♭2
Every nation, tongue and tribe,
     Dm7   Am7
Every ocean in between will cry,
B♭2   Gm7
     will cry.

CHORUS:

     F
Praise God from whom all blessings flow,
     C/E
Praise Him, all creatures here below.
     Dm7   B♭2
To Him all the glory be - longs,
     F
Praise Him above you heavenly host.
     C/E
Praise Father, Son and Holy Ghost,
     Dm7
Let all the earth sing along.

CHORUS ENDING:

B♭2
     Come join the song.
(F   Gm7   Dm7   C   F   Gm7   Dm7   C)
                                 1st time only

VERSE 2:

F   F/A   B♭2
Gathered 'round the throne above,
     Dm7   Am7   B♭2
We'll be swept up in the mel - ody,
F   F/A   B♭2
Hearts will overflow with love,
     Dm7   Am7
We'll be singing out a sym - phony,
B♭2   Gm7
     we'll sing.

(REPEAT CHORUS)

BRIDGE:

B♭2   Gm7   F/A
     Come join the song that fills eter - nity,
     B♭2   C7
Sung throughout all his - tory,
     Gm7
As an - gels shout
     F/A   B♭2
and kings lay down their crowns,
     B♭dim
We bow down.
     F/A   C/E
Praise God from whom all blessings flow,
     Cm/E♭   B♭2/D
Praise Him, all creatures here below.
     F   C/E
Praise Him above you heavenly host.
     Cm/E♭   B♭2/D
Praise Father, Son and Holy Ghost,

FINAL CHORUS:

     G
Praise God from whom all blessings flow,
     D/F♯
Praise Him, all creatures here below.
     Em7   C2
To Him all the glory be - longs,
     G
Praise Him above you heavenly host.
     D/F♯
Praise Father, Son and Holy Ghost,
     Em7
Let all the earth sing along.
C2
     Come join the song.

ENDING:

G   Am7   Em7   D
               Come join the song.

(REPEAT ENDING TWICE)

G   Am7   Em7   D   G

Copyright © 2006 Thankyou Music (PRS) (adm. worldwide by EMI CMG Publishing excluding the UK and Europe which is adm. by kingswaysongs.com)/ Alletrop Music (BMI). All rights reserved. Used by permission. CCLI Song No. 4879967

Let God Arise

CHRIS TOMLIN, ED CASH and JESSE REEVES

KEY OF (A)

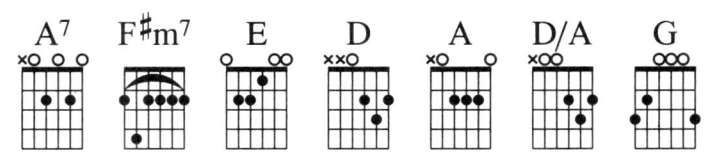

A7   F#m7   E   D   A   D/A   G

VERSE 1:

   A7
Hear the ho - ly roar of God resound,

Watch the waters part before us now.

     F#m7
Come and see what He has done for us,

 E
Tell the world of His great love,

PRE-CHORUS:

   D F#m7 E
Our God is a God who saves.

   D F#m7 E
Our God is a God who saves.

CHORUS:

     A   D/A
Let God arise, Let God arise.

      A7
Our God reigns now and forever,

   D/A
He reigns now and forever.

(G A7 D G A7 D) *1st time only*

CONTINUED...

VERSE 2:

   A7
His en - emies will run for sure,

The church will stand, She will endure.

    F#m7
He holds the keys of life, our Lord,

   E
Death has no sting, no final word,

(REPEAT PRE-CHORUS)

(REPEAT CHORUS TWICE)

INSTRUMENTAL:

D F#m7 E D F#m7 E

(REPEAT PRE-CHORUS TWICE)

(REPEAT CHORUS TWICE)

ENDING:

G A7 D G A7 D

G A7 D G A7 D

A

Copyright © 2006 worshiptogether.com Songs / sixsteps Music (ASCAP) (admin. by EMI CMG Publishing) / Alletrop Music (BMI)
All rights reserved. Used by permission. CCLI Song No. 4822413

Love Came Down
BEN CANTELON

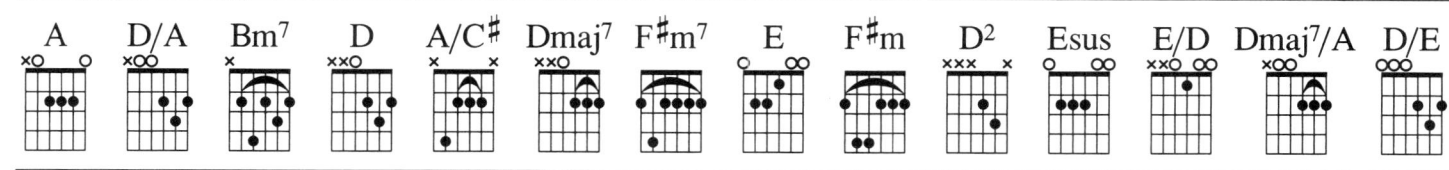

Chords: A D/A Bm7 D A/C# Dmaj7 F#m7 E F#m D2 Esus E/D Dmaj7/A D/E

Capo 1 (A)

VERSE 1:

(D/A)   A   D/A
   When I call   on Your name, You an - swer;
      A   D/A
When I fall,   You are there by my side.
       A   D/A
You deliv - ered me out of dark   - ness,
        A   D/A
Now I stand   in the hope of new life.

VERSE 1 ENDING 1:

      A   D/A   A
Yeah,   stand in the hope of new life with You.

(REPEAT VERSE 1)

VERSE 1 ENDING 2:

       Bm7   A   D
By grace   I'm free; You res - cued me.
Bm7   A/C#   D
All I am is   Yours.

CHORUS:

A
   I've found a love greater than life itself.
Dmaj7(/A)   *4th time only*
   I've found a hope stronger and nothing compares.
F#m7   D
   I once was lost, now I'm alive in You,

CHORUS ENDING 1:

       A   Dmaj7
I'm alive in You.   Thank You, Lord.
A   D
  I'm alive in You.

VERSE 2:

         A   D
You're my God   and my firm founda - tion.
      A   D
It is You   whom I'll trust at all times.
        A   D
I give glo - ry and praise, adora - tion
          A   D
To my Sav - ior Who's seated on   high.

(REPEAT CHORUS)

CHORUS ENDING 2:

(D)
   I found love. Oh, sing...

CONTINUED...

(REPEAT CHORUS)

CHORUS ENDING 3:

             (A)   *Last time only*
I'm alive in You.

BRIDGE:

E   F#m   D   A
         I'm alive in You.   I'm alive in You, Lord.
E   F#m7   D2   A
         Thank You, Lord.   Thank You, Lord.
            E   F#m7
I'm singing: Love came down and rescued me.
Dmaj7   A
   I thank You, yes,   I thank You.
   Esus   F#m7
I once was blind but now I see.
Dmaj7   A
   I see You, yes,   I see You.
   Esus   F#m7
And love came down and rescued me.
Dmaj7   A
   I thank You, yes,   I thank You.
   E   F#m7
I once was blind but now I see.
Dmaj7   A   E   F#m7
   I see You, yes,   I see You, Lord.
Dmaj7   A   E   F#m7   D
   I see You,   I see You, Lord.
E/D   A   Bm7   A/C#   D
     By grace   I'm free. You res - cued me.
Bm7   A/C#   D
All I am is   Yours.
        Bm7   A/C#   D
By grace   I'm free. You res - cued me.
Bm7   A/C#   Dmaj7
All I am is   Yours.

(REPEAT CHORUS)

CHORUS ENDING 4:

                 D/E
I'm loving You, Lord. We sing:...

(REPEAT CHORUS & CHORUS ENDING 3)

Copyright © 2006 Thankyou Music (PRS) (adm. by EMI CMG Publishing, excluding the UK and Europe which is adm. by kingswaysongs.com)
All rights reserved. Used by permission. CCLI Song No. 4943316

Made To Worship

CHRIS TOMLIN, STEPHAN SHARP and ED CASH

KEY OF (C)

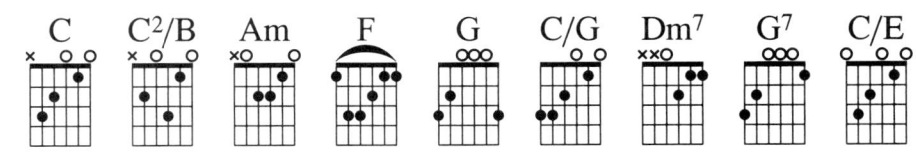

C   C²/B   Am   F   G   C/G   Dm⁷   G⁷   C/E

VERSE 1:

C   C²/B
Be - fore the day, be - fore the light,
Am   F   G
Be - fore the world revolved around the sun.
C   C²/B
God on high stepped down in - to time,
                  Am
And wrote the sto - ry
             F   G
of His love for everyone.

PRE-CHORUS:

F   G
 He has filled our hearts with wonder,
F   C/G   F
 so that we al - ways re - member:

CHORUS:

C
You and I were made to worship,
F
You and I are called to love,
Dm⁷   G⁷
You and I are forgiven and free.
        C
When you and I embrace surrender,
       F
When you and I choose to believe,
    Dm⁷   G⁷
Then you and I will see

(you and I will see) *3rd time only*

who we were meant to be.

VERSE 2:

C   C²/B
 All we are and all we have,
Am   F
Is all a gift from God that we receive.
C   C²/B
Brought to life we open up   our eyes,
             Am   F   G
To see the maj - esty and glory of the King.

CONTINUED...

(REPEAT PRE-CHORUS)

(REPEAT CHORUS)

BRIDGE:

Dm⁷
 Even the rocks cry out,
C/E
 even the heavens shout,
F   G⁷
 At the sound of His Holy name.
Dm⁷
 So let every voice sing out,
C/E
 let every knee bow down,
F   G⁷
 He is worthy of all our praise.

(REPEAT CHORUS TWICE)

ENDING:

         F   Dm⁷   G⁷
Yeah,   we were meant to be,   oo.
              C   F
You and I,   you and I,
      Dm⁷   G⁷
yeah,   yeah, oo.
                              C
We were meant to be.

Copyright © 2006 worshiptogether.com Songs / sixsteps Music (ASCAP) (adm. by EMI CMG Publishing) / Alletrop Music (BMI) / Stenpan Music (ASCAP)
All rights reserved. Used by permission. CCLI Song No. 4794118

O Church Arise

STUART KENNEDY and KEITH GETTY

KEY OF (D)

A⁷sus   D   G/B   A/C#   D/F#   G   Asus   A   Bm   Dsus

CONTINUED...

VERSE 1:

   A⁷sus   D   G/B A/C#
O Church, a - rise, and put your armor on;

     D/F# G   Asus A   D
Hear the call of   Christ, our Cap   -   tain.

   A⁷sus D   G/B A/C#
For now the weak can say that they are strong

    D/F# G   Asus A   D
In the strength that God has giv   -   en.

    D/F# G   D/F# A
With shield of faith and belt of   truth,

    D/F# G   D/F# Bm   A
We'll stand a - gainst the dev   -   il's   lies;

   A⁷sus D   G/B A/C#
An army   bold, whose battle cry is   love,

    D/F# G
Reaching out to   those

 Asus A   D   Dsus   D
in dark   -   ness.

VERSE 2:

   A⁷sus D   G/B A/C#
Our call to   war, to love the captive soul.

    D/F# G   Asus A   D
But to rage a - gainst the cap   -   tor.

   A⁷sus D   G/B A/C#
And with the sword that makes the wounded whole

    D/F# G   Asus A   D
We will fight and faith and va   -   lor.

    D/F# G   D/F# A
When faced with trials on every   side.

    D/F# G   D/F# Bm   A
We know the outcome is   se   -   cure.

   A⁷sus D   G/B A/C#
And Christ will have the prize for which He died,

    D/F# G
And in - heri   -   tance

 Asus A   D   Dsus   D
of na   -   tions.

VERSE 3:

   A⁷sus D   G/B A/C#
Come see the cross, where love and mercy meet.

    D/F# G   Asus A   D
As the Son of   God is strick   -   en.

   A⁷sus D   G/B A/C#
Then see His foes lie crushed be - neath His feet,

    D/F# G   Asus A   D
For the Conquer - or has ris   -   en.

    D/F# G   D/F# A
And as the   stone is rolled a - way.

    D/F# G   D/F# Bm   A
And Christ e - merges from   the   grave.

   A⁷sus D   G/B A/C#
This victory   march continues till the   day

    D/F# G
Every eye and heart

 Asus A   D   Dsus   D
shall see   Him.

VERSE 4:

   A⁷sus D   G/B A/C#
So Spirit,   come, put strength in every   stride,

    D/F# G   Asus A   D
Give grace for every hur   -   dle.

   A⁷sus D   G/B A/C#
That we may run with faith to win the prize

    D/F# G   Asus A   D
Of a servant good and faith   -   ful.

    D/F# G   D/F# A
As saints of old still line the way.

    D/F# G   D/F# Bm   A
Re - telling   triumphs of   His   grace.

   A⁷sus D   G/B A/C#
We hear their calls and hunger for the day,

    D/F#
When with Christ

  G   Asus A   D   Dsus   D
we stand in glo   -   ry.

Copyright © 2005 Thankyou Music (PRS) (adm. by EMI CMG Publishing excluding UK & Europe which is adm. by kingswaysongs.com).
All right reserved. Used by permission. CCLI Song No. 4611992

On The Third Day

MATT MAHER and MARC BYRD

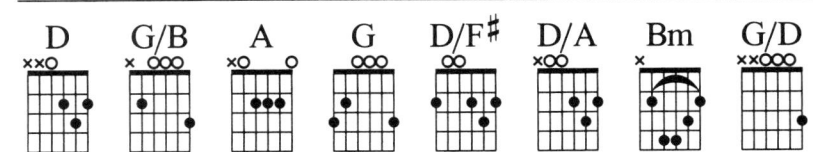

Capo 1 (D)

VERSE 1:

      D
Creation brings an offering,

 G/B   A
    As autumn leaves   turn to gold,

 G   D
    The trees bow down   in highest praise,

 G/B   A
    Now made bare   before Your throne.

 G   D/F#
The western sky an amber blaze,

 G   D/A   G/B
    At the end of the day,

    D/A   A   D
For ev - 'rything must die   to rise again.

VERSE 2:

      D
The winter's chill, a bitter cold,

 G/B   A
    As sin and shame   leave us to fall,

 G   D
    The clouds now full   of newborn snow,

 G/B   A
    For grace to come   and save us all,

 G   D/F#
Within the darkest night of man,

 G   D/A   G/B
    Was found Your saving hand,

    D/A   A   D
For ev - 'rything must die   to rise again.

CHORUS 1:

    G   D   D/A
On the third day, behold   the King,

    G   Bm   A
On the third day, death has   no sting,

    G   Bm   A   D
On the third day, we're for - given and rec - onciled.

VERSE 3:

     D
The earth it groans in labor pains,

 G/B   A
    As flowers stretch   to heaven above,

CONTINUED...

 G   D
Your creatures sing   the prophet's song,

 G/B   A
    To be a gift   of selfless love.

 G   D/F#
The sun is rising in the east,

 G   D/A   G/B
And Your spirit is unleashed,

    D/A   A   D
For ev - 'rything must die   to rise again.

VERSE 4:

     D
And so we wait in joyful hope,

 G/B   A
    For You to come   and take us home,

 G   D
And so we join   beneath the cross,

 G/B   A
    In suffering   from whence we go.

 G   D/F#
The greatest act of sovereign grace,

 G   D/A   G/B
In the universe displayed,

    D/A   A   D
For ev - 'rything must die   to rise again.

(REPEAT CHORUS 1)

CHORUS 2:

    G   D   D/A
On the third day, the saints   rejoice,

    G   Bm   A
On the third day, we lift   our voice,

    G   Bm   A   D
On the third day, u - nited and glo - rified.

(REPEAT CHORUS 1 & CHORUS 2)

ENDING:

 G/D   D

Copyright © 2006 Thankyou Music (PRS) (adm. worldwide by EMI CMG Publishing excluding the UK and Europe which is adm. by kingswaysongs.com)
spiritandsong.com Publishing/Meaux Mercy/Blue Raft Music (BMI) (adm. by EMI CMG Publishing)
All rights reserved. Used by permission. CCLI Song No. 4724023

Resurrection Day

MATT MAHER

KEY OF (G)

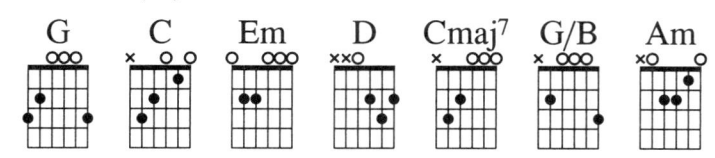

G C Em D Cmaj7 G/B Am

VERSE 1:

G
  It's the weight of Your glory,

Brings the proud to their knees,

And the light of revelation,

Lets the blind man see.

C
  It's the power of the cross,

Breaks away death's embrace,

And we celebrate our freedom,

Dancing on an empty grave.

PRE-CHORUS:

Em   D
Roll away the stone,

Cmaj7   D
Roll away the   stone.

CHORUS:

    G   G/B   C   D
We sing for joy,   we shout Your name,

    G   G/B   Em   D
We cele - brate Your resurrection   day.

    G   G/B   C   D
We sing for joy,   we shout Your name,

    G   G/B   C   D   G
We cele - brate Your resur - rection   day.

GUITAR SOLO:

G   C   G   C   G   C   G   C

CONTINUED...

VERSE 2:

G
  You declare what is holy,

You declare what is good,

In the sight of all the nations,

You declare that You are God.

C
  It's the power in Your Blood,

Breaks away sin's embrace,

And we celebrate our freedom,

Dancing on our broken chains.

(REPEAT PRE-CHORUS & CHORUS)

Em   D   Am   Em   D   Am

(REPEAT CHORUS TWICE)

(REPEAT GUITAR SOLO)

G

Copyright © 2005 Thankyou Music (PRS) (adm. worldwide by EMI CMG Publishing excluding the UK and Europe which is adm. by kingswaysongs.com)/ spiritandsong.com Publishing (BMI) (adm. by EMI CMG Publishing) All rights reserved. Used by permission. CCLI Song No. 4669786

Shine

MATT REDMAN

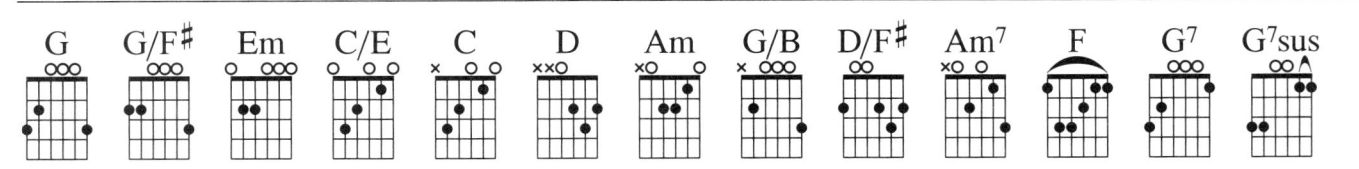

VERSE:

      G   G/F#
Lord we have seen the rising sun,
  Em   C/E Em
Awakening the early dawn,
  C   G D
And we're rising up to give You praise.
       G   G/F#
Lord we have seen the stars and moon,
     Em   C/E Em
See how they shine, they shine for You.
  C   G D
And You're calling us to do the same,

PRE-CHORUS:

    Am
So we rise up with a song,
   G/B
And we rise up with a cry,
    C
And we're giv - ing You our lives.

CHORUS 1:

      G
We will shine like stars in the universe,
    D/F#
Holding out Your truth in the darkest place.
   Am7
We'll be living for Your glory,
    C
Jesus we'll be living for Your glory.

(REPEAT VERSE, PRE-CHORUS & CHORUS 1)

CHORUS 2

      G
We will burn so bright with Your praise, oh, God,
    D/F#
And declare Your light to this broken world.
  F
We'll be living for Your glory,
    C
Jesus, we'll be living for Your glory.

CONTINUED...

BRIDGE:

      Am
Like the sun so radiantly,
      G/B
Sending light for all to see,
     C
Let Your Ho - ly Church arise.
    Am
Ex - ploding into life,
     G/B
Like a su - pernova's light,
     C
Set Your Ho - ly Church on fire,

(REPEAT BRIDGE)

     G
We will shine.
     G7
We will shine.

(REPEAT CHORUS 1, CHORUS 2 & PRE-CHORUS)

    G G7sus G7
Jesus, we will shine.

Copyright © 2006 Thankyou Music (PRS) (adm. worldwide by EMI CMG Publishing, excluding the UK and Europe, which is adm. by kingswaysongs.com).
All rights reserved. Used by permission. CCLI Song No. 4831435

Sound Of Melodies

LEELAND MOORING, JACK MOORING and STEVE WILSON

KEY OF (A)

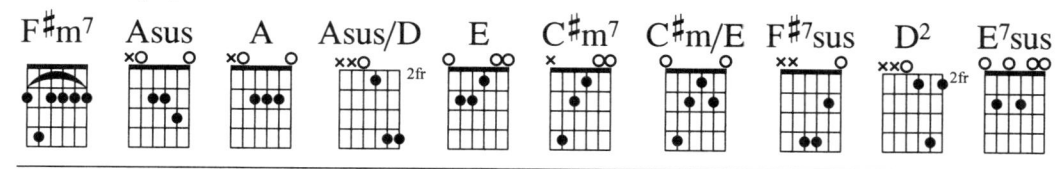

F#m7 Asus A Asus/D E C#m7 C#m/E F#7sus D2 E7sus

VERSE 1:

F#m7   Asus   A
We who were called to be Your people,

F#m7   Asus   A
Struggling sinners and thieves.

   F#m7   Asus   A
We're lifted up from the ashes,

   F#m7   Asus   A
And out came the song of the re - deemed,

F#m7   Asus/D   A
   The song of the redeemed.

F#m7   Asus/D

CHORUS:

              A
Can you hear the sound of melodies,

        E   C#m7
Oh, the sound of melodies rising up to You,

     C#m/E   F#7sus D2
Rising up   to   You,   God?

     A
The sound of melodies,

        E   C#m7
Oh, the sound of melodies rising up to You,

     C#m/E   F#7sus D2   A
Rising up   to   You,   God?

VERSE 2:

    F#m7   Asus/D   A
Oh, we have caught a reve - lation,

    F#m7   Asus/D   A
That nothing can separate us from.

    F#m7   Asus/D   A
The love we re - ceived through sal - vation,

    F#m7   Asus/D   A
It fills your daughters and Your sons,

F#m7   Asus/D   A
   Your daughters and Your sons.

F#m7   Asus/D

CONTINUED...

(REPEAT CHORUS)

BRIDGE:

                                        E
The sound of Your love, the sound of Your love,

              F#m7   D2
Is what You're   hear - ing.

A   E
  The sound of Your sons, the sound of Your sons,

              F#m7   D2
You've won Your   chil - dren.

A   E
  The sound of Your love, the sound of Your love,

              F#m7   D2
Is what You're   hear - ing.

A   E
  Your daughters in love, Your daughters in love,

              F#m7   D2
You've won Your   chil - dren.

CHANNEL:

        A
The sound of melodies,

         E7sus   E   C#m7
Oh, the sound of melo - dies rising up to You.

          E   F#m7   D2   A
Rising up to You,   God,

E   C#m7   E   F#m7 D2
  Rising up to You,   God.

REFRAIN:

     A   E
La, la, la, la, la, la, la, la, la, la, la, la.

          C#m7   C#m/E   F#7sus D2
La, la, la, la, la, la, la, la, la,   la,   la.

(REPEAT REFRAIN)

A

Speak, O Lord

KEITH GETTY and STUART TOWNEND

KEY OF (C)

F/A G/B C² F C Am C/E G G/F Gsus/F G⁹/F C²/E Gsus F²

CONTINUED...

VERSE 1:

F/A　G/B　C²　　　F　　　　C
Speak, O　　Lord, as we come to You,
　　　　　F　　　　　C　　　Am　　G/B
To re - ceive the food　of Your holy word.
F/A　G/B　C²　　F　　　　C
Take　Your　truth, plant it deep in us;
　　　　　F　　　C/E F　　G　　C
Shape and fashion us　　　in Your like-ness,
C/E　　G　　G/F　C/E
That the light of　　Christ
　　　　Gsus/F　G⁹/F　　C²/E
might be seen　　　　　to-day,
　　　　G　G/F　C/E　　　Am　　Gsus　G
In our acts of　love and our deeds of faith.
F/A　G/B　C²　　　F　　　　C
Speak, O　　Lord, and ful-fill in us
　　　　F　　　C/E
all your purposes,
　F　　　Gsus　G　C
For Your glo　-　ry.
F²

C²/E　　　　　F²　　　　　　Gsus　　　　G

VERSE 2:

F/A　G/B　C²　　F　　　C
Teach us　　Lord full o-bedience,
　　　F　　　　C　　　Am　G/B
Holy rev-erence, true hu-mility.
F/A　G/B　C²　　F　　　　C
Test　our　thoughts and our attitudes,
　　　F　　　C/E F　　G　　C
In the radiance　　　of Your puri - ty.
C/E　　G　　G/F　C/E
Cause our faith to　rise,
　　　　Gsus/F　G⁹/F　　C²/E
Cause our eyes　　　to see,
　　　G　G/F　C/E　　　Am　　Gsus　G
Your ma-jes-tic　love and au-thor - i - ty.
F/A　G/B　C²　　F　　　　C
Words of　power that can never fail;
　　　F　　　C/E F　　Gsus　G　C
Let their truth pre-vail　over un - belief.
F²

C²/E　　　　　F²　　　　　　Gsus　　　　G

VERSE 3:

F/A　G/B　C²　　　F　　　　C
Speak, O　　Lord, and re-new our minds;
　　　F　　　　C
Help us grasp the heights
　　　　Am　　　G/B
of Your plans for us.
F/A　G/B　C²　　　F　　　　C
Truths un - changed from the dawn of time,
　　　F　　　C/E F　　G　　C
That will echo down　　through e-terni-ty.
C/E　　G　　G/F　C/E
And by grace we'll　stand
　　　　Gsus/F　G⁹/F　　C²/E
on Your prom　-　　is-es;
　　　G　G/F　C/E　　　Am　　Gsus　G
And by faith we'll　walk as You walk with us.
F/A　G/B　C²　　　F　　　　C
Speak, O　　Lord, till Your church is built,
　　　F　　　C/E F　　　Gsus　G　C
And the earth is filled　　with Your glo - ry.
F²

C²/E　　　　　F²　　　　　　Gsus　　　　G

C

Copyright © 2005 Thankyou Music (PRS) (adm. worldwide by EMI CMG Publishing excluding the UK & Europe which is adm. by kingswaysongs.com).
All rights reserved. Used by permission. CCLI Song No. 4615235

Tears Of The Saints

LEELAND MOORING and JACK MOORING

Capo 4 (Em)

VERSE 1:

Bm⁷   Em
There are many prodigal sons,
  C
On our city streets they run,
       D
Searching for shel - ter.
       Em
There are homes broken down,
  C
People's hopes have fallen to the ground,
   D   Am⁷
From fail - ures. This is an e - mergency!

CHORUS:

G/B   C
   There are tears from the saints,
     G   D
For the lost and unsaved,
              Am⁷
We're crying for them come back home,
          C   D
We're crying for them come back home,
      C
And all Your children will stretch out their hands,
        G
And pick up   the crippled man,
         Am⁷
Father we will lead them home,
      C   D   Bm⁷
Father we will lead them home,

INTERLUDE 1:

Em   C   D

(CONTINUED...)

VERSE 2:

Bm⁷   Em
There are schools full of hatred,
  C   D
Even churches have forsaken love and mer - cy.
       Em
May we see this generation,
  C
In its state of desperation.
        D   Am⁷
For Your glo - ry. This is an e - mergency!

(REPEAT CHORUS)

INTERLUDE 2:

Em   D   Gsus   G

BRIDGE:

D   Gsus   G
Sinners, reach out   your hands!
D   Gsus   G
Children in Christ   you stand!
D   Gsus   G
Sinners, reach out   your hands!
D   Em   C   Am
Children in Christ   you stand!

(REPEAT CHORUS)

ENDING:

C
   And all Your children will stretch out their hands,
        G   D
And pick up   the crippled man,
         Am⁷
Father we will lead them home,
      C
Father we will lead them home,

D   Bm⁷   C

Copyright © 2005 Meaux Mercy (BMI) / Meaux Jeaux Music (SESAC) (adm. by EMI CMG Publishing)
All rights reserved. Used by permission. CCLI Song No. 4768694

The Wonder Of The Cross

VICKY BEECHING

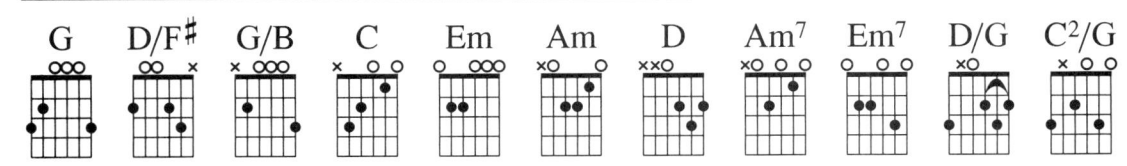

Capo 1 (G)

VERSE 1:

      G   D/F# G
O precious sight, my Savior stands,
     G/B
Dying for me with outstretched hands.
     C   D/F# Em
O precious sight, I love to gaze,
        Am   D/F# Em
Remembering   sal - vation's day,
        Am   D/F# G
Remembering   sal - vation's day.
               D/F# G
Though my eyes linger on this scene,
        G/B
May passing time and years not steal
     C   D/F# Em
The power with which it impacts me,
     Am   D/F# Em
The freshness of its myster - y,
     Am   D/F# G
The freshness of its myster - y.

CHORUS:

G   D
  May I never lose the wonder,
  Am⁷   G
The wonder of the cross.
    Em⁷   D/F#
May I see it like the first time
     Am⁷   Em⁷
Standing as a sinner lost,
      C   G/B
Undone by mercy and left speechless,
    Am⁷   Em⁷
Watching wide eyed at the cost.
    C   D/F# Em⁷
May I never lose the wonder,

CHORUS ENDING 1:

  Am D/F# G
The wonder of the cross.

CONTINUED...

VERSE 2:

        G   D/F# G
Behold the Godman cruci - fied,
     G/B
The perfect sinless sacrifice.
        C   D/F# Em
As blood ran down those nails and wood,
   Am   D/F# Em
History   was split in two, yes,
   Am   D/F# G
History   was split in two.
        D/F# G
Behold the empty wooden tree,
     G/B
His body gone, alive and free.
    C   D/F# Em
We sing with ever - lasting joy,
    Am   D/F# Em
For sin and death have been de - stroyed, yes,
    Am   D/F# G
Sin and death have been de - stroyed.

(REPEAT CHORUS)

CHORUS ENDING 2:

  Am D/F# Em⁷   D/F# G
The wonder of the cross.

Am⁷   G/B   C   D   Em⁷   D/F#

G   Am⁷ G/B C

(REPEAT CHORUS & CHORUS ENDING 1)

G   D/G   G   C²/G

G   D/G   G   C²/G

G

Copyright © 2007 Thankyou Music (PRS) (adm. worldwide by EMI CMG Publishing, excluding the UK and Europe, which is adm. by kingsway songs.com)
All right reserved. Used by permission. CCLI song #4886507.

To The Only God

CHRIS TOMLIN

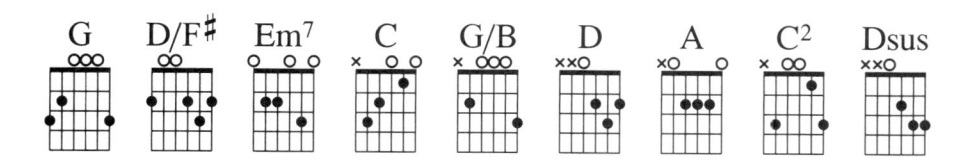

Capo 1 (G)

VERSE:

G   D/F#   Em⁷
To the on - ly God

         C   G/B
who is a - ble to keep   us,

C   D
Able us to keep us from falling.

G   D/F#   Em⁷
To the on - ly God

VERSE ENDING:

      C   G/B
be all glo - ry and hon - or,

Em⁷   A
Majesty and po - wer,

C   D   (G) *1st time only*
For all ages now and forevermore.

(REPEAT VERSE & VERSE ENDING)

BRIDGE:

C²   Dsus   C²   Dsus
    Forever - more.

(REPEAT VERSE ENDING)

ENDING:

G
  Forevermore.

Copyright © 2007 Worshiptogether.com Song/sixsteps Music (ASCAP) (adm. by EMI CMG Publishing).
All rights reserved. Used with permission. CCLI Song No. 4879284

Unwavering

MATT MAHER

KEY OF (E)

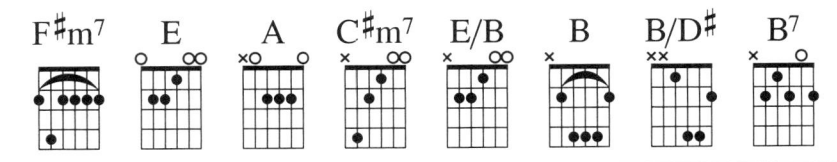

F#m7   E   A   C#m7   E/B   B   B/D#   B7

VERSE 1:

F#m7   E   A   E
    Blessed are the poor, the kingdom is theirs.
         C#m7   F#m7
Alive in the promise to be dead to the   world.
              E   A   E
Blessed are the meek in awe of You Father,
   A   E/B   E   A   E
The Word at Your right hand, spirit of truth.

CHORUS:

             A   E
Unwavering is Your voice,
         B   E
unwavering is Your hand,
         C#m7 B/D#   E
Unwavering is   the   heart
   C#m7   B
that bled for the sins of man.
             A   E   B   C#m7
Unwavering is Your will, unwavering is Your plan,
    A   E/B   B
The fount of sal - vation
          *(E   A   E)   *last time C#m7
on which we will stand.

(B7   E   A   E   C#m7   A)   *1st time only*

VERSE 2:

F#m7   E   A   E
    Blessed are the righteous on bended knee,
        C#m7   F#m7
Found in this freedom, committed to   You.
              E   A   E
Blessed are those who see the heights of glory,
  A   E/B B   E   A   E
Found in the valley,   and suffering for You.

CONTINUED...

(REPEAT CHORUS TWICE)

A   E/B
The fount of sal - vation
  B   A   B   A   B
on which we will stand.

BRIDGE:

                    A   B
Send us out to be Your hands and   feet,
                    A   B
Send us out to be Your hands and feet,
                    A   B
Send us out to be Your hands and   feet,
                    A   B
Send us out to   be Your hands and   feet.
                    A   B
Send us out to be Your hands and   feet,
                    A   B
Send us out to be Your hands and   feet,
                    A   B
Send us out to be Your hands and   feet.

A   B   A   B

Copyright © 2006 Thankyou Music (PRS) (adm. worldwide by EMI CMG Publishing, excluding Europe, which is adm. by kingswaysongs.com)/ spiritandsong.com Publishing (BMI) All rights reserved. Used by permission. CCLI Song No. 4669827

We Remember

MARC BYRD and LEELAND MOORING

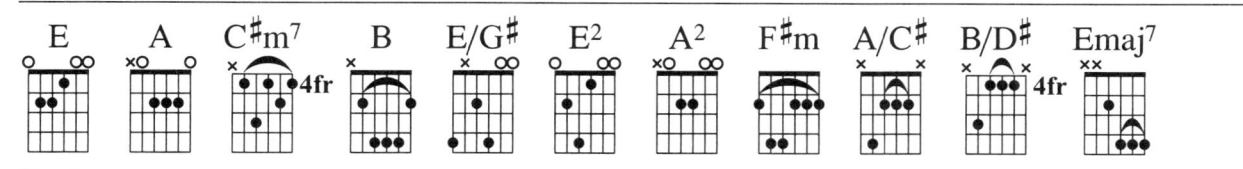

Chords: E A C#m7 B E/G# E2 A2 F#m A/C# B/D# Emaj7

Capo 2 (E)

VERSE 1:

      E
We worship You, Lord,

                          A
In the splendor of Your holiness,

                          C#m7
In the beauty of Your righteous - ness;

 B   A
Holy, ho - ly!

           E
We offer You thanks

                          A
For the endless love You have displayed,

                    C#m7
For the sacrifice You freely gave;

  B   A
Worthy, wor - thy!

PRE-CHORUS:

       B C#m7   A
You are ho - ly, pre - cious Lamb of God.

 B   E/G#   A
Forev - er You will reign,

Forever You will reign.

        B C#m7 A   E/G# A
King of glo - ry, ris - en Son of God.

 B   E/G#
Forev - er You will reign,

 A
Forev - er You will reign.

(E2   A2) *1st time only*

CONTINUED...

VERSE 2:

      E
Father of light,

                 A
In radiance and majesty

                               C#m7
Sent Your Son to set the captive free;

 B   A
Holy, ho - ly!

      E
Infinite love,

                          A
On the cross You saved us from our sin,

                           C#m7
Conquered death and will return a - gain;

 B   A
Worthy, wor - thy!

(REPEAT PRE-CHORUS)

CHORUS:

       F#m   E/G#   A   B
We re - member, we re - member the cross.

      A/C# B/D#   A/C#   B/D#
We re - member, we re - member the cost.

       F#m   E/G#
We re - member, Lord,

        A   B
we re - member the cross.

      A/C# B/D#   A/C#   B/D#
We re - member, we re - member the cost.

(REPEAT PRE-CHORUS)

ENDING:

       F#m   E/G#   A   B
We re - member, we re - member the cross.

      A/C# Emaj7   A/C#   B/D#
We re - member, we re - member the cost.

Copyright © 2006 Meaux Mercy/Blue Raft Music (BMI) (adm. by EMI CMG Publishing)
All right reserved. Used by permission. CCLI #4255918

Yes And Amen

Matt Redman, Robert Marvin and Josiah Bell

KEY OF (G)

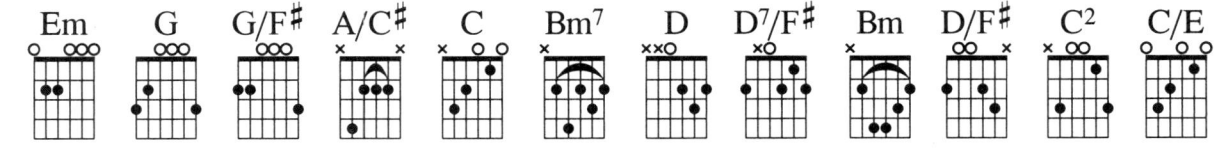

Chord diagrams: Em G G/F# A/C# C Bm7 D D7/F# Bm D/F# C2 C/E

VERSE 1:

Em
    Hear Your people saying yes,
                            G
Hear Your people saying yes   to You.
Em
    Yes to anything You ask,
                         G
Yes to anything we're called   to do.
Em
    Hear Your people say amen,
                         G
Hear Your people say amen   to You.
Em
    Let Your kingdom come on earth,
                         G
Let it be just like we prayed   to You.

CHORUS 1:

Yes and amen to everything that's in Your heart,
        G/F#
Yes and a - men to everything that You have planned.
    A/C#
We live to see Your will be done,
    C   G
And see Your perfect kingdom come on earth,
    Bm7
on the earth.

VERSE 2:

Em   D   Em
    All the promis - es are yes,
        D7/F#   G
All the promis - es are yes   in You.
Em   D   Em
    Every good and perfect gift,
                        G
Every blessing that we have   was You.

(REPEAT CHORUS 1)

CONTINUED...

CHORUS 2:

               G
Yes and a - men, we're taking up our cross for You.
              G/F#
Give us the strength to take these dreams

and follow through.
    A/C#
We live to see Your will be done,
    C   G
And see Your perfect kingdom come on earth,
    Bm*   *2nd time, Bm7
On the earth.

VERSE 3:

Em   D   Em
    Hear Your people saying yes,
        D/F#   G   D/F# G Bm
Hear Your people saying yes   to You.
Em   D   Em
    Yes to any - thing You ask,
        D/F#   G   D/F# G Bm
Yes to any - thing we're called   to do.
Em   D   Em
    Hear Your people say amen,
        D/F#   G   D/F# G Bm
Hear Your people say amen   to You.
Em   D   Em
    Let Your kingdom come on earth,
        D/F#   G   D/F# G
Let it be just like we prayed   to You.

(REPEAT CHORUS 1 & 2)

G   D G   C   G   C2 D/F#

Em   D/F# G   D/F# G   C/E C2

ENDING:

(D/F#)*   Em   D/F#   G
Yes and a - men,
D/F#   G   C2
Yes and a - men.   *D/F# *not played 1st time*

(REPEAT ENDING 3 TIMES)

    D/F#   Em   D/F#   G

Copyright © 2006 Thankyou Music (PRS) (adm. worldwide by EMI CMG Publishing, excluding the UK and Europe, which is adm. by kingswaysongs.com) / Meaux Mercy (adm. by EMI CMG Publishing) / JLCB Music (BMI) All rights reserved. Used by permission. CCLI Song No. 4835967

You Are God

CHARLIE HALL

KEY OF (G)

VERSE 1:

G   G/F#   Em⁷   G/D
   You're closer   than our troubles,

C   G/B   C   D
   More present than   any danger,

G   G/F#   Em⁷   G/D
   More grand than gold and silver.

C   G/B   C   D
   You are   God,   You are   God.

G   G/F#   Em⁷   G/D

C²   G/B   C²   D

VERSE 2:

G   G/F#   Em⁷   G/D
   You're the joy of   man's de - sire;

C   G/B   C   D
   You are Father,   Satis - fier.

G   G/F#   Em⁷   G/D
   We are stunned with wide eyed wonder.

C   G/B   C   D
   You are   God,   You are   God.

G   G/F#   Em⁷   G/D

C²   G/B   C²   D

CONTINUED...

CHORUS:

G   D/F#
   Fill our hearts   with love and faith.

Em⁷   G/D
   You fight for us,   You make us brave.

C²   G/B   C²   Dsus
   You are   God,   You are God.

G   D/F#
   You walk with us,   You lead us up.

Em⁷   G/D   C²
   Faith, hope and love   wakes up with dawn.

        G/B   C²   Dsus
You are God,   You are God.

(G/B   Cmaj⁷   G/D

G/B   Cmaj⁷   G/D) *1st time only*

BRIDGE:

     G/B   Cmaj⁷   G/D
And life   flows from God,

           G/B   Cmaj⁷   G/D
It flows from God.

(REPEAT BRIDGE & CHORUS)

G

Copyright © 2007 worshiptogether.com Songs/sixsteps Music (ASCAP) (adm. by EMI CMG Publishing)
All rights reserved. Used by permission. CCLI Song No. 4925303

You Are My God (Like A Whisper)

BRENTON BROWN

KEY OF (E)

E   E/D   A   B   A/B   A/C#   B/D#

VERSE 1:

E   E/D
   Like a whisper,   like a love song,

 A
I   can hear Your voice, I can hear Your voice.

E   E/D
   Like a father   to his newborn,

 A   E
I   can hear Your voice calling   me:

CHORUS 1:

         A   B   E
"You are My   child, you are My   child, and I love   you.

         A   B   E
You are My   child, you are My   child, and I love   you."

VERSE 2:

E   E/D
   Like a promise,   like a thank you,

 A
I   will sing this song, I will sing this song.

E   E/D
   For the way You   make my heart new,

 A   E
I   will sing this song to   You.

CHORUS 2:

         A   B   E
You are my   God, You are my   God, and I love   You.

         A   B   E
You are my   God, You are my   God, and I love   You.

BRIDGE:

          A   A/B
There is no   higher call, there's no great - er reward

           A/C#   A/B
Than to know   You, God, to be known   as Yours.

          A   A/B
There is no   better goal, nothing I'm   longing for

            A/C#   B/D#
Can compare   with the truth that forev - er more:

(REPEAT CHORUS 2)

Copyright © 2005 Thankyou Music (PRS) (adm. worldwide by EMI CMG Publishing, excluding the UK and Europe which is administered by kingswaysongs.com) All rights reserved. Used by permission. CCLI Song No. 4707590

Your Glory Endures Forever

CHARLIE HALL

KEY OF (G)

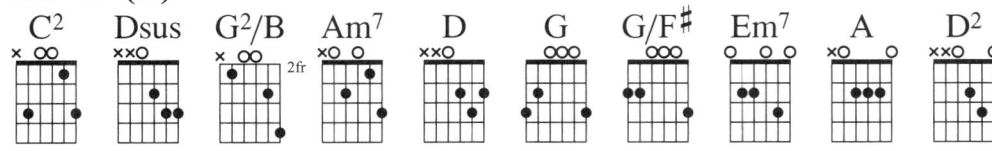

C²   Dsus   G²/B   Am⁷   D   G   G/F♯   Em⁷   A   D²

VERSE:

  C²   Dsus   G²/B   C²
And You ride on wings of wind, You are be - ginning and the end.
                      Dsus   G²/B   Am⁷
Mountains melting in Your flame, creation pulsing out Your name.

PRE-CHORUS:

                 D
And You are forever,   and You are forever

CHORUS:

G   G/F♯   C²
  Your glory endures forever,   Your beauty out - shines the heavens.
Em⁷   D   A   C²
  And we will de - clare Your wonders,   Your splendor, Your   majesty.

VERSE:

                Dsus   G²/B   C²
Earth rotating in Your hand, galax - ies in Your com - mand.
                          Dsus   G²/B   Am⁷
You make and sustain the breath of man, Your deeds go on forever.

(REPEAT PRE-CHORUS)

(REPEAT CHORUS TWICE)

BRIDGE:

Am⁷   Dsus   G²/B   C²
  You are forever,   You are forever,   You are forever,
Dsus   G²/B   A   C²
  You are forever,   You are forever,   You are forever.

(REPEAT CHORUS TWICE)

ENDING:

G   G/F♯   C²   Em⁷   D   A   C²

G   G/F♯   C²
Glory, and honor, and praise. Glory, and honor, and praise.
Em⁷   D²
Glory, and honor, and praise
C²
  And You ride on wings of wind, You are beginning and the end.

Copyright © 2005 worshiptogether.com Songs / sixsteps Music (ASCAP) (adm. by EMI CMG Publishing)
All rights reserved. Used by permission. CCLI Song No. 4653620

Cut Capo Instructions
by Mitch Bohannon

The cut capo is designed to be placed on the 2nd fret with strings tuned to standard tuning (E A D G B E). It can be used in conjunction with a full capo (discussed later). The capo serves two purposes. First, it allows for chord "voicings" different from standard open chords. Secondly, use of the cut capo often calls for very simple fingerings which makes the chords easier for beginning players.

Place the capo on the fret board from the top so that it covers strings 5, 4, and 3. Make sure it is next to the fret bar. This will provide better intonation and allow the player to reach the bass note with more ease.

Using the capo on by itself on the second fret, you will be playing in the key of "E." A simple chord progression used in the song "I Could Sing of Your Love Forever" looks like this…

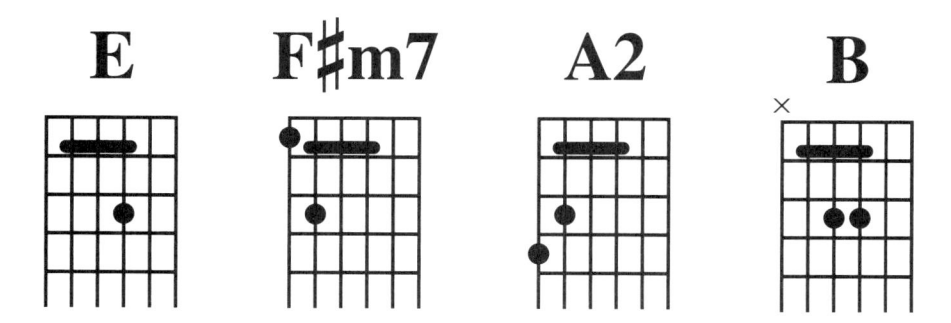

E   F♯m7   A2   B

The fingerings are much more simple than standard fingerings. The 1st and 2nd strings ring continuously, providing a "droning" sound effect which also allows for more time in chord changes. For the **F♯m7** chord, simply reach around the capo with the index finger (#1) and use fingers #3 and #4 on the 5th and 4th strings. (It will become more comfortable after you play it a few times.)

STRUMMING/RHYTHM

Chords played with the cut capo are almost *all* 6-string chords which means you can strum all six strings giving a very full sound. Hammer-ons are also very easy in that you're only fingering a couple of strings. To "hammer-on" simply strum the open strings and then quickly snap your finger(s) into the chord position. Combining hammer-ons with palm muting it becomes very easy to create an easy acoustic rhythm drive.

TRANSPOSING – PLAYING IN DIFFERENT KEYS

Transposing the capo to another key is the same as playing in the key of "E" and using a standard capo…

Full capo fret	Short-cut capo fret	Key
1	3	F
2	4	F♯ / G♭
3	5	G
4	6	G♯ / A♭
5	7	A

This means that the same progression used above (**E, F♯m7, A2, B**) played with a full capo on fret 3 and the cut capo on fret 5 would transpose to: **G, Am7, C2, D**.

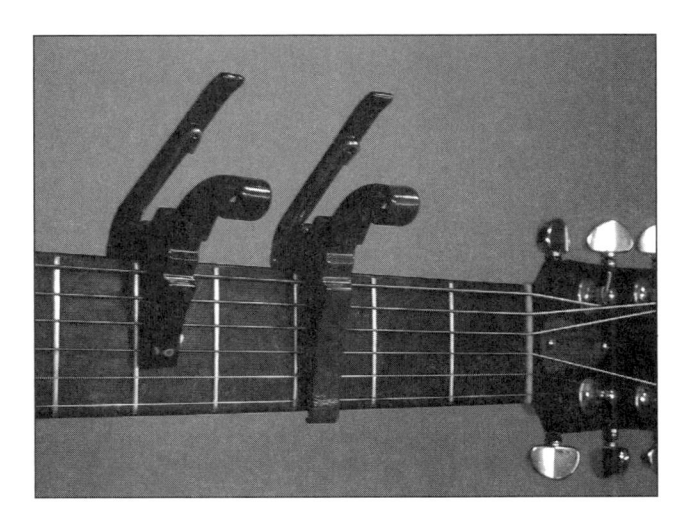

The above picture shows the position of the capos when playing in the key of "G." To transpose chords (change to a different key), remember that every fret is a half-step. The key of "G" is three (3) half-steps up from "E." To transpose to this key, each chord in the key of "E" would move up three (3) half-steps.

The cut capo charts in this book were designed to match the key of the sheet music. However, songs can often be transposed to make them easier to play or sing. Specifically, songs in the key of "D" are easier to play with the capo in the key of "E."

VARIATIONS IN CHORD DIAGRAMS

Some chords represented on the cut capo chord diagrams may include or exclude certain notes. The reason for this is because many cut capo chords are simplified due to the limitations in fingering that are inherent to its use. The unique sound produced by the cut capo more than makes up for this alteration. Example: with the first two strings open (B & E), an "**A**" chord is technically an "**A2**" because of the added "B". In addition, a "**B**" chord is technically a "**Bsus**" because of the added "E". When using the cut capo charts a song that contains an "**A**" and an "**A2**" will have the same fingering represented for both chords.

There are also some chords with alternate bass notes that do not work well with the cut capo. In this case, you may see a chord symbol with an alternate bass note, but the diagram will not reflect this bass note. We have chosen to leave the alternate bass note on the cut capo chord symbol to represent the writers' original intention, and give you the ability to be creative. So, if you like, you can try to figure out a way to include the bass note, either by using alternate fingering with the cut capo, or by fingering the chord above the cut capo with a "bar" type application.

We have given you a way to begin, but encourage you to be creative and explore new ideas. We hope this opens you up to many new and innovative chord shapes and sounds.

Cut capos are available for purchase in the store at worshiptogether.com

A Greater Song

PAUL BALOCHE and MATT REDMAN

E   C#m7   D/F#   D   F#m7   E/G#   A   G   Bm7

Cut Capo 2 (A)

VERSE 1:

 E C#m7 D/F# D
  Who could imagine a mel - ody,

E   C#m7   D
True enough to tell of Your mer - cy?

 E C#m7 D/F# D
  Who could imagine a har - mony,

E   C#m7   D
Sweet enough to tell of Your love?

PRE-CHORUS:

    F#m7
I see the heav - ens proclaiming You

 E/G#
day after day,

    A   D
And I know in my heart that there must be a way...

CHORUS 1:

     A   E/G#
To sing a great - er song,

  F#m7   D
A great - er song to You on the earth.

     A   E/G#
To sing a great - er song,

  F#m7   D
A great - er song to You on the earth.

VERSE 2:

 E C#m7 D/F# D
  Who could imagine a sym - phony,

E   C#m7   D
Grand enough to tell of Your glo - ry?

 E C#m7 D/F# D
  Our high - est praise but a fee - ble breath,

E   C#m7   D
A whisper of Your thunderous worth.

CONTINUED...

(REPEAT PRE-CHORUS)

(REPEAT CHORUS 1)

CHORUS 2:

A   E/G#
Hallelujah, we want to lift You higher.

G   D
Hallelujah, we want to lift You higher.

A   E/G#
Hallelujah, we want to lift You higher.

G   D
Hallelujah, we want to lift You higher.

F#m7 G Bm7 G

F#m7 D Bm7 G

(REPEAT PRE-CHORUS)

(REPEAT CHORUS 2 TWICE)

Copyright © 2006 Thankyou Music (PRS) (adm. worldwide by EMI CMG Publishing, excluding the UK and Europe, which is adm. by kingswaysongs.com)/ Integrity's Hosanna! Music (ASCAP) (c/o Integrity Media, Inc.) All rights reserved. Used by permission. CCLI Song No. 4662336

Adoration (Down In Adoration Falling)

THOMAS AQUINAS
Additional verse and chorus by MATT MAHER

Chords: A Bm/A D/A E/A E/G# F#m7 Esus D Bm7 E7 E C#m7 A/B A/E A/D A/C# D/F#

Capo 4, Cut Capo 6 (A)

VERSE:

A   Bm/A
Down in ado - ration falling,
D/A   Bm/A   A
This great sacra - ment we hail;
     D/A
Over ancient forms departing,
           E/A
Newer rites of grace pre - vail;
A   Bm/A
Faith for all de - fects supplying
D/A   Bm/A   A
Where the feeble senses   fail.

PRE-CHORUS:

A
To the everlasting Father,
E/G#
And the Son who reigns on high,
F#m7
With the Spirit blest proceeding
Esus
Forth from each eternally,
D
Be salvation, honor, blessing;
Bm7   E7   A
Might and endless majes - ty.

CHORUS 1:

(A)   D   E
 Jesus lamb of God, saving love for all,
      D   E
Lord of heaven and earth, Father's love for all;
F#m7   C#m7   D
I   bow   to   You.

CHORUS 2:

         E   D
Jesus lamb of God, saving love for all,
      E
Lord of heaven and earth,
F#m7   C#m7   D   (E   A   ) *Play first time only.*
I   bow   to   You, (bow to You, I bow to You.)

CONTINUED...

INTERLUDE:

A   Bm7   A/B   F#m7

A/E   A/D   Bm7

BRIDGE:

A   E/G#
Pour upon us Lord of Mercy,
F#m7   Esus   D2
Spirit of Thy selfless   love;
F#m7   A/C#
Make us of one true heart yearning
D   F#m7   E/G#
For the glory of   Thy   Son;
A   Bm7
Jesus, fire of justice blazing;
F#m7   D   E   A
Gladdening light for - ever   more.

(REPEAT CHORUS 1)

(REPEAT CHORUS 2 THREE TIMES)

ENDING:

          A   Bm7   A/C#
I bow to You, bow to You, I bow to You,
       D/F#   E   A
Bow to You,   I   bow to You.

D/A   A

Copyright © 2003 Thankyou Music (PRS) (adm. worldwide by EMI CMG Publishing, excluding the UK and Europe, which is adm. by kingswaysongs.com) /spiritandsong.com (BMI) (adm. by EMI CMG Publishing) All rights reserved. Used by permission. CCLI Song No. 4729949

Amazing Grace (My Chains Are Gone)

Words and Music by JOHN NEWTON, JOHN P. REES and EDWIN OTHELLO EXCELL
Arrangement and additional chorus by CHRIS TOMLIN and LOUIE GIGLIO

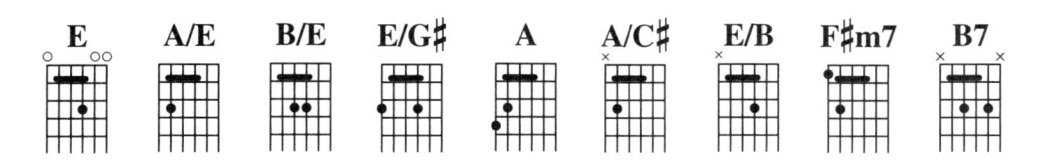

E   A/E   B/E   E/G♯   A   A/C♯   E/B   F♯m7   B7

Capo 1, Cut Capo 3 (E)

VERSE 1:

    E   A/E   E
Amaz - ing Grace, how   sweet the sound,
                    B/E
That saved a wretch like   me.
     E   E/G♯   A   E
I once was lost, but now am found,
             B/E   E
Was blind but now I see.

VERSE 2:

     E   A/E   E
'Twas Grace that taught my heart to fear,
                B/E
And Grace my fears re - lieved.
    E   E/G♯   A   E
How pre - cious did that Grace appear,
         B/E   E
The hour I first believed.

CHORUS:

   E/G♯ A   E/G♯
My chains are gone, I've been set   free,
      A/C♯   E/B
My God, my Savior has ransomed   me.
  E/G♯ A   E/G♯
And like a flood His mercy   reigns,
      F♯m7   B7   E
Unending love,   Amazing Grace.

CONTINUED...

VERSE 3:

     E   A/E   E
The Lord has promised good   to me,
               B/E
His word my hope secures.
     E   E/G♯   A   E
He will my   shield and por - tion be,
          B/E   E
As long as   life endures.

(REPEAT CHORUS TWICE)

VERSE 4:

A/E   E   A/E   E
   The earth shall soon dissolve   like snow,
             B/E
The sun forbear to shine.
     E   E/G♯   A   E
But God who called me here below,
          B/E   E
Will be for - ever mine,
          B/E   E
Will be for - ever mine,
         B/E   E
You are for - ever   mine.

Public Domain. Arr. Copyright © 2006 worshiptogether.com Songs/sixsteps Music (ASCAP) (adm. by EMI CMG Publishing)
All rights reserved. Used by permission. CCLI Song No. 4768151

Be Lifted High

LEELAND MOORING

Capo 2, Cut Capo 4 (E)

VERSE 1:

E	E/G#	A	E/G#
Sin and its ways grow old,

F#m	F#m/E	B
All of my heart turns to stone.

C#m	E/B
And I'm left with no strength

G#m/B	B	E/G#
to arise,

F#m	Bsus	B	Esus	E
I need to be lift - ed high.

VERSE 2:

E	E/G#	A	E/G#
Sin and its ways lead to pain,

F#m	F#m/E	B
Left here with hurt and shame.

C#m	E/B	B	E/G#
So no longer will I leave Your side,

F#m	Bsus	B	Esus	E
Jesus, You be lift - ed high.

CHORUS:

A	E/G#	A	E/G#
You be lifted high, You be lifted high,

F#m	F#m/E	B/D#
You be lifted high in my life,

C#m	G#m	A
oh God.

F#m	F#m/E	B/D#
And I fall to my knees so it's You

C#m	G#m	A
that they see, not I,

F#m	Bsus	B	Esus	E
Jesus, You be lift - ed high.

CONTINUED...

VERSE 3:

E	E/G#
And even now that I'm in - side

A	E/G#
Your hands,

F#m	F#m/E	B
Help me not to grow pride - ful again.

C#m	E/B	G#m/B	B	E/G#
Don't let me forsake sac - rifice,

F#m	Bsus	B	Esus	E
Jesus, You be lift - ed high.

VERSE 4:

E	E/G#
And if I'm blessed with the rich - es

A	E/G#
of kings,

F#m	F#m/E	B
How could I ever think that it was me?

C#m	E/B
For You brought me from dark - ness

G#m/B	B	E/G#
to light,

F#m	Bsus	B	Esus	E
Jesus, You be lift - ed high.

(REPEAT CHORUS TWICE)

F#m	Bsus	B	B/E	E	B/E	E
Jesus, You be lift - ed high.

Copyright © 2006 Meaux Mercy (BMI) (adm. by EMI CMG Publishing)
All rights reserved. Used by permission. CCLI Song No. 4831442

Be Praised

MICHAEL GUNGOR

[Chord diagrams: B7, F#m7, Emaj7, G#m7, F#, B, C#m7, F#sus, E6, F#/A#, G#m/B]

Cut Capo 2 (B)

CONTINUED...

VERSE 1:

  B7   F#m7
Prais - es to the One from whom it all began,

  B7
The One who formed the stars

      F#m7
and who gave life to man.

  Emaj7
He set the world in motion,

  G#m7
creat - ed sky and ocean.

  Emaj7
And here I stand beloved and called by name.

CHORUS 1:

F#   B   F#m7
 Be praised, be praised!

C#m7   F#sus
Lis - ten to creation lift - ing up Your name.

F#   B   F#m7   C#m7
 Be praised, be praised, be praised!

Emaj7   E6

VERSE 2:

  B7   F#m7
Prais - es to the One from whom it all began,

  B7
The One who gave Himself

  F#m7
to save sin - ful man.

  Emaj7
You scorned the shame of Your cross.

  G#m7
My sin, my blame is now gone.

  Emaj7
And here I stand beloved and called by name.

(REPEAT CHORUS 1)

BRIDGE:

  G#m7   F#/A# G#m/B   Emaj7   C#m7
Oh, oh, oh, oh.

  G#m7   F#/A# G#m/B   Emaj7   C#m7
Oh, oh, oh, oh.

VERSE 3:

  B   F#m7
All prais - es to the One from whom it all began,

  B
The One who conquered death

      F#m7
and who will come again.

  Emaj7
The na - tions will behold You

  G#m7
as ev - 'rything becomes new,

  Emaj7
and there I'll stand

           F#
beloved and called by name.

CHORUS 2:

  B   F#m7
Be praised, be praised!

C#m7
Lis - ten to Your people

F#sus   F#
lift - ing up Your name.

  B   F#m7   C#m7
Be praised, be praised, be praised!

Emaj7
(Oh!) *lyric 1st time only*

(REPEAT CHORUS 2)

E6   B

Copyright © 2007 worshiptogether.com Songs (ASCAP) (adm. by EMI CMG Publishing)
All right reserved. Used by permission. CCLI Song No. 4954903

Beautiful News

MATT REDMAN

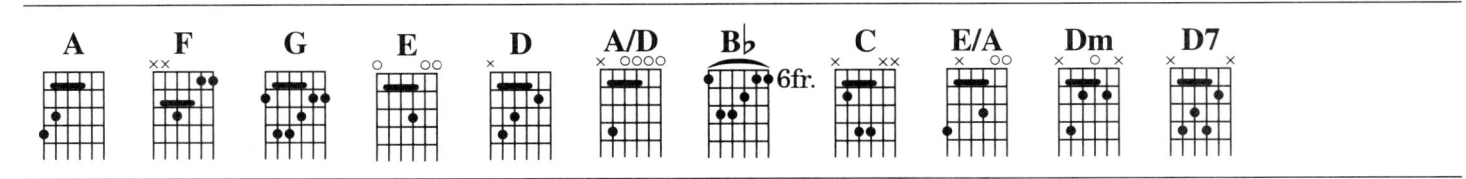

Cut Capo 2 (A)

VERSE:

A
Joy is the theme of my song,

And the beat of my heart,

               F   G
And that joy is found in You.

A
For You showed the pow'r of Your cross,

And Your great saving love,

             F   G
And my soul woke up to You.

E   D
  I heard Your beautiful news,

E   D
  Grace so amazing, so true.

CHORUS:

D   A/D
  Shout it out, let the peo - ple sing,

   Bb
Some - thing so powerful should

C
Shake the whole wide world.

A   E/A
  Make it loud, make it lou - der still,

F
Sav - ior, we're singing now

G
To celebrate Your beautiful news.

(A   F G)*   (A)**
*(1st time only)   **(3rd time only)

(REPEAT VERSE)

(REPEAT CHORUS TWICE)

CONTINUED...

BRIDGE:

Dm   C   A
  There's a God who came down to save,

Dm   C   A
  Showed the world His amaz - ing grace.

Dm   C   A
  There's a God who came down to save,

    F   D   D7
And He calls your name.

CHORUS:

A
  Shout it out, let the people sing,

   F
Some - thing so powerful should

G
shake the whole wide world.

(Shake the whole wide world,

Shake the whole wide world,

Shake the whole wide world.)

(REPEAT CHORUS)

ENDING:

A   F   G
           To celebrate Your beautiful news,

A   F   G   A
           beautiful news.

Copyright © 2006 Thankyou Music (PRS) (adm. worldwide by EMI CMG Publishing, excluding the UK and Europe, which is adm. by kingswaysongs.com).
All rights reserved. Used by permission. CCLI Song No. 4836007

Captivated

VICKY BEECHING

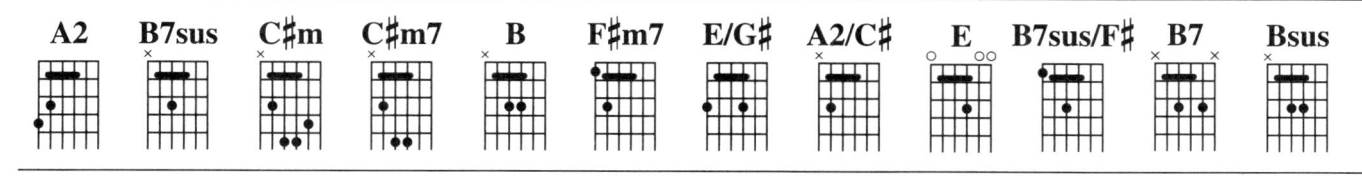

Chords: A2, B7sus, C#m, C#m7, B, F#m7, E/G#, A2/C#, E, B7sus/F#, B7, Bsus

Cut Capo 2 (E)

VERSE 1:
A²   B⁷sus   C#m
  Your laughter it echoes   like a joyous thunder,
A²   C#m B⁷sus
  Your whisper it warms me like a summer breeze.
A²   B⁷sus   C#m⁷
  Your anger is fiercer   than the sun in its splendor,
A²   C#m⁷   B
  You're close and   yet full of mystery.
                F#m⁷   E/G#
And ever since the   day
               A²
that I saw Your   face,
    F#m⁷   E/G#   A²   B⁷sus
Try as I   may,   I cannot look away,
      A²/C#   B⁷sus
I cannot look away...

CHORUS:
E   B⁷sus/F# E/G#   A²
Capti - vated by   You,
    E   B⁷sus/F# E/G#   A²
I am capti - vated by   You.
C#m B   A²   E/G#
May my life be one unbroken gaze,

CHORUS ENDING 1:
F#m⁷   B⁷   E
Fixed upon the beau - ty of   Your face.
B⁷sus/F#   E/G#   A²

VERSE 2:
A²   B⁷sus   C#m
  Beholding is becoming,   so as You fill my gaze,
A²   C#m   B⁷sus
  I become more like You   and my heart is changed.
A²   B⁷sus   C#m⁷
  Beholding is becoming,   so as You fill my view,
A²   C#m⁷   B
  Transform me into the   likeness of You.
       F#m⁷   E/G#   A²
This is what I   ask,   for all my   days,
    F#m⁷   E/G#   A²   B⁷sus
That I   may   never look away,
     A²/C#   B⁷sus
never look away...

CONTINUED...

(REPEAT CHORUS)

CHORUS ENDING 2:
B⁷sus/F#   E/G#
Fixed upon Your beauty,
A²
Fixed upon Your beauty.

BRIDGE:
Bsus   A²   E/G#
  No other could ever be as beautiful,
Bsus   B   A²   E/G#
  No other could ever steal my heart   away.
Bsus   A²   E/G#
  No other could ever be as beautiful,
Bsus   A²   E/G#
  No other could ever steal my heart   away.
F#m⁷   E/G#   A²

            C#m⁷   B⁷sus/F#   E/G#   A²
I just can't look away...

(REPEAT CHORUS)

ENDING:
B⁷sus/F#   E/G#
Fixed upon the beauty,
A²   C#m⁷
Fixed upon the beauty,
B⁷sus/F#   Bsus B
Fixed upon the beau - ty
   E   B⁷sus/F#
of   Your face.
E/G#   A²   E
   The beau - ty of Your face.
B⁷sus/F#   E/G#   A²

Copyright ©2005 Thankyou Music (PRS) (adm. worldwide by worshiptogether.com Songs excluding the UK and Europe, which is adm. by kingswaysongs.com).
All rights reserved. Used by permission. CCLI Song No. 4673703

Carried To The Table

LEELAND MOORING, MARC BYRD and STEVE HINDALONG

Chords: Bm7, D/A, G2, A, D/F#, Em7, Asus, D, D/C#, G2/B, Dsus, G2/F#, G2/D

Cut Capo 2 (A)

VERSE 1:

Bm7   D/A
Wounded and forsaken,
   G2   A
I was shattered by the fall,
Bm7   D/A
Broken and forgotten,
   G2   D/F#
feeling lost and all alone.
Em7
Summoned by the King
   Asus   A
into   the master's courts,
Em7
Lifted by the Savior
   Asus   A
and cradled in His arms.

CHORUS OPENING 1:

    D/F#   G2   D/F#
I was carried to the ta - ble,

CHORUS:

Em7   A   D   D/C#
   seated where   I don't belong,
G2/B   D/F#   G2   D/F#
   Carried to the ta - ble,
Em7   A   D
   swept a - way by His love.
   Em7   Dsus   Asus
And I don't see my bro - kenness any - more,
A   Em7   Dsus   Asus
   When I'm seated at the ta - ble of the Lord.
   A   D/F#   G2   G2/F#
I'm carried to the ta - ble,
Em7   A   (D   D/C#)*
   the table of the Lord.   *1st time only*

VERSE 2:

Bm7   D/A
Fighting thoughts of fear,
   G2   A
wond'ring why He called my name,
   Bm7   D/A
Am I good enough to share this cup,
   G2   D/F#
this world has left me lame.

(CONTINUED...)

Em7
Even in my weakness,
   Asus   A
the Savior called my name.
Em7
In His Holy presence,
   Asus   A
I'm healed and una - shamed.

CHORUS OPENING 2:

    D/F#   G2   D/F#
As I'm carried to the ta - ble,

(REPEAT CHORUS)

INTERLUDE 1:

G2/B   D/A   G2/B   D/A

G2/B   D/A   Em7

CHORUS OPENING 3:

   A   D/F#   G2
I'm carried to the ta - ble

(REPEAT CHORUS)

INTERLUDE 2:

G2/D   D   G2/D   D

G2/D   D   Em7   A

ENDING:

G2/D   D
   You carried me   my God,
G2/D   D
   You carried me.
G2/D   D
   You carried me   my God,
Em7   A
   You carried me.

(REPEAT ENDING FIVE TIMES AND FADE)

Copyright © 2006 Meadowgreen Music Company (ASCAP)/Meaux Mercy/Blue Raft Music (BMI) (adm. by EMI CMG Publishing)
All rights reserved. Used by permission. CCLI Song No. 4681678

Closer

CHARLIE HALL, KENDALL COMBES, DUSTIN RAGLAND and BRIAN BERGMAN

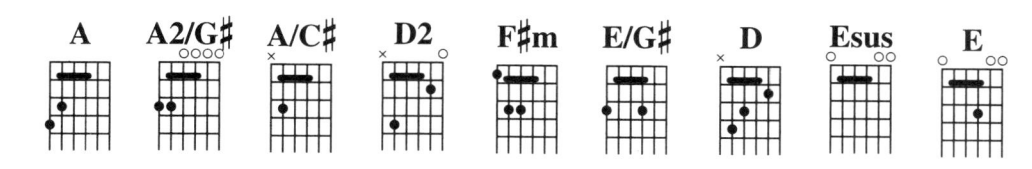

Capo 1, Cut Capo 3 (A)

VERSE:

A   A2/G#   A/C# D2
Beautiful are the words   spoken to me,

A   A2/G#   A/C#   D2

A   A2/G#   A/C#   D2
Beautiful is the one   who is speaking.

A   A2/G#   A/C#   D2

(REPEAT VERSE)

CHORUS 1:

A   A2/G#   A/C#   D2
Come in close,

A   A2/G#   A/C#   D2
come in close   and speak,

A   A2/G#   A/C#   D2
Come in close,   come closer to me.

A   A2/G#   A/C#   D2

(REPEAT VERSE)

(REPEAT CHORUS 1)

INTERLUDE:

A   A2/G#   A/C#   D2

(CONTINUED...)

BRIDGE:

A   A2/G#
And the power of Your words

A/C#   D2
Are filled with grace and mercy.

A   A2/G#   A/C#   D2
Let them fall on my ears and break my stony heart.

(REPEAT BRIDGE)

CHORUS 2:

F#m   E/G#   A   D
Come in close,   come in close and speak,

F#m   Esus   D2
Come in close,   come closer to me.

Esus   E   *Sung 2nd time only
     (Come closer to me.)*

(REPEAT CHORUS 2)

(REPEAT INTERLUDE)

(REPEAT BRIDGE TWICE)

(REPEAT CHORUS TWICE)

ENDING:

A

Copyright © 2005 worshiptogether.com Songs/sixsteps Music (ASCAP) (adm. by EMI CMG Publishing)
All rights reserved. Used by permission. CCLI # 4665302

Created To Worship

VICKY BEECHING

Cut Capo 2 (E)

VERSE 1:

A²   B   C#m⁷
   You formed us from   the dust,

A²   B   C#m⁷
   You breathed Your breath   in us.

A²   B   C#m⁷   F#m¹¹
   We are the work   of Your hands.

A²   B   C#m⁷
   Now we breathe back   to You

A²   B   C#m⁷
   Love songs of grat - itude,

A²   B   C#m⁷   F#m¹¹
   A - doring You   with all we have.

CHORUS:

                    A²   C#m⁷
'Cause we were creat - ed

B   E   A²   C#m⁷
   To worship Your   name,

B   E   A²   C#m⁷
   And we were crea - ted

B   E   A²   C#m⁷   B
   To bring You our   praise.

VERSE 2:

A²   B   C#m⁷
   If we don't wor - ship You,

A²   B   C#m⁷
   We'll search for sub - stitutes

A²   B   C#m⁷   F#m¹¹
   To fill the void   in our souls.

A²   B   C#m⁷
   Wor - shiping oth - er things

A²   B   C#m⁷
   De - stroys our lib - erty.

A²   B   C#m⁷   F#m¹¹
   But as we praise   You, we are free.

CONTINUED...

(REPEAT CHORUS)

BRIDGE:

               A²   C#m⁷
So we will wor - ship,

B   E   A²   C#m⁷
   And so we will   praise.

B   E   F#m⁷
   You are Creat - or

E/G#   A²
   For all our days.

A²   C#m⁷   A²   C#m⁷

ENDING:

A²   C#m⁷
   For this is what we were made to do,

A²   C#m⁷
   This is what we were made to do.

A²   C#m⁷
   This is what we were made to do,

A²   Bsus   B
   So we lift up our praise to You.

A²   C#m⁷   A²   C#m⁷   A²

Copyright © 2004 Thankyou Music (PRS) (adm. worldwide by EMI CMG Publishing excluding the UK and Europe which is adm. by kingswaysongs.com).
All rights reserved. Used by permission. CCLI Song No. 3994713

Everything

TIM HUGHES

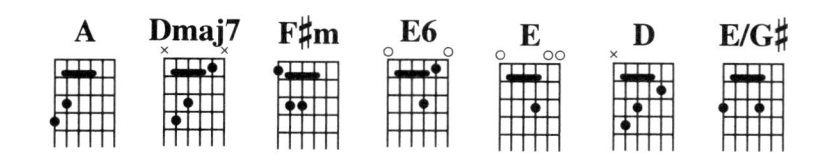

A Dmaj7 F♯m E6 E D E/G♯

Capo 3, Cut Capo 5 (A)

VERSE 1:

       A   Dmaj7
God in my liv - ing, there in my breath - ing.

      F♯m   E6
God in my wak - ing, God in my sleep - ing

      A   Dmaj7
God in my rest - ing, there in my work - ing.

      F♯m   E6
God in my think - ing, God in my speak - ing.

CHORUS:

     Dmaj7 E   F♯m E
Be my ev - 'rything,   be my every - thing.

     Dmaj7 E   A
Be my ev - 'rything,   be my every - thing.

VERSE 2:

      A   Dmaj7
God in my hop - ing, there in my dream - ing.

     F♯m   E6
God in my watch - ing, God in my wait - ing.

      A   Dmaj7
God in my laugh - ing, there in my weep - ing.

     F♯m   E6
God in my hurt - ing, God in my heal - ing.

(REPEAT CHORUS)

BRIDGE:

D   E
  Christ in me, Christ in me,

F♯m
   Christ in me the hope of glory,

CONTINUED...

BRIDGE ENDING 1:

D   E   F♯m
  You   are everything.

(REPEAT BRIDGE)

BRIDGE ENDING 2:

D   E   F♯m   E/G♯
  Be my every - thing.

(REPEAT CHORUS TWICE)

(REPEAT VERSE 2)

(REPEAT BRIDGE & BRIDGE ENDING 1)

ENDING CHORUS 1:

         Dmaj7   E
You are every - thing,

         F♯m   E
You are every - thing.

         Dmaj7   E
You are every - thing,

         A
You are every - thing.

ENDING CHORUS 2:

        Dmaj7   E
Jesus every - thing,

        F♯m   E
Jesus every - thing.

        Dmaj7   E   A
Jesus every - thing, Jesus every - thing.

Copyright © 2005 Thankyou Music (PRS) (adm. worldwide by EMI CMG Publishing excluding the UK and Europe which is adm. by kingswaysongs.com)
All rights reserved. Used by permission. CCLI Song No. 4685258

Forever Holy

BEN CRIST

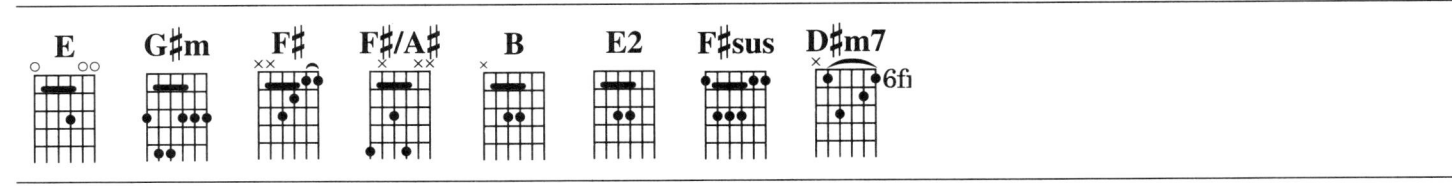

Cut Capo 2 (B)

VERSE 1:

| E | G#m | F# | F#/A# | E | G#m | F# | F#/A# |
God, You stand when all has fall - en.

| E | G#m | F# | F#/A# | E | G#m | F# | F#/A# |
You em - brace the long for - got - ten.

PRE-CHORUS:

E   F#
I guess it's just hard to believe

E   F#
The grace You pour out on me.

E   F#
I guess I'm just starting to see

E   F#
How You're working in me.

CHORUS:

B   F#/A#
This is what makes my head spin;

G#m   F#
You're forever holy.

E   G#m
God of all cre - ation,

E   F#
Pour Your life in - to me.

B   F#/A#
This is so over - whelming,

G#m   F#
You're forever holy.

E   G#m
God of my sal - vation,

E   F#
Clothe me in Your glory, yeah.

(E2   G#m   F#sus F# D#m7) *1st time only*

CONTINUED...

VERSE 2:

| E2 | G#m | F# | D#m7 | E2 | G#m | F# | D#m7 |
God, You hold when all is break - ing.

| E2 | G#m | F# | D#m7 | E2 | G#m | F# | D#m7 |
You re - store the tired and ach - ing.

(REPEAT PRE-CHORUS & CHORUS)

BRIDGE:

E   F#sus   E   F#sus

                          E   F#sus
Clothe me in Your glory.

                          E   F#sus
Clothe me in Your glory.

(REPEAT CHORUS TWICE)

ENDING:

E   F#   E
Clothe me in Your glory.

Copyright © 2006 Spinning Audio Vortex, Inc. (BMI) (adm. by EMI CMG Publishing)
All rights reserved. Used by permission. CCLI Song No. 4943330

Give Me Jesus

JEREMY CAMP

A   F#m7   D2   C#m7   D

Capo 3, Cut Capo 5 (A)

VERSE 1:

    A   F#m7
In the morn - ing when I rise,

    D2   A
In the morn - ing when I rise,

   F#m7   D2
In the morn - ing when I rise,

   A
Give me Je - sus.

CHORUS:

   C#m7 F#m7
Give me Jesus,

   D2 A
Give me Jesus,

    F#m7 D2
You can have all this world,

CHORUS TAG:

     A
Just give me Je - sus.

VERSE 2:

A   F#m7
When I am alone,

D2   A
When I am alone,

F#m7   D2
When I am alone,

   A
Give me Je - sus.

(REPEAT CHORUS & CHORUS TAG)

CONTINUED...

INTERLUDE:

A F#m7 D2 A
       Jesus,

   F#m7   D2 A
Give me Jesus.

VERSE 3:

A   F#m7
When I come to die,

D2   A
When I come to die,

F#m7   D2
When I come to die,

    A
Give me Je - sus.

(REPEAT CHORUS & CHORUS TAG)

(REPEAT CHORUS)

ENDING:

    F#m7 D2
You can have all this world,

    F#m7 D2
You can have all this world,

     A
Just give me Je - sus.

F#m7 D A F#m7 D A

  F#m7 D2 A
Jesus.

Copyright © 2006 Thirsty Moon River Publishing / Stolen Pride Music (ASCAP) (adm. by EMI CMG Publishing)
All rights reserved. Used by permission. CCLI Song No. 4874344

Give You Glory

JEREMY CAMP

Capo 5, Cut Capo 7 (A)

VERSE 1:

      A
We have raised a thousand voices,

   F#m
Just to lift Your holy name,

    D
And we will raise thousands more,

       E
To sing of Your beauty in this place.

A
None can even fathom,

  F#m
No, not one define Your worth,

D
As we marvel in Your presence

  E
To the ends of the earth.

CHORUS:

      A
We give You glory,

                F#m
Lifting up our hands and singing Holy,

     D
You alone are worthy,

           Dm
We just want to touch   Your heart Lord,

Touch Your heart.

A   F#m
Glory, lifting up our voice and singing Holy,

    D
You alone are worthy,

           Dm
We just want to touch   Your heart Lord,

Touch Your heart.

CONTINUED...

VERSE 2:

     A
As we fall down before You,

    F#m
With our willing hearts we seek,

    D
In the greatness of Your glory,

   E
It's so hard to even speak.

       A
There is nothing we can offer,

  F#m
No, nothing can repay,

   D
So we give You all our praises,

  E
And lift our voice to sing.

(REPEAT CHORUS)

BRIDGE:

F#m   D   E
Our hope is drenched in You,

F#m   D   E
Our faith has been re - newed.

F#m   D   E
We trust in Your every word,

C   D   E
Nothing else can even measure up to You.

(REPEAT CHORUS THREE TIMES)
A

Copyright © 2006 Thirsty Moon River Publishing / Stolen Pride Music (ASCAP) (adm. by EMI CMG Publishing)
All rights reserved. Used by permission. CCLI Song No. 4874337

God Of Justice

TIM HUGHES

A2   B   E/G#   E   C#m7   B/D#   Bsus   F#m   C#m   F#m7   E/B

Cut Capo 2 (E)

VERSE 1:

A²　　　　B　　　E/G#　A²
　God of jus - tice, Sav - ior to　　all.
　　　　　　　B　　　E/G#　A²
Came to res - cue the weak and the poor.
　　　　　　B　　E　A²
Chose to serve and not be served.
B　　　E/G#　　　C#m7

PRE-CHORUS 1:

C#m7　　　　B/D#
Jesus, You have called us,
A²　　　　　　　　　　　　　　　　B
Freely we've received, now freely we will　give.

CHORUS:

　　　　　E (E/B)*　　　　B/D# (B)*
We must　go, Live to feed the hungry, *3rd time only
　　　　C#m7　　　　　　A²
Stand beside the broken,　We must go.
　　　　E　　　　　　　　　B/D#
Stepping forward,　Keep us from just　　singing,
　　　　C#m7　　　　　A²
Move us into action, we must go.

VERSE 2:

A²　　　B　　E
To act just - ly, ev-ery day.
A²　　　　B　　　E/G#
　Loving mer - cy, in ev - ery way.
A²　　　　B　　　E/G#
　Walking hum - bly, before You, God.
A²　　B　　E/G#

PRE-CHORUS 2:

　　　C#m7　　　　　　B/D#
You have shown us what You　　require,
A²　　　　　　　　　　　　　　　　B
Freely we've received, now freely we will　give.

(REPEAT CHORUS)

CONTINUED...

BRIDGE:

(Bsus) *A²
　　　　　Fill us up and send us out, *1st time only
Bsus　　　　　　　　　E/G#
　　Fill us up and send us out,
A²　　　　　　　　　　　　　Bsus　　E/G#
　　Fill us up and send us out Lord.

(REPEAT BRIDGE FOUR TIMES)

INSTRUMENTAL:

F#m   C#m   E   B   F#m7   C#m7   E   B

CHANNEL:

　　　　　F#m7　　　　　　C#m7
A change is　made, loving mer - cy.
　　　　　　E　　　B
We must go,　we must go
　　　　　　F#m7　　　　　C#m7
to the bro - ken and the hurt - ing,
　　　　　　F#m7　　　B
We must go,　we must go.

(REPEAT CHORUS)

ENDING (INSTRUMENTAL):

E   B/D#   C#m7   A²

E   B/D#   C#m7   A²

E   B/D#   C#m7   A²

E/B   B   C#m   A²

E/B   B   C#m   A²

E   B/D#   C#m7   A²

E   B/D#   C#m7   A²   E

Copyright © 2005 Thankyou Music (PRS) (adm. worldwide by EMI CMG Publishing excluding the UK and Europe which is adm. by kingswaysongs.com)
All rights reserved. Used by permission. CCLI Song No. 4447128

Great God Of Wonders

ANDY BROMLEY

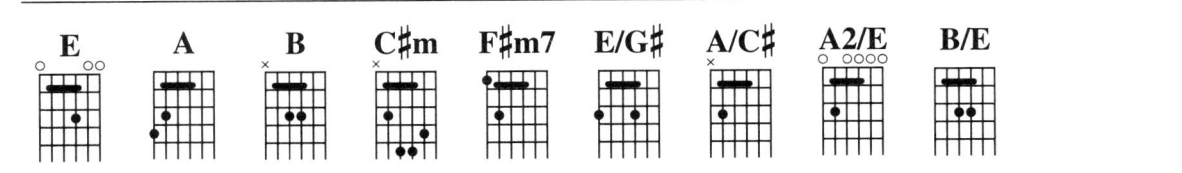

Cut Capo 2 (E)

VERSE:

E
Great God of wonders, Great God in power,

   A
The heavens are declaring glories of Your name,

B A   E
   Glories of Your name.

Great God of Zion, Great God in beauty,

   A
The nations are gathering to worship at Your feet,

B A   E
   To worship at Your feet.

PRE-CHORUS:

B   C#m
  From the rising to the setting sun,

      A
Your name   will be praised.

F#m7
God above all gods,

E/G#
King above all kings,

A   B
Lord of heaven and earth.

CHORUS 1:

          E   A   B
We give to You praise, praise, praise.

A/C#
   Give You

E   A   B   (E) *1st time only*
  praise, praise, praise.

(REPEAT VERSES)

(REPEAT PRE-CHORUS)

(REAPET CHRUS)

CONTINUED...

BRIDGE:

          E   B
You are the   great God a - bove all gods,

          A   B
You are the   great King a - bove all kings

          E   B
You are the   great Lord of heaven and earth,

         A   B
We give You   praise.

(REPEAT BRIDGE)

CHORUS 2:

         E   A2/E   B/E
We give You praise,   praise,   praise.

         E   A2/E   B
We give You praise,   praise,   praise.

(REPEAT CHORUS 1)

E   A   B   A/C#

ENDING:

          B
Only Lord, worthy all our praise, Lord Jesus.

           A   E
Hallelujah, Lord, Hallelu.

Copyright © 2004 Thankyou Music (PRS) (adm. worldwide by EMI CMG Publishing excluding the UK and Europe, which is adm. by kingswaysongs.com)
All rights reserved. Used by permission. CCLI Song No. 4443115

Here And Now

MATT MAHER

Chords: C#m, Amaj7, Bsus, E2, F#m7, B, E, Am2, G#m7, B/D#, E/G#, B/F#

Capo 4, Cut Capo 6 (E)

VERSE 1:

   C#m   Amaj7
No more waiting, Your love's ex - haling.
   Bsus   E2
You are   here and re - turning.
   F#m7   B
We're coming home, and all are one.

CHORUS:

        E   Am2
Here and now;   the proud made low - ly.
        E   Am2
Here and now;   the Lamb made might - y.
        C#m   G#m7
Here and now;   the slave to free - dom.
        A   B
Here and now;   the coming King - dom.

CHORUS ENDING 1:

       E   Am2
Here and now.

E   Am2
   (The cross is)

VERSE 2:

   C#m   Amaj7
The cross is happening, the world is ending,
   Bsus   E2
Dead and a - live, we are be - ginning,
   F#m7   B
We're coming home, and all are one.

(REPEAT CHORUS TWICE)

CONTINUED...

CHORUS ENDING 2:

(B)
   Here and now.

BRIDGE:

E   C#m B/D# E   E/G# A E/G#   B/F#
Tears of   glad - ness, in the sad - ness,
   C#m B/D# E   E/G# A
We're fall - ing   and vic - torious.
   C#m B/D# E   E/G# A E/G#   B/F#
Bless'd and   brok - en, the flood - gates o - pen,
   C#m B/D# E   E/G# A
The sun is   ris - ing to shine
B   C#m B/D# E

(REPEAT CHORUS TWICE)

(REPEAT CHORUS ENDING 2)

ENDING:

E   Am2   E   Am2
  It's here   and now,   it's here   and now.
E   Am2   E

The Highest And The Greatest

NICK HERBERT and TIM HUGHES

Capo 1, Cut Capo 3 (A)

VERSE 1:

    C#m   D   E   A
Wake every heart and every tongue,

    C#m   D   E   A
To sing the new e - ternal song,

    E   D   A/C#   D
And crown Him King of Glory now,

    E   D   F#m   E/G#
Con - fess Him Lord of all.

CHORUS:

    A
You are the high - est,

    E
You are the great - est,

    Bm7   A   E
You are the Lord of all.

    A(F#m)*
Angels will worship,

    E(E/G#)*   *3rd time only
Nations will bow down,

    Bm7   A   D
To the Lord of all.

VERSE 2:

    C#m   D   E   A
A day will come when all will sing,

    C#m   D   E   A
And glori - fy our matchless King,

    E   D   A/C#   D
Your name un - rivaled stands a - lone

    E   D   F#m   E/G#
You are the Lord of all.

(REPEAT CHORUS)

CONTINUED...

BRIDGE:

    Bm7   A/C#
Let every heart, let every tongue,

    D
Sing of Your name, sing of Your name.

    Bm7   A/C#
Let every heart, let every tongue,

    D
Sing, sing, sing.

(REPEAT BRIDGE)

(REPEAT CHORUS THREE TIMES)

1st time, harmony tacet until last C chord.

CHANNEL:

    D   E   F#m   D
Lifting You high, higher and higher, Lord.

ENDING:

    D
Lifting You high, higher and higher,

    E
Lifting You high, higher and higher,

    F#m   D
Lifting You high, higher and higher, Lord.

(REPEAT ENDING FOUR TIMES & FADE)

Copyright © 2007 Thankyou Music (PRS) (adm. worldwide by EMI CMG Publishing excluding the UK and Europe which is adm. by kingswayongs.com)
All rights reserved. Used by permission. CCLI Song No. 4769758

How Can I Keep From Singing

CHRIS TOMLIN, MATT REDMAN and ED CASH

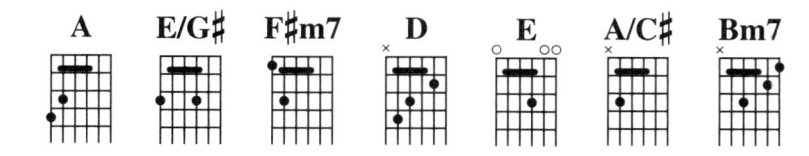

Chord diagrams: A, E/G#, F#m7, D, E, A/C#, Bm7

Cut Capo 2 (A)

VERSE 1:
    A   E/G#
There is an endless song, echoes in my soul,
 F#m7   D
I hear the music ring.
   E   A   E/G#
And though the storms may come, I am holding on,
F#m7 E/G# A F#m7 D
To the rock I cling.

CHORUS:
A   E
How can I keep from singing Your praise?
   D   A/C#
How can I ever say e - nough,
    D   E
How a - mazing is Your love?
A   E
How can I keep from shouting Your name?
   D   A/C#
I know I am loved by the King,

CHORUS TAG:
     D   E   A
And it makes my heart want to sing.

VERSE 2:
    A   E/G#
I will lift my eyes in the darkest night,
 F#m7   D
For I know my Savior lives.
   E A
And I will walk with You
     E/G#
Knowing You see me through,
F#m7 E/G# A F#m7 D
And sing the songs You give.

(REPEAT CHORUS & CHORUS TAG)

CONTINUED...

BRIDGE:
    Bm7   A/C#   D   E
I can sing in the troubled times, sing when I win.
    Bm7   A/C#
I can sing when I lose my step
   D   E
and I fall down a - gain.
    Bm7   A/C#
I can sing 'cause You pick me up,
D   E
Sing 'cause You're there.
    Bm7   A/C#
I can sing 'cause You hear me Lord,
    D   E
When I call to You in pray - er.
    Bm7   A/C#
I can sing with my last breath,
D   E   Bm7   A/C#
Sing for I know that I'll sing with the angels,
     D   E
And the saints around the throne.

(REPEAT CHORUS)

ENDING:
     D   E
And it makes my heart,
    D   A/C#
I am loved by the King,
     D   E
And it makes my heart,
    D   A/C#
I am loved by the King,
     D   E   A
And it makes my heart want to sing.
Yeah, I can sing.

Copyright © 2006 worshiptogether.com Songs / sixsteps Music (ASCAP) (adm. by EMI CMG Publishing) / Alletrop Music (BMI)/
Thankyou Music (PRS) (adm. worldwide by EMI CMG Publishing, excluding the UK and Europe, which is adm. by kingswaysongs.com)
All rights reserved. Used by permission. CCLI Song No. 4822372

I Stand For You

JOHN ELLIS

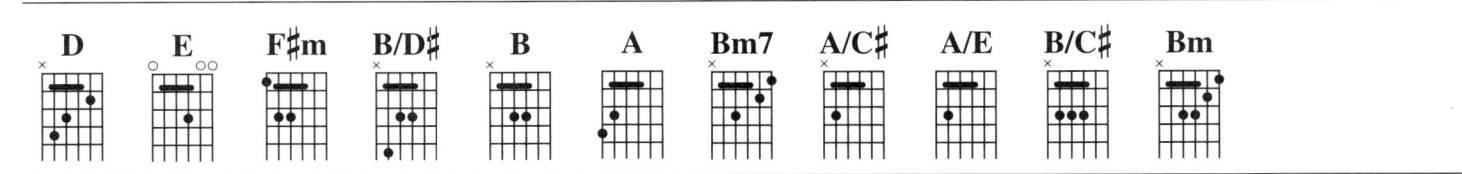

Capo 3, Cut Capo 5 (A)

VERSE 1:
    D E   F#m E
Jesus, I stand for You,
                D   E   B/D# B
No matter what you lead me through.
           D   E   A   B
They will chase me out and close me down,
          D   E   A
But Jesus, I'll stand for You.

CHORUS:
       D   E   A   F#m
I'll always stand, I'll always stand,
       D   E   A
I'll always stand for You.
      D   E   A   B
In all this world, You're all that's true,
     D   E   A
I'll always stand for You.

CHORUS TAG:
D   F#m E   D
  For You, yeah.

VERSE 2:
    D   E   F#m E
Jesus, I've stood my ground,
            D   E   B/D# B
When unbelief was all a - round.
        D   E   A   B
I have felt the sting re - jection brings,
        D   E   A
But Jesus, I'll still stand for You.

(REPEAT CHORUS)

CONTINUED...

BRIDGE:
         D   Bm7   E   A/C#
A time will come when every - one
         D   Bm7   E   A
Will turn their eyes on the risen Son
          D   A   D   A/E
But un - til that day, this world will turn a - way,
        B/D#   B/C# B
And so I take Your hand,
     D   E   A
I'll always stand for You.

INTERLUDE:
(A)   D   F#m   E
(for You.) For You, yeah.
B/D#   B   D   E   A
  I will always, I will always, always.
       D   E   A   B
Guilty of dis - grace, But You took my place,
         D   Bm   A
So Jesus, I'll always stand for You.

(REPEAT CHORUS)

ENDING:
     D   F#m   E   A
For You. Always stand for you.

Copyright © 2004 Birdwing Music/Near Bliss Music/Mouthfulofsongs (ASCAP) (adm. by EMI CMG Publishing)
All rights reserved. Used by permission. CCLI Song No. 4255224

I Will Remember You

BRENTON BROWN

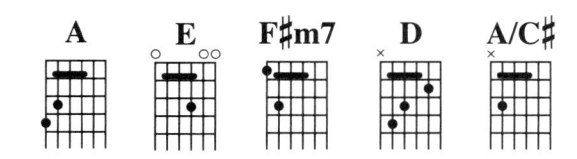

A E F#m7 D A/C#

Cut Capo 2 (A)

CHORUS 1:

    A   E
I will remem - ber You,
   F#m7   D
always re - member You,
    A   E
I will remem - ber You,
      F#m7 D
and all You've done for me.

VERSE 1:

A E F#m7   D
 I will not forget all Your ben - efits,
A   E   F#m7 D
 Even when the storm surrounds my soul.
A   E
 How You com - fort me,
F#m7 D
  heal all my diseases,
A   E
 How You lift me up
  F#m7   D
on ea - gle's wings.

(REPEAT CHORUS 1 TWICE)

VERSE 2:

A E F#m7   D
 I will not forget all Your ben - efits,
A   E   F#m7 D
 How You've cho - sen and adopt - ed me.
A   E
 Orphaned by my sin,
F#m7   D
  Your grace has let me in,
A   E
 And never once
   F#m7   D
have You aban - doned me.

CONTINUED...

(REPEAT CHORUS 1 TWICE)

BRIDGE:

A/C#   D   E
  I have tast - ed and I've seen
      F#m7
how You fa - ther faithfully,
A/C#   D
  How You shep - herd those
    E   F#m7
who fear Your name.
A/C#   D   E
  When the shad - ow's start to fall
     F#m7
and my heart begins to fail,
A/C#   D   E F#m7
  I will lift my eyes to You again.

CHORUS 2:

       A
And I will remem - ber You, always remember You,

I will remember You and all You've done for me.
      A/C#
I will remember You,
   F#m7   D
always re - member You,
    A A/C#
I will remem - ber You
      F#m7 D
and all You've done for me.

(REPEAT CHORUS 1 TWICE)

ENDING:

A E F#m7 D
Yeah.

A E   F#m7 D A
   All You've done for me, yeah.

Copyright © 2006 Thankyou Music (PRS) (adm. worldwide by EMI CMG Publishing excluding the UK and Europe, which is adm. by kingswaysongs.com)
All rights reserved. Used by permission. CCLI Song No. 4707387

Join The Song

VICKY BEECHING and ED CASH

Capo 1, Cut Capo 3 (E)

CONTINUED...

VERSE 1:

E   E/G#   A2
One day every voice   will sing,
C#m7   G#m7   A2
Every beggar, prince   and king,
E   E/G#   A2
Every nation, tongue   and tribe,
  C#m7   G#m7
Every ocean in between   will cry,
 A2   F#m7
   will cry.

CHORUS:

         E
Praise God from whom all blessings flow,
    B/D#
Praise Him, all creatures here below.
   C#m7   A2
To Him all the glory be - longs,
       E
Praise Him above you heavenly host.
       B/D#
Praise Father, Son and Holy Ghost,
    C#m7
Let all the earth sing along.

CHORUS ENDING:

A2
   Come join the song.
(E   F#m7   C#m7   B   E   F#m7   C#m7   B)
                                        1st time only

VERSE 2:

E   E/G#   A2
Gathered 'round the throne   above,
        C#m7   G#m7   A2
We'll be swept up in the mel - ody,
E   E/G#   A2
Hearts will overflow   with love,
        C#m7   G#m7
We'll be singing out a sym - phony,
 A2   F#m7
   we'll sing.

(REPEAT CHORUS)

BRIDGE:

A2   F#m7   E/G#
   Come join the song   that fills eter - nity,
         A2   B7
Sung   throughout all his - tory,
       F#m7
As an - gels shout
         E/G#   A2
and kings   lay down their crowns,
            Adim
We bow down.
         E/G#   B/D#
Praise God from whom all blessings flow,
    Bm/D   A2/C#
Praise Him, all creatures here below.
       E   B/D#
Praise Him above you heavenly host.
    Bm/D   A2/C#
Praise Father, Son and Holy Ghost,

FINAL CHORUS:

         F#
Praise God from whom all blessings flow,
    C#/E#
Praise Him, all creatures here below.
   D#m7   B2
To Him all the glory be - longs,
       F#
Praise Him above you heavenly host.
    C#/E#
Praise Father, Son and Holy Ghost,
    D#m7
Let all the earth sing along.
B2
   Come join the song.

ENDING:

F#   G#m7   D#m7   C#
                    Come join   the song.

(REPEAT ENDING TWICE)

F#   G#m7   D#m7   C#   F#

Copyright © 2006 Thankyou Music (PRS) (adm. worldwide by EMI CMG Publishing excluding the UK and Europe which is adm. by kingswaysongs.com)/ Alletrop Music (BMI). All rights reserved. Used by permission. CCLI Song No. 4879967

Let God Arise

CHRIS TOMLIN, ED CASH and JESSE REEVES

Cut Capo 2 (A)

VERSE 1:

A⁷
Hear the ho - ly roar of God resound,

Watch the waters part before us now.

F♯m⁷
Come and see what He has done for us,

E
Tell the world of His great love,

PRE-CHORUS:

    D   F♯m⁷   E
Our God is a God who saves.

    D   F♯m⁷   E
Our God is a God who saves.

CHORUS:

        A   D/A
Let God arise, Let God arise.

          A⁷
Our God reigns now and forever,

   D/A
He reigns now and forever.

(G A⁷ D   G A⁷ D)   *1st time only*

CONTINUED...

VERSE 2:

A⁷
His en - emies will run for sure,

The church will stand, She will endure.

F♯m⁷
He holds the keys of life, our Lord,

E
Death has no sting, no final word,

(REPEAT PRE-CHORUS)

(REPEAT CHORUS TWICE)

INSTRUMENTAL:
D F♯m⁷ E   D F♯m⁷ E

(REPEAT PRE-CHORUS TWICE)

(REPEAT CHORUS TWICE)

ENDING:
G A⁷ D   G A⁷ D

G A⁷ D   G A⁷ D

A

Copyright © 2006 worshiptogether.com Songs / sixsteps Music (ASCAP) (admin. by EMI CMG Publishing) / Alletrop Music (BMI)
All rights reserved. Used by permission. CCLI Song No. 4822413

Love Came Down

BEN CANTELON

Capo 1, Cut Capo 3 (A)

VERSE 1:

(D/A)   A   D/A
    When I call   on Your name, You an - swer;
              A   D/A
When I fall,   You are there by my side.
            A   D/A
You deliv - ered me out of dark   - ness,
            A   D/A
Now I stand   in the hope of new life.

VERSE 1 ENDING 1:

        A   D/A   A
Yeah,   stand in the hope of new life with You.

(REPEAT VERSE 1)

VERSE 1 ENDING 2:

       Bm7   A   D
By grace   I'm free; You res - cued me.
Bm7   A/C#   D
All I am is   Yours.

CHORUS:

A
   I've found a love greater than life itself.
Dmaj7(/A) 4th time only
   I've found a hope stronger and nothing compares.
F#m7   D
     I once was lost, now I'm alive in You,

CHORUS ENDING 1:

            A   Dmaj7
I'm alive in You. Thank You, Lord.
    A   D
I'm alive in You.

VERSE 2:

            A   D
You're my God   and my firm founda - tion.
          A   D
It is You   whom I'll trust at all times.
          A   D
I give glo - ry and praise, adora - tion
         A   D
To my Sav - ior Who's seated on   high.

(REPEAT CHORUS)

CHORUS ENDING 2:

(D)
   I found love. Oh, sing...

CONTINUED...

(REPEAT CHORUS)

CHORUS ENDING 3:

            (A)   Last time only
I'm alive in You.

BRIDGE:

E   F#m D   A
    I'm alive in You.   I'm alive in You, Lord.
E   F#m7 D2   A
    Thank You, Lord. Thank You, Lord.
             E   F#m7
I'm singing: Love came down and rescued me.
Dmaj7   A
     I thank You, yes,   I thank You.
  Esus   F#m7
I once was blind but now I see.
Dmaj7   A
     I see You, yes,   I see You.
  Esus   F#m7
And love came down and rescued me.
Dmaj7   A
     I thank You, yes,   I thank You.
  E   F#m7
I once was blind but now I see.
Dmaj7   A   E   F#m7
     I see You, yes,   I see You, Lord.
Dmaj7   A   E F#m7 D
     I see You, I see You, Lord.
E/D   A   Bm7   A/C#   D
    By grace   I'm free. You res - cued me.
Bm7   A/C#   D
All I am is   Yours.
          Bm7   A/C#   D
    By grace   I'm free. You res - cued me.
Bm7   A/C#   Dmaj7
All I am is   Yours.

(REPEAT CHORUS)

CHORUS ENDING 4:

                          D/E
I'm loving You, Lord. We sing:...

(REPEAT CHORUS & CHORUS ENDING 3)

Copyright © 2006 Thankyou Music (PRS) (adm. by EMI CMG Publishing, excluding the UK and Europe which is adm. by kingswaysongs.com)
All rights reserved. Used by permission. CCLI Song No. 4943316

Made To Worship

CHRIS TOMLIN, STEPHAN SHARP and ED CASH

A   A2/G#   F#m   D   E   A/E   Bm7   E7   A/C#

Capo 3, Cut Capo 5 (A)

VERSE 1:

     A   A2/G#
Be - fore the day, be - fore the light,
  F#m   D E
Be - fore the world revolved around the sun.
  A   A2/G#
God on high stepped down in -   to time,
                  F#m
And wrote the sto - ry
                          D   E
of His love for everyone.

PRE-CHORUS:

D   E
  He has filled our hearts with wonder,
D   A/E   D
  so that we al - ways re - member:

CHORUS:

A
You and I were made to worship,
D
You and I are called to love,
Bm7   E7
You and I are forgiven and free.
     A
When you and I embrace surrender,
    D
When you and I choose to believe,
  Bm7   E7
Then you and I will see

(you and I will see) *3rd time only*

who we were meant to be.

VERSE 2:

A   A2/G#
  All we are and all we have,
 F#m   D
Is all a gift from God that we receive.
A   A2/G#
Brought to life we open up   our eyes,
        F#m   D E
To see the maj - esty and glory of the King.

CONTINUED...

(REPEAT PRE-CHORUS)

(REPEAT CHORUS)

BRIDGE:

Bm7
  Even the rocks cry out,
A/C#
  even the heavens shout,
D   E7
  At the sound of His Holy name.
Bm7
  So let every voice sing out,
A/C#
  let every knee bow down,
D   E7
  He is worthy of all our praise.

(REPEAT CHORUS TWICE)

ENDING:

        D   Bm7   E7
Yeah,   we were meant to be,   oo.
                A   D
You and I,   you and I,
             Bm7   E7
yeah,   yeah, oo.

                          A
We were meant to be.

Copyright © 2006 worshiptogether.com Songs / sixsteps Music (ASCAP) (adm. by EMI CMG Publishing) / Alletrop Music (BMI) / Stenpan Music (ASCAP)
All rights reserved. Used by permission. CCLI Song No. 4794118

O Church Arise

STUART KENNEDY and KEITH GETTY

Capo 5, Cut Capo 7 (A)

VERSE 1:

E⁷sus　A　　　　　D/F♯　E/G♯
O Church, a - rise, and put your armor on;

　A/C♯　D　　　Esus　E　A
Hear the call of　Christ, our Cap　-　tain.

E⁷sus　A　　　　　D/F♯　E/G♯
For now the weak can say that they are strong

　A/C♯　D　　　Esus　E　A
In the strength that God has giv　-　en.

　A/C♯　D　　A/C♯　E
With shield of faith and belt of　truth,

　A/C♯　D　　　A/C♯　F♯m　E
We'll stand a - gainst the dev　-　il's　lies;

E⁷sus　A　　　　　D/F♯　E/G♯
An army　bold, whose battle cry is　love,

　A/C♯　D
Reaching out to　those

　Esus　E　　A　Asus　A
in dark　-　ness.

VERSE 2:

　E⁷sus　A　　　　　D/F♯　E/G♯
Our call to　war, to love the captive soul.

　A/C♯　D　　　Esus　E　A
But to rage a - gainst the cap　-　tor.

E⁷sus　A　　　　　D/F♯　E/G♯
And with the sword that makes the wounded whole

　A/C♯　D　　　Esus　E　A
We will fight and faith and va　-　lor.

　A/C♯　D　　A/C♯　E
When faced with trials on every　side.

　A/C♯　D　　　A/C♯　F♯m　E
We know the outcome is　　se - cure.

E⁷sus　A　　　　　D/F♯　E/G♯
And Christ will have the prize for which He died,

　A/C♯　D
And in - heri - tance

　Esus　E　　A　Asus　A
of na　-　tions.

CONTINUED...

VERSE 3:

E⁷sus　A　　　　　D/F♯　E/G♯
Come see the cross, where love and mercy meet.

　A/C♯　D　　　Esus　E　A
As the Son of　God is strick　-　en.

E⁷sus　A　　　　　D/F♯　E/G♯
Then see His　foes lie crushed be - neath His feet,

　A/C♯　D　　　Esus　E　A
For the Conquer - or has ris　-　en.

　A/C♯　D　　A/C♯　E
And as the　stone is rolled a - way.

　A/C♯　D　　　A/C♯　F♯m　E
And Christ e - merges from　the　grave.

E⁷sus　A　　　　　D/F♯　E/G♯
This victory　march continues till the　day

　A/C♯　D
Every eye and heart

　Esus　E　　A　Asus　A
shall see　　Him.

VERSE 4:

　E⁷sus　A　　　　　D/F♯　E/G♯
So Spirit,　come, put strength in every　stride,

　A/C♯　D　　　Esus　E　A
Give grace for every hur　-　dle.

E⁷sus　A　　　　　D/F♯　E/G♯
That we may run with faith to win the prize

　A/C♯　D　　　Esus　E　A
Of a servant good and faith　-　ful.

　A/C♯　D　　A/C♯　E
As saints of old still line the way.

　A/C♯　D　　　A/C♯　F♯m　E
Re - telling　triumphs of　His　grace.

E⁷sus　A　　　　　D/F♯　E/G♯
We hear their calls and hunger for the day,

　A/C♯
When with Christ

　D　Esus　E　A　Asus　A
we stand in glo　-　ry.

Copyright © 2005 Thankyou Music (PRS) (adm. by EMI CMG Publishing excluding UK & Europe which is adm. by kingswaysongs.com)
All right reserved. Used by permission. CCLI Song No. 4611992

On The Third Day

MATT MAHER and MARC BYRD

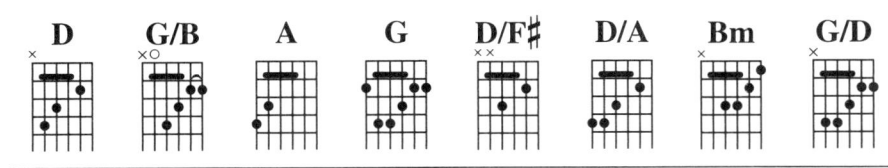

[Chord diagrams: D, G/B, A, G, D/F#, D/A, Bm, G/D]

Capo 1, Cut Capo 3 (D)

VERSE 1:
      D
Creation brings an offering,
  G/B   A
    As autumn leaves   turn to gold,
G   D
   The trees bow down   in highest praise,
G/B   A
   Now made bare   before Your throne.
G   D/F#
   The western sky an amber blaze,
G   D/A   G/B
   At the end of the day,
   D/A   A   D
For ev - 'rything must die   to rise again.

VERSE 2:
     D
The winter's chill, a bitter cold,
G/B   A
   As sin and shame   leave us to fall,
G   D
   The clouds now full   of newborn snow,
G/B   A
   For grace to come   and save us all,
G   D/F#
   Within the darkest night of man,
G   D/A   G/B
   Was found Your saving hand,
   D/A   A   D
For ev - 'rything must die   to rise again.

CHORUS 1:
       G   D   D/A
On the third day, behold   the King,
       G   Bm   A
On the third day, death has   no sting,
       G   Bm   A   D
On the third day, we're for - given and rec - onciled.

VERSE 3:
    D
The earth it groans in labor pains,
G/B   A
   As flowers stretch   to heaven above,

CONTINUED...
     G   D
   Your creatures sing   the prophet's song,
G/B   A
   To be a gift   of selfless love.
G   D/F#
   The sun is rising in the east,
G   D/A   G/B
   And Your spirit is unleashed,
   D/A   A   D
For ev - 'rything must die   to rise again.

VERSE 4:
      D
And so we wait in joyful hope,
G/B   A
   For You to come   and take us home,
G   D
   And so we join   beneath the cross,
G/B   A
   In suffering   from whence we go.
G   D/F#
   The greatest act of sovereign grace,
G   D/A   G/B
   In the universe displayed,
   D/A   A   D
For ev - 'rything must die   to rise again.

(REPEAT CHORUS 1)

CHORUS 2:
       G   D   D/A
On the third day, the saints   rejoice,
       G   Bm   A
On the third day, we lift   our voice,
       G   Bm   A   D
On the third day, u - nited and glo - rified.

(REPEAT CHORUS 1 & CHORUS 2)

ENDING:
G/D   D

Copyright © 2006 Thankyou Music (PRS) (adm. worldwide by EMI CMG Publishing excluding the UK and Europe which is adm. by kingswaysongs.com)
spiritandsong.com Publishing/Meaux Mercy/Blue Raft Music (BMI) (adm. by EMI CMG Publishing)
All rights reserved. Used by permission. CCLI Song No. 4724023

Resurrection Day

MATT MAHER

Chords: E A C#m B Amaj7 E/G# F#m

Capo 3, Cut Capo 5 (E)

VERSE 1:

E
  It's the weight of Your glory,

Brings the proud to their knees,

And the light of revelation,

Lets the blind man see.

A
  It's the power of the cross,

Breaks away death's embrace,

And we celebrate our freedom,

Dancing on an empty grave.

PRE-CHORUS:

C#m   B
Roll away the stone,

Amaj7   B
Roll away the   stone.

CHORUS:

     E   E/G#   A   B
We sing for joy,   we shout Your name,

     E   E/G#   C#m   B
We cele - brate Your resurrection   day.

     E   E/G#   A   B
We sing for joy,   we shout Your name,

     E   E/G#   A   B   E
We cele - brate Your resur - rection   day.

GUITAR SOLO:

E   A   E   A   E   A   E   A

CONTINUED...

VERSE 2:

E
  You declare what is holy,

You declare what is good,

In the sight of all the nations,

You declare that You are God.

A
  It's the power in Your Blood,

Breaks away sin's embrace,

And we celebrate our freedom,

Dancing on our broken chains.

(REPEAT PRE-CHORUS & CHORUS)

C#m B   F#m   C#m B   F#m

(REPEAT CHORUS TWICE)

(REPEAT GUITAR SOLO)

E

Copyright © 2005 Thankyou Music (PRS) (adm. worldwide by EMI CMG Publishing excluding the UK and Europe which is adm. by kingswaysongs.com)/ spiritandsong.com Publishing (BMI) (adm. by EMI CMG Publishing) All rights reserved. Used by permission. CCLI Song No. 4669786

Shine

MATT REDMAN

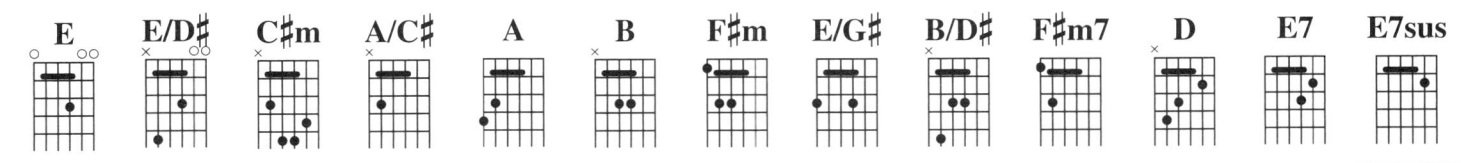

Chords: E E/D# C#m A/C# A B F#m E/G# B/D# F#m7 D E7 E7sus

Capo 3, Cut Capo 5 (E)

VERSE:

              E   E/D#
Lord we have seen the rising sun,

     C#m   A/C# C#m
Awakening the early dawn,

     A   E   B
And we're rising up to give You praise.

              E   E/D#
Lord we have seen the stars and moon,

         C#m   A/C# C#m
See how they shine, they shine for You.

     A   E   B
And You're calling us to do the same,

PRE-CHORUS:

    F#m
So we rise up with a song,

    E/G#
And we rise up with a cry,

          A
And we're giv - ing You our lives.

CHORUS 1:

        E
We will shine like stars in the universe,

       B/D#
Holding out Your truth in the darkest place.

    F#m7
We'll be living for Your glory,

       A
Jesus we'll be living for Your glory.

(REPEAT VERSE, PRE-CHORUS & CHORUS 1)

CHORUS 2

      E
We will burn so bright with Your praise, oh, God,

      B/D#
And declare Your light to this broken world.

  D
We'll be living for Your glory,

      A
Jesus, we'll be living for Your glory.

CONTINUED...

BRIDGE:

     F#m
Like the sun so radiantly,

    E/G#
Sending light for all to see,

         A
Let Your Ho - ly Church arise.

    F#m
Ex - ploding into life,

     E/G#
Like a su - pernova's light,

         A
Set Your Ho - ly Church on fire,

(REPEAT BRIDGE)

      E
We will shine.

      E7
We will shine.

(REPEAT CHORUS 1, CHORUS 2 & PRE-CHORUS)

          E   E7sus   E7
Jesus, we will shine.

Copyright © 2006 Thankyou Music (PRS) (adm. worldwide by EMI CMG Publishing, excluding the UK and Europe, which is adm. by kingswaysongs.com)
All rights reserved. Used by permission. CCLI Song No. 4831435

Sound Of Melodies

LEELAND MOORING, JACK MOORING and STEVE WILSON

Cut Capo 2 (A)

VERSE 1:

F#m7　　Asus　　　A
We who were called to be Your people,

F#m7　　Asus　　A
Struggling sinners and thieves.

　F#m7　　Asus　　A
We're lifted　up from the ashes,

　F#m7　　Asus　　　A
And out came the song of the re - deemed,

F#m7　Asus/D　　　A
The song of the redeemed.

F#m7　Asus/D

CHORUS:

　　　　　　A
Can you hear the sound of melodies,

　　　E　　　　　　C#m7
Oh, the sound of melodies rising up to You,

　C#m/E　　F#7sus　D2
Rising up　to　You,　God?

　　A
The sound of melodies,

　　　E　　　　　　C#m7
Oh, the sound of melodies rising up to You,

　C#m/E　　F#7sus　D2　A
Rising up　to　You,　God?

VERSE 2:

　F#m7　Asus/D　　A
Oh, we have caught a reve - lation,

　F#m7　　Asus/D　A
That nothing can separate us from.

　F#m7　　Asus/D　　　　A
The love we re - ceived through sal - vation,

　F#m7　Asus/D　　　A
It fills your daughters and Your sons,

F#m7　　Asus/D　　　A
　Your daughters and Your　sons.

F#m7　　Asus/D

CONTINUED...

(REPEAT CHORUS)

BRIDGE:

　　　　　　　　　　　　　　　　E
The sound of Your love, the sound of Your love,

　　　　　　F#m7　　D2
Is what You're　hear - ing.

A　　　　　　　　　　　　　　　E
The sound of Your sons, the sound of Your sons,

　　　　　　F#m7　　D2
You've won Your　chil - dren.

A　　　　　　　　　　　　　　　　E
The sound of Your love, the sound of Your love,

　　　　　　F#m7　　D2
Is what You're　hear - ing.

A　　　　　　　　　　　　　　　E
Your daughters in love, Your daughters in love,

　　　　　　F#m7　　D2
You've won Your　chil - dren.

CHANNEL:

　　A
The sound of melodies,

　　　E7sus　　　E　　　C#m7
Oh, the sound of melo - dies rising up to You.

　　　E　F#m7　D2　A
Rising up to You,　God,

E　　　　　C#m7　　E　F#m7　D2
　Rising up to You,　God.

REFRAIN:

A　　　　　　　　　　　E
La, la, la, la, la, la, la, la, la, la, la, la.

C#m7　　　C#m/E　　F#7sus　D2
La, la, la, la, la, la, la, la, la,　la,　la,　la.

(REPEAT REFRAIN)

A

Copyright © 2006 Meaux Mercy (BMI) / Meaux Jeaux (SESAC) (adm. by EMI CMG Publishing)
All rights reserved. Used by permission. CCLI Song No. 4669425

Speak, O Lord

KEITH GETTY and STUART TOWNEND

Capo 3, Cut Capo 5 (A)

VERSE 1:

D/F♯ E/G♯ A²   D   A
Speak, O   Lord, as we come to You,
      D   A   F♯m   E/G♯
To re - ceive the food   of Your holy word.
D/F♯ E/G♯ A²   D   A
Take Your truth, plant it deep in us;
             D   A/C♯ D   E   A
Shape and fashion us   in Your like-ness,
A/C♯   E   E/D   A/C♯
That the light of   Christ
        Esus/D E⁹/D   A²/C♯
might be seen   to-day,
      E   E/D A/C♯   F♯m   Esus   E
In our acts of   love and our deeds of faith.
D/F♯ E/G♯ A²   D   A
Speak, O   Lord, and ful-fill in us
           D   A/C♯
all your purposes,
D   Esus   E A
For Your glo -   ry.
D²

A²/C♯   D²   Esus   E

VERSE 2:

D/F♯ E/G♯ A²   D   A
Teach us   Lord full o-bedience,
      D   A   F♯m E/G♯
Holy rev-erence, true hu-mility.
D/F♯ E/G♯ A²   D   A
Test   our   thoughts and our attitudes,
      D   A/C♯ D   E   A
In the radiance   of Your puri - ty.
A/C♯   E   E/D   A/C♯
Cause our faith to   rise,
        Esus/D E⁹/D   A²/C♯
Cause our eyes   to see,
      E   E/D A/C♯   F♯m   Esus   E
Your ma-jes-tic   love and au-thor - i - ty.
D/F♯ E/G♯ A²   D   A
Words of   power that can never fail;
      D   A/C♯ D Esus   E   A
Let their truth pre-vail   over un -   belief.
D²

A²/C♯   D²   Esus   E

CONTINUED...

VERSE 3:

D/F♯ E/G♯ A²   D   A
Speak, O   Lord, and re-new our minds;
      D   A
Help us grasp the heights
     F♯m   E/G♯
of Your plans for us.
D/F♯ E/G♯ A²   D   A
Truths un - changed from the dawn of time,
      D   A/C♯ D   E   A
That will echo down   through e-terni-ty.
A/C♯   E   E/D   A/C♯
And by grace we'll stand
        Esus/D E⁹/D   A²/C♯
on Your prom -   is-es;
      E   E/D A/C♯   F♯m   Esus   E
And by faith we'll   walk as You walk with us.
D/F♯ E/G♯ A²   D   A
Speak, O   Lord, till Your church is built,
      D   A/C♯ D   Esus E A
And the earth is filled   with Your glo -   ry.
D²

A²/C♯   D²   Esus   E

A

Copyright © 2005 Thankyou Music (PRS) (adm. worldwide by EMI CMG Publishing excluding the UK & Europe which is adm. by kingswaysongs.com)
All rights reserved. Used by permission. CCLI Song No. 4615235

Tears Of The Saints

LEELAND MOORING and JACK MOORING

[Chord diagrams: C#m7, F#m, D, E, Bm7, A/C#, A, Asus]

Capo 2, Cut Capo 4 (F#m)

VERSE 1:

C#m7   F#m
   There are many prodigal sons,
    D
On our city streets they run,
           E
Searching for shel - ter.
       F#m
There are homes broken down,
        D
People's hopes have fallen to the ground,
       E   Bm7
From fail - ures. This is an e - mergency!

CHORUS:

A/C#   D
   There are tears from the saints,
       A   E
For the lost and unsaved,
         Bm7
We're crying for them come back home,
              D   E
We're crying for them come back home,
           D
And all Your children will stretch out their hands,
          A
And pick up   the crippled man,
           Bm7
Father we will lead them home,
              D   E   C#m7
Father we will lead them home,

INTERLUDE 1:

F#m   D   E

VERSE 2:

C#m7   F#m
   There are schools full of hatred,
         D   E
Even churches have forsaken love and mer - cy.
           F#m
May we see this generation,
       D
In its state of desperation.
              E   Bm7
For Your glo - ry. This is an e - mergency!

(REPEAT CHORUS)

INTERLUDE 2:

F#m   E   Asus   A

BRIDGE:

E   Asus   A
Sinners, reach out   your hands!
E   Asus   A
Children in Christ   you stand!
E   Asus   A
Sinners, reach out   your hands!
E   F#m   D   Bm
Children in Christ   you stand!

(REPEAT CHORUS)

ENDING:

D
   And all Your children will stretch out their hands,
          A   E
And pick up   the crippled man,
           Bm7
Father we will lead them home,
           D
Father we will lead them home,
              E   C#m7   D

Copyright © 2005 Meaux Mercy (BMI) / Meaux Jeaux Music (SESAC) (adm. by EMI CMG Publishing)
All rights reserved. Used by permission. CCLI Song No. 4768694

The Wonder Of The Cross

VICKY BEECHING

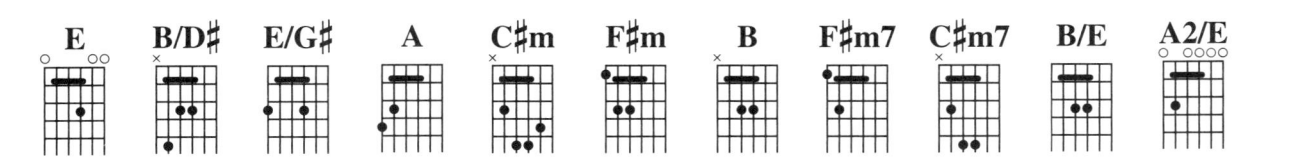

[Chord diagrams: E, B/D#, E/G#, A, C#m, F#m, B, F#m7, C#m7, B/E, A2/E]

Capo 4, Cut Capo 6 (E)

VERSE 1:

      E   B/D# E
O precious sight, my Savior stands,
    E/G#
Dying for me with outstreched hands.
     A   B/D# C#m
O precious sight, I love to gaze,
      F#m B/D# C#m
Remembering   sal - vation's day,
      F#m B/D# E
Remembering   sal - vation's day.
          B/D# E
Though my eyes linger on this scene,
    E/G#
May passing time and years not steal
     A   B/D# C#m
The power with which it impacts me,
     F#m B/D# C#m
The freshness of its myster - y,
     F#m B/D# E
The freshness of its myster - y.

CHORUS:

E   B
  May I never lose the wonder,
F#m7   E
The wonder of the cross.
  C#m7   B/D#
May I see it like the first time
    F#m7   C#m7
Standing as a sinner lost,
    A   E/G#
Undone by mercy and left speechless,
  F#m7   C#m7
Watching wide eyed at the cost.
  A   B/D# C#m7
May I never lose the wonder,

CHORUS ENDING 1:

  F#m B/D# E
The wonder of the cross.

CONTINUED...

VERSE 2:

     E   B/D# E
Behold the Godman cruci - fied,
    E/G#
The perfect sinless sacrifice.
     A   B/D# C#m
As blood ran down those nails and wood,
    F#m B/D# C#m
History   was split in two, yes,
    F#m B/D# E
History   was split in two.
     B/D# E
Behold the empty wooden tree,
    E/G#
His body gone, alive and free.
     A   B/D# C#m
We sing with ever - lasting joy,
    F#m B/D# C#m
For sin and death have been de - stroyed, yes,
    F#m B/D# E
Sin and death have been de - stroyed.

(REPEAT CHORUS)

CHORUS ENDING 2:

  F#m B/D# C#m7 B/D# E
The wonder of the cross.

F#m7 E/G# A   B   C#m7 B/D#

E   F#m7 E/G# A

(REPEAT CHORUS & CHORUS ENDING 1)

E   B/E   E   A2/E

E   B/E   E   A2/E

E

Copyright © 2007 Thankyou Music (PRS) (adm. worldwide by EMI CMG Publishing, excluding the UK and Europe, which is adm. by kingsway songs.com)
All right reserved. Used by permission. CCLI song #4886507.

To The Only God

CHRIS TOMLIN

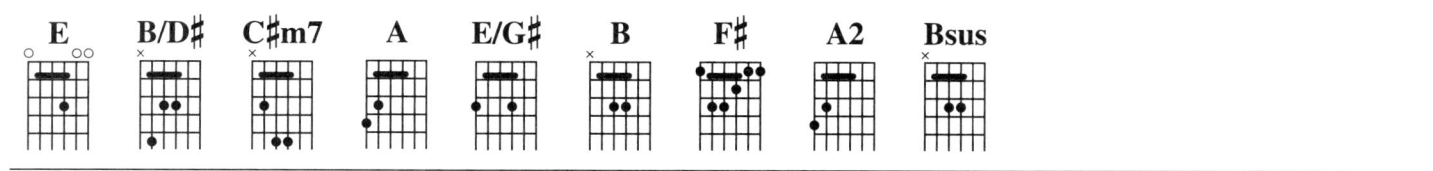

Chords: E B/D# C#m7 A E/G# B F# A2 Bsus

Capo 4, Cut Capo 6 (E)

VERSE:

E   B/D#   C#m7
To the on - ly God

       A   E/G#
who is a - ble to keep   us,

A   B
Able us to keep   us from falling.

E   B/D#   C#m7
To the on - ly God

VERSE ENDING:

       A   E/G#
be all glo - ry and hon - or,

C#m7   F#
Majesty and po - wer,

A   B   (E) *1st time only*
For all ages now   and forevermore.

(REPEAT VERSE & VERSE ENDING)

BRIDGE:

A2   Bsus   A2   Bsus
       Forever - more.

(REPEAT VERSE ENDING)

ENDING:

E
  Forevermore.

Copyright © 2007 Worshiptogether.com Song/sixsteps Music (ASCAP) (adm. by EMI CMG Publishing).
All rights reserved. Used with permission. CCLI Song No. 4879284

Unwavering

MATT MAHER

F#m7   E   A   C#m7   E/B   B   B/D#   B7

Cut Capo 2 (E)

CONTINUED...

VERSE 1:

F#m7   E   A   E
Blessed are the poor, the kingdom is theirs.

        C#m7   F#m7
Alive in the promise to be dead to the   world.

             E   A   E
Blessed are the meek in awe of You Father,

A   E/B   E   A   E
The Word at Your right hand, spirit of truth.

CHORUS:

           A   E
Unwavering is Your voice,

           B   E
unwavering is Your hand,

           C#m7   B/D#   E
Unwavering is   the   heart

C#m7   B
that bled for the sins of man.

           A   E   B   C#m7
Unwavering is Your will, unwavering is Your plan,

A   E/B   B
The fount of sal - vation

          *(E   A   E)   *last time C#m7
on which we will stand.

(B7   E   A   E   C#m7   A)   *1st time only*

VERSE 2:

F#m7   E   A   E
Blessed are the righteous on bended knee,

      C#m7   F#m7
Found in this freedom, committed to   You.

            E   A   E
Blessed are those who see the heights of glory,

A   E/B   B   E   A   E
Found in the valley,   and suffering for You.

(REPEAT CHORUS TWICE)

A   E/B
The fount of sal - vation

B   A   B   A   B
on which we will stand.

BRIDGE:

                 A   B
Send us out to be Your hands and   feet,

                 A   B
Send us out to be Your hands and feet,

                 A   B
Send us out to be Your hands and   feet,

              A   B
Send us out to   be Your hands and   feet.

                 A   B
Send us out to be Your hands and   feet,

                 A   B
Send us out to be Your hands and   feet,

                 A   B
Send us out to be Your hands and   feet.

A   B   A   B

Copyright © 2006 Thankyou Music (PRS) (adm. worldwide by EMI CMG Publishing, excluding Europe, which is adm. by kingswaysongs.com)/
spiritandsong.com Publishing (BMI) All rights reserved. Used by permission. CCLI Song No. 4669827

We Remember

MARC BYRD and LEELAND MOORING

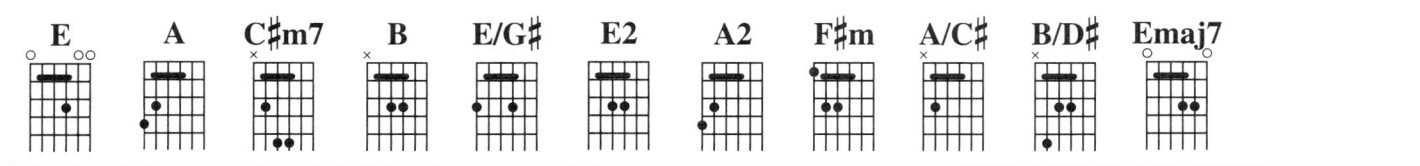

Chords: E A C#m7 B E/G# E2 A2 F#m A/C# B/D# Emaj7

Capo 2, Cut Capo 4 (E)

VERSE 1:

     E
We worship You, Lord,

          A
In the splendor of Your holiness,

          C#m7
In the beauty of Your righteous - ness;

B **A**
Holy, ho - ly!

     E
We offer You thanks

          A
For the endless love You have displayed,

        C#m7
For the sacrifice You freely gave;

B **A**
Worthy, wor - thy!

PRE-CHORUS:

   B **C#m7** **A**
You are ho - ly, pre - cious Lamb of God.

 B   **E/G#** **A**
Forev - er You will reign,

Forever You will reign.

    B **C#m7** **A**   **E/G#** **A**
King of glo - ry, ris - en Son of God.

 B   **E/G#**
Forev - er You will reign,

 A
Forev - er You will reign.

(**E2**   **A2**) *1st time only*

VERSE 2:

    E
Father of light,

       A
In radiance and majesty

          C#m7
Sent Your Son to set the captive free;

B **A**
Holy, ho - ly!

    E
Infinite love,

         A
On the cross You saved us from our sin,

         C#m7
Conquered death and will return a - gain;

B **A**
Worthy, wor - thy!

(REPEAT PRE-CHORUS)

CHORUS:

   F#m **E/G#** **A**   **B**
We re - member, we re - member the cross.

   A/C# **B/D#** **A/C#** **B/D#**
We re - member, we re - member the cost.

   F#m **E/G#**
We re - member, Lord,

   A   **B**
we re - member the cross.

   A/C# **B/D#** **A/C#** **B/D#**
We re - member, we re - member the cost.

(REPEAT PRE-CHORUS)

ENDING:

   F#m **E/G#** **A**   **B**
We re - member, we re - member the cross.

   A/C# **Emaj7** **A/C#** **B/D#**
We re - member, we re - member the cost.

Copyright © 2006 Meaux Mercy/Blue Raft Music (BMI) (adm. by EMI CMG Publishing)
All right reserved. Used by permission. CCLI #4255918

Yes And Amen

Matt Redman, Robert Marvin and Josiah Bell

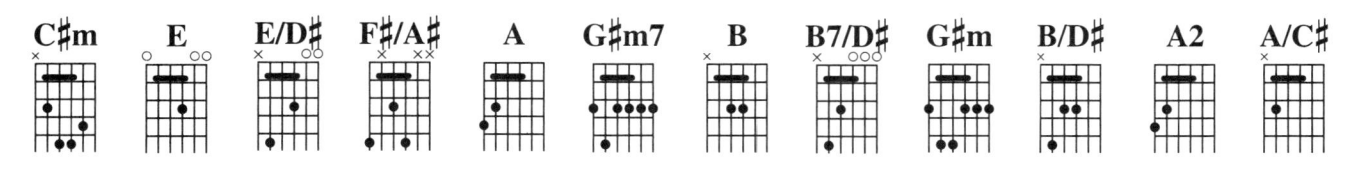

Chords: C#m, E, E/D#, F#/A#, A, G#m7, B, B7/D#, G#m, B/D#, A2, A/C#

Capo 3, Cut Capo 5 (E)

VERSE 1:

C#m
    Hear Your people saying yes,
                             E
Hear Your people saying yes   to You.
C#m
    Yes to anything You ask,
                             E
Yes to anything we're called   to do.
C#m
    Hear Your people say amen,
                             E
Hear Your people say amen   to You.
C#m
    Let Your kingdom come on earth,
                             E
Let it be just like we prayed   to You.

CHORUS 1:

Yes and amen to everything that's in Your heart,
        E/D#
Yes and a - men to everything that You have planned.
    F#/A#
We live to see Your will be done,
     A   E
And see Your perfect kingdom come on earth,
      G#m7
on the earth.

VERSE 2:

C#m   B   C#m
    All the promis - es are yes,
         B7/D#   E
All the promis - es are yes   in You.
C#m   B   C#m
    Every good and perfect gift,
                             E
Every blessing that we have   was You.

(REPEAT CHORUS 1)

CONTINUED...

CHORUS 2:

            E
Yes and a - men, we're taking up our cross for You.
            E/D#
Give us the strength to take these dreams
and follow through.
    F#/A#
We live to see Your will be done,
     A   E
And see Your perfect kingdom come on earth,
      G#m*   *2nd time, G#m7
On the earth.

VERSE 3:

C#m   B   C#m
    Hear Your people saying yes,
          B/D#   E   B/D# E G#m
Hear Your people saying yes   to You.
C#m   B   C#m
    Yes to any - thing You ask,
          B/D#   E   B/D# E G#m
Yes to any - thing we're called   to do.
C#m   B   C#m
    Hear Your people say amen,
          B/D#   E   B/D# E G#m
Hear Your people say amen   to You.
C#m   B   C#m
    Let Your kingdom come on earth,
          B/D#   E   B/D# E
Let it be just like we prayed   to You.

(REPEAT CHORUS 1 & 2)

E   B   E   A   E   A2   B/D#

C#m B/D# E B/D# E   A/C# A2

ENDING:

(B/D#)*   C#m   B/D#   E
Yes and a - men,
B/D#   E   A2
Yes and a - men.   *B/D# not played 1st time

(REPEAT ENDING 3 TIMES)

B/D#   C#m   B/D#   E

Copyright © 2006 Thankyou Music (PRS) (adm. worldwide by EMI CMG Publishing, excluding the UK and Europe, which is adm. by kingswaysongs.com) / Meaux Mercy (adm. by EMI CMG Publishing) / JLCB Music (BMI) All rights reserved. Used by permission. CCLI Song No. 4835967

You Are God

CHARLIE HALL

Capo 3, Cut Capo 5 (E)

VERSE 1:

E   E/D#   C#m7   E/B
 You're closer   than our troubles,

A   E/G#   A   B
 More present than any danger,

E   E/D#   C#m7   E/B
 More grand than gold and silver.

A   E/G#   A   B
 You are   God, You are   God.

E   E/D#   C#m7   E/B

A²   E/G#   A²   B

VERSE 2:

E   E/D#   C#m7   E/B
 You're the joy of   man's de - sire;

A   E/G#   A   B
 You are Father,   Satis - fier.

E   E/D#   C#m7   E/B
 We are stunned with wide eyed wonder.

A   E/G#   A   B
 You are   God, You are   God.

E   E/D#   C#m7   E/B

A²   E/G#   A²   B

CONTINUED...

CHORUS:

E   B/D#
 Fill our hearts   with love and faith.

C#m7   E/B
 You fight for us,   You make us brave.

A²   E/G#   A²   Bsus
 You are   God,   You are God.

E   B/D#
 You walk with us,   You lead us up.

C#m7   E/B   A²
 Faith, hope and love   wakes up with dawn.

       E/G#   A²   Bsus
You are God,   You are God.

  (E/G#   Amaj7   E/B

E/G#   Amaj7   E/B)   *1st time only*

BRIDGE:

        E/G# Amaj7   E/B
And life   flows from God,

             E/G# Amaj7   E/B
It flows from God.

(REPEAT BRIDGE & CHORUS)

E

Copyright © 2007 worshiptogether.com Songs/sixsteps Music (ASCAP) (adm. by EMI CMG Publishing)
All right reserved. Used by permission. CCLI Song No. 4925303

You Are My God (Like A Whisper)

BRENTON BROWN

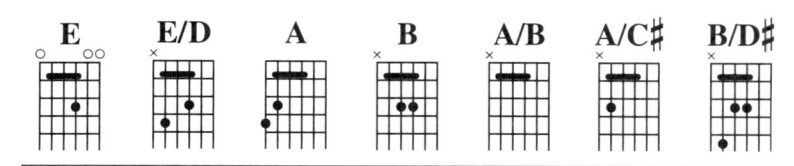

[Chord diagrams: E, E/D, A, B, A/B, A/C#, B/D#]

Cut Capo 2 (E)

VERSE 1:

E   E/D
  Like a whisper,   like a love song,
A
I   can hear Your voice, I can hear Your voice.
E   E/D
  Like a father   to his newborn,
A   E
I   can hear Your voice calling   me:

CHORUS 1:

        A   B   E
"You are My   child, you are My   child, and I love   you.
       A   B   E
You are My   child, you are My   child, and I love   you."

VERSE 2:

E   E/D
  Like a promise,   like a thank you,
A
I   will sing this song, I will sing this song.
E   E/D
  For the way You   make my heart new,
A   E
I   will sing this song to   You.

CHORUS 2:

      A   B   E
You are my   God, You are my   God, and I love   You.
      A   B   E
You are my   God, You are my   God, and I love   You.

BRIDGE:

        A   A/B
There is no   higher call, there's no great - er reward
        A/C#   A/B
Than to know   You, God, to be known   as Yours.
        A   A/B
There is no   better goal, nothing I'm   longing for
         A/C#   B/D#
Can compare   with the truth that forev - er more:

(REPEAT CHORUS 2)

Copyright © 2005 Thankyou Music (PRS) (adm. worldwide by EMI CMG Publishing, excluding the UK and Europe which is administered by kingswaysongs.com) All rights reserved. Used by permission. CCLI Song No. 4707590

Your Glory Endures Forever

CHARLIE HALL

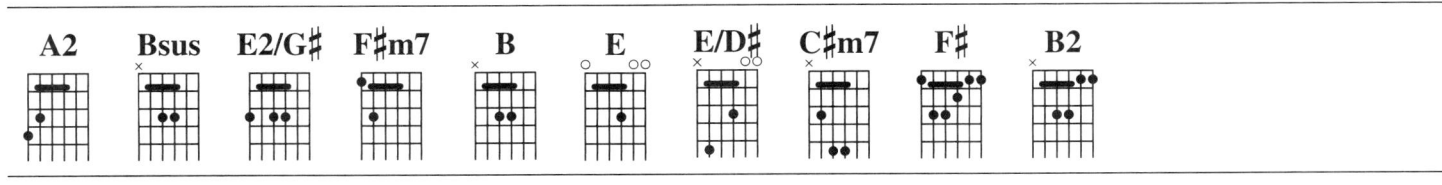

A2 Bsus E2/G# F#m7 B E E/D# C#m7 F# B2

Capo 3, Cut Capo 5 (E)

VERSE:

A²   Bsus   E²/G#   A²
   And You ride on wings of wind, You are be - ginning and the end.
                      Bsus   E²/G#   F#m⁷
Mountains melting in Your flame, creation pulsing out Your name.

PRE-CHORUS:

                          B
And You are forever,   and You are forever

CHORUS:

E   E/D#   A²
   Your glory endures forever,   Your beauty out - shines the heavens.
C#m⁷   B   F#   A²
   And we will de - clare Your wonders, Your splendor, Your   majesty.

VERSE:

              Bsus   E²/G#   A²
Earth rotating in Your hand, galax - ies in Your com - mand.
                           Bsus   E²/G#   F#m⁷
You make and sustain the breath of man, Your deeds go on forever.

(REPEAT PRE-CHORUS)

(REPEAT CHORUS TWICE)

BRIDGE:

F#m⁷   Bsus   E²/G#   A²
   You are forever,   You are forever, You are forever,
Bsus   E²/G#   F#   A²
   You are forever, You are forever,   You are forever.

(REPEAT CHORUS TWICE)

ENDING:

E   E/D#   A²   C#m⁷   B   F#   A²

E   E/D#   A²
Glory, and honor, and praise. Glory, and honor, and praise.
C#m⁷   B²
Glory, and honor, and praise
A²
   And You ride on wings of wind, You are beginning and the end.

Copyright © 2005 worshiptogether.com Songs / sixsteps Music (ASCAP) (adm. by EMI CMG Publishing)
All rights reserved. Used by permission. CCLI Song No. 4653620

A Greater Song
PAUL BALOCHE and MATT REDMAN

Who could imagine a melody,
True enough to tell of Your mercy?
Who could imagine a harmony,
Sweet enough to tell of Your love?

I see the heavens proclaiming You day after day,
And I know in my heart that there must be a way...

To sing a greater song,
A greater song to You on the earth.
To sing a greater song,
A greater song to You on the earth.

Who could imagine a symphony,
Grand enough to tell of Your glory?
Our highest praise but a feeble breath,
A whisper of Your thunderous worth.

Hallelujah, we want to lift You higher.
Hallelujah, we want to lift You higher.

© 2006 Thankyou Music (PRS) (adm. worldwide by EMI CMG Publishing, excluding the UK and Europe, which is adm. by kingswaysongs.com) / Integrity's Hosanna! Music (ASCAP) All rights reserved. Used by permission. CCLI Song No. 4662336

Adoration (Down In Adoration Falling)
Written by THOMAS AQUINAS.
Additional verse and chorus by MATT MAHER

Down in adoration falling, this great sacrament we hail;
Over ancient forms departing, newer rites of grace prevail;
Faith for all defects supplying where the feeble senses fail.

To the everlasting Father, and the Son who reigns on high,
With the Spirit blest proceeding forth from each eternally,
Be salvation, honor, blessing; might and endless majesty.

Jesus lamb of God, saving love for all,
Lord of heaven and earth, Father's love for all;
I bow to You.
Jesus lamb of God, saving love for all,
Lord of heaven and earth,
I bow to You, bow to You, I bow to You.

Pour upon us Lord of Mercy, spirit of Thy selfless love;
Make us of one true heart yearning for the glory of Thy Son;
Jesus, fire of justice blazing; gladdening light forever more.

Copyright © 2003 Thankyou Music/spiritandsong.com (adm. by EMI CMG Publishing)
All rights reserved. Used by permission. CCLI Song No. 4729949

Amazing Grace (My Chains Are Gone)

JOHN NEWTON, JOHN P. REES and EDWIN OTHELLO EXCELL
Arrangement and additional chorus CHRIS TOMLIN and LOUIE GIGLIO

Amazing Grace, how sweet the sound,
That saved a wretch like me.
I once was lost, but now am found,
Was blind but now I see.

'Twas Grace that taught my heart to fear,
And Grace my fears relieved.
How precious did that Grace appear,
The hour I first believed.

My chains are gone, I've been set free,
My God, my Savior has ransomed me.
And like a flood His mercy reigns,
Unending love, Amazing Grace.

The Lord has promised good to me,
His word my hope secures.
He will my shield and portion be,
As long as life endures.

The earth shall soon dissolve like snow,
The sun forbear to shine.
But God who called me here below,
Will be forever mine,
Will be forever mine,
You are forever mine.

Public Domain. Arr. Copyright (c) 2006 worshiptogether.com Songs/sixsteps Music/ASCAP (EMI CMG Publishing)
All rights reserved. Used by permission. CCLI Song No. 4768151

Be Lifted High
LEELAND MOORING

Sin and its ways grow old,
All of my heart turns to stone.
And I'm left with no strength to arise,
I need to be lifted high.

Sin and its ways lead to pain,
Left here with hurt and shame.
So no longer will I leave Your side,
Jesus, You be lifted high.

You be lifted high, You be lifted high,
You be lifted high in my life, oh God.
And I fall to my knees so it's You that they see, not I,
Jesus, You be lifted high.

And even now that I'm inside Your hands,
Help me not to grow prideful again.
Don't let me forsake sacrifice,
Jesus, You be lifted high.

And if I'm blessed with the riches of kings,
How could I ever think that it was me?
For You brought me from darkness to light,
Jesus, You be lifted high.

Copyright © 2006 Meaux Mercy (adm. by EMI CMG Publishing)
All rights reserved. Used by permission. CCLI Song No. 4831442

Be Praised
MICHAEL GUNGOR

Praises to the One from whom it all began,
The One who formed the stars and who gave life to man.
He set the world in motion, created sky and ocean.
And here I stand beloved and called by name.

Be praised, be praised!
Listen to creation lifting up Your name.
Be praised, be praised, be praised!

Praises to the One from whom it all began,
The One who gave Himself to save sinful man.
You scorned the shame of Your cross.
My sin, my blame is now gone.
And here I stand beloved and called by name.

Oh, oh, oh, oh.
Oh, oh, oh, oh.

All praises to the One from whom it all began,
The One who conquered death and who will come again.
The nations will behold You as everything becomes new,
and there I'll stand beloved and called by name.

Be praised, be praised!
Listen to Your people lifting up Your name.
Be praised, be praised, be praised! Oh!

Copyright © 2007 worshiptogether.com Songs (ASCAP) (adm. by EMI CMG Publishing)
All right reserved. Used by permission. CCLI 495903

Beautiful News
MATT REDMAN

Joy is the theme of my song,
And the beat of my heart,
And that joy is found in You.
For You showed the pow'r of Your cross,
And Your great saving love,
And my soul woke up to You.
I heard Your beautiful news,
Grace so amazing, so true.

Shout it out, let the people sing,
Something so powerful should shake the whole wide world.
Make it loud, make it louder still,
Savior, we're singing now to celebrate Your beautiful news.

There's a God who came down to save,
Showed the world His amazing grace.
There's a God who came down to save,
And He calls your name.

© 2006 Thankyou Music (PRS) (adm. worldwide by EMI CMG Publishing, excluding the UK and Europe, which is adm. by kingswaysongs.com) All rights reserved. Used by permission. CCLI Song No. 4836007

Captivated
VICKY BEECHING

Your laughter it echoes like a joyous thunder,
Your whisper it warms me like a summer breeze.
Your anger is fiercer than the sun in its splendor,
You're close and yet full of mystery.
Ever since the day that I saw Your face,
Try as I may, I cannot look away, I cannot look away...

Captivated by You,
I am captivated by You.
May my life be one unbroken gaze,
Fixed upon the beauty of Your face.

Beholding is becoming, so as You fill my gaze,
I become more like You and my heart is changed.
Beholding is becoming, so as You fill my view,
Transform me into the likeness of You.
This is what I ask, for all my days,
That I may never look away, never look away...

No other could ever be as beautiful,
No other could ever steal my heart away.
I just can't look away...

Copyright ©2005 Thankyou Music/PRS (adm. worldwide by worshiptogether.com Songs excluding the UK and Europe, which is admin. by kingswaysongs.com). All rights reserved. Used by permission.

Carried To The Table

LEELAND MOORING, MARC BYRD and STEVE HINDALONG

Wounded and forsaken, I was shattered by the fall,
Broken and forgotten, feeling lost and all alone.
Summoned by the King into the master's courts,
Lifted by the Savior and cradled in His arms.

I was (As I'm) carried to the table, seated where I don't belong,
Carried to the table, swept away by His love.
And I don't see my brokenness anymore,
When I'm seated at the table of the Lord.
I'm carried to the table, the table of the Lord.

Fighting thoughts of fear, wond'ring why He called my name,
Am I good enough to share this cup, this world has left me lame.
Even in my weakness, the Savior called my name.
In His Holy presence, I'm healed and unashamed.

You carried me my God, You carried me.
You carried me my God, You carried me.

Copyright © 2006 Meadowgreen Music Company/ASCAP/Meaux Mercy/Blue Raft Music/BMI (adm. by EMI CMG Publishing)
All rights reserved. Used by permission. CCLI Song No. 4681678

Closer

*CHARLIE HALL, KENDALL COMBES,
DUSTIN RAGLAND and BRIAN BERGMAN*

Beautiful are the words spoken to me,
Beautiful is the one who is speaking.

Come in close, come in close and speak,
Come in close, come closer to me.

And the power of Your words
Are filled with grace and mercy.
Let them fall on my ears and break my stony heart.

Copyright © 2005 worshiptogether.com Songs/sixsteps Music/ASCAP (adm. by EMI CMG Publishing)
All rights reserved. Used by permission. CCLI # 4665302

Created to Worship
VICKY BEECHING

You formed us from the dust
You breathed Your breath in us
We are the work of Your hands
Now we breathe back to You
Love songs of gratitude
Adoring You with all we have

'Cause we were created to worship Your name
And we were created to bring You our praise

If we don't worship You
We'll search for substitutes
To fill the void in our soul
Worshipping other things
Destroys our liberty
But as we praise You we are free

'Cause we were created to worship Your name
And we were created to bring You our praise

So we will worship, so we will praise
You our Creator for all our days

For this is what we were made to do
This is what we were made to do
This is what we were made to do
So we lift our praise to You

Copyright © 2004 Thankyou Music. Administered worldwide by worshiptogether.com Songs excluding the UK and Europe (adm. by Kingsway Music).
All rights reserved. Used by permission. CCLI Song No. 3994713

Everything
TIM HUGHES

God in my living, there in my breathing.
God in my waking, God in my sleeping.
God in my resting, there in my working.
God in my thinking, God in my speaking.

Be my everything, be my everything.
Be my everything, be my everything.

God in my hoping, there in my dreaming.
God in my watching, God in my waiting.
God in my laughing, there in my weeping.
God in my hurting, God in my healing.

Christ in me, Christ in me,
Christ in me the hope of glory,
You are everything.
Christ in me, Christ in me,
Christ in me the hope of glory,
Be my everything.

You are everything, You are everything.
Jesus everything, Jesus everything.

Copyright © 2005 Thankyou Music (adm. worldwide by worshiptogether.com Songs, excluding the UK and Europe, which is adm. by Kingswaysongs.com) All rights reserved. Used by permission. CCLI Song No. 4685258

Forever Holy
BEN CRIST

God, You stand when all has fallen.
You embrace the long forgotten.

I guess it's just hard to believe
The grace You pour out on me.
I guess I'm just starting to see
How You're working in me.

This is what makes my head spin;
You're forever holy.
God of all creation,
Pour Your life into me.
This is so overwhelming,
You're forever holy.
God of my salvation,
Clothe me in Your glory, yeah.

God, You hold when all is breaking.
You restore the tired and aching.

Clothe me in Your glory.
Clothe me in Your glory.

Copyright © 2006 Spinning Audio Vortex, Inc. (BMI (adm. by EMI CMG Publishing)
All right reserved. Used by permission. CCLI 4943330

Give Me Jesus
JEREMY CAMP

In the morning when I rise,
In the morning when I rise,
In the morning when I rise,
Give me Jesus.

Give me Jesus,
Give me Jesus,
You can have all this world,
Just give me Jesus.

Jesus, give me Jesus.

When I am alone,
When I am alone,
When I am alone,
Give me Jesus.

When I come to die,
When I come to die,
When I come to die,
Give me Jesus.

You can have all this world,
You can have all this world,
Just give me Jesus.
Jesus.

Copyright © 2006 Thirsty Moon River Publishing / Stolen Pride Music (ASCAP) (adm. by EMI CMG Publishing)
All rights reserved. Used by permission. CCLI Song No. 4874344

Give You Glory
JEREMY CAMP

We have raised a thousand voices,
Just to lift Your holy name,
And we will raise thousands more,
To sing of Your beauty in this place.
None can even fathom,
No, not one define Your worth,
As we marvel in Your presence
To the ends of the earth.

We give You glory,
Lifting up our hands and singing Holy, You alone are worthy,
We just want to touch Your heart Lord, touch Your heart.
Glory, lifting up our voice and singing Holy, You alone are worthy,
We just want to touch Your heart Lord, touch Your heart.

As we fall down before You,
With our willing hearts we seek,
In the greatness of Your glory,
It's so hard to even speak.
There is nothing we can offer,
No, nothing can repay,
So we give You all our praises,
And lift our voice to sing.

Our hope is drenched in You,
Uur faith has been renewed.
We trust in Your every word,
Nothing else can even measure up to You.

Copyright © 2006 Thirsty Moon River Publishing / Stolen Pride Music / ASCAP (adm. by EMI CMG Publishing)
All rights reserved. Used by permission. CCLI Song No. 4874337

God Of Justice
TIM HUGHES

God of justice, Savior to all.
Came to rescue the weak and the poor.
Chose to serve and not be served.

Jesus, You have called us,
Freely we've received, now freely we will give.

We must go, live to feed the hungry,
Stand beside the broken, we must go.
Stepping forward, keep us from just singing,
Move us into action, we must go.

To act justly, every day.
Loving mercy, in every way.
Walking humbly, before You, God.

You have shown us what You require,
Freely we've received, now freely we will give.

Fill us up and send us out,
Fill us up and send us out,
Fill us up and send us out Lord.

A change is made, loving mercy.
We must go, we must go to the broken and the hurting,
We must go, we must go.

Copyright © 2005 Thankyou Music (PRS) (adm. worldwide by EMI CMG Publishing excluding the UK and Europe which is adm. by kingswaysongs.com) All rights reserved. Used by permission. CCLI Song No. 4447128

Great God Of Wonders

ANDY BROMLEY

Great God of wonders, Great God in power,
The heavens are declaring glories of Your name,
Glories of Your name.

Great God of Zion, Great God in beauty,
The nations are gathering to worship at Your feet,
To worship at Your feet.

From the rising to the setting sun,
Your name will be praised.
God above all gods,
King above all kings,
Lord of heaven and earth.

We give to You praise, praise, praise.
Give You praise, praise, praise.

You are the great God above all gods,
You are the great King above all kings.
You are the great Lord of heaven and earth,
We give You praise.

Copyright © 2004 Thankyou Music (adm. worldwide by worshiptogether.com Songs, excluding the UK and Europe, which is adm. by Kingswaysongs.com) All rights reserved. Used by permission. CCLI Song No. 4443115

Here and Now
MATT MAHER

No more waiting, Your love's exhaling.
You are here and returning.
We're coming home, and all are one.

Here and now; the proud made lowly.
Here and now; the Lamb made mighty.
Here and now; the slave to freedom.
Here and now; the coming Kingdom.
Here and now.

The cross is happening, the world is ending,
Dead and alive, we are beginning,
We're coming home, and all are one.

Tears of gladness, in the sadness,
We're falling and victorious.
Bless'd and broken, the floodgates open,
The sun is rising to shine.

It's here and now, it's here and now.

© 2005 Thankyou Music (PRS), administered worldwide by worshiptogether.com Songs excluding the UK and Europe which is admin. by Kingswaysongs.com / Spiritandsong.com Publishing (BMI), administered by EMI CMG Publishing.
All rights reserved. Used by permission. CCLI # 4666930.

The Highest And The Greatest
NICK HERBERT and TIM HUGHES

Wake every heart and every tongue,
To sing the new eternal song,
And crown Him King of Glory now,
Confess Him Lord of all.

You are the highest,
You are the greatest,
You are the Lord of all.
Angels will worship,
Nations will bow down,
To the Lord of all.

A day will come when all will sing,
And glorify our matchless King,
Your name unrivaled stands alone,
You are the Lord of all.

Let every heart, let every tongue,
Sing of Your name, sing of Your name.
Let every heart, let every tongue,
Sing, sing, sing.

Lifting You high, higher and higher, Lord.

© 2007 Thankyou Music (admin. worldwide by EMI CMG Publishing, excluding Europe, which is admin. by kingswaysongs.com) (PRS)
All rights reserved. Used by permission. CCLI # 4769758

How Can I Keep From Singing
CHRIS TOMLIN, MATT REDMAN and ED CASH

There is an endless song, echoes in my soul,
I hear the music ring.
And though the storms may come, I am holding on,
To the rock I cling.

How can I keep from singing Your praise,
How can I ever say enough?
How amazing is Your love?
How can I keep from shouting Your name?
I know I am loved by the King,
And it makes my heart want to sing.

I will lift my eyes in the darkest night,
For I know my Savior lives.
And I will walk with You knowing You'll see me through,
And sing the songs You give.

I can sing in the troubled times, sing when I win.
I can sing when I lose my step, and fall down again.
I can sing 'cause You pick me up, sing 'cause You're there.
I can sing 'cause You hear me, Lord, when I call You in prayer.
I can sing with my last breath, sing for I know,
That I'll sing with the angels and the saints around the throne.

Copyright © 2006 worshiptogether.com Song / sixsteps Music / ASCAP (admin. by EMI CMG Publishing) Thankyou Music / PRS (administered worldwide by EMI CMG-Publishing, excluding the UK and Europe, which is administered by kingswaysongs.com) Alletrop Music / BMI. All rights reserved. Used by permission. CCLI Song No. 4822372

I Stand For You

JOHN ELLIS

Jesus, I stand for You,
No matter what you lead me through.
They will chase me out and close me down,
But Jesus, I'll stand for You.

I'll always stand,
I'll always stand,
I'll always stand for You.
In all this world,
You're all that's true,
I'll always stand for You.

Jesus, I've stood my ground,
When unbelief was all around.
I have felt the sting rejection brings,
But Jesus, I'll still stand for You.

A time will come when everyone
Will turn their eyes on the risen Son
But until that day,
this world will turn away,
And so I take Your hand,
I'll always stand for You.

Guilty of disgrace,
But You took my place,
So Jesus, I'll always stand for You.

Copyright ©2005 Birdwing Music/Near Bliss Music/Mouthfulofsongs/ASCAP (adm. by EMI CMG Publishing).
All rights reserved. Used by permission.

I Will Remember You
BRENTON BROWN

I will remember You, always remember You,
I will remember You and all You've done for me.

I will not forget all Your benefits,
Even when the storm surrounds my soul.
How You comfort me, heal all my diseases,
How You lift me up on eagle's wings.

I will not forget all Your benefits,
How You've chosen and adopted me.
Orphaned by my sin, Your grace has let me in,
And never once have You abandoned me.

I have tasted and I've seen how You father faithfully,
How You shepherd those who fear Your name.
When the shadow's start to fall and my heart begins to fail,
I will lift my eyes to You again.

Copyright ©2006 Thankyou Music (PRS) (adm. worldwide by EMI CMG Publishing excluding the UK and Europe, which is adm. by kingswaysongs.com) All rights reserved. Used by permission. CCLI Song No. 4707387

Join The Song
VICKY BEECHING and ED CASH

One day every voice will sing,
Every beggar, prince and king,
Every nation, tongue and tribe,
Every ocean in between will cry, will cry.

Praise God from whom all blessings flow,
Praise Him, all creatures here below.
To Him all the glory belongs,
Praise Him above you heavenly host.
Praise Father, Son and Holy Ghost,
Let all the earth sing along.

Come join the song.

Gathered 'round the throne above,
We'll be swept up in the melody,
Hearts will overflow with love,
We'll be singing out a symphony, we'll sing.

Come join the song that fills eternity,
Sung throughout all history,
As angels shout and kings lay down their crowns,
We bow down.

Copyright © 2006 Thankyou Music (PRS) (adm. worldwide by EMI CMG Publishing excluding the UK and Europe which is adm. by kingswaysongs.com) Alletrop Music (BMI). All rights reserved. Used by permission. CCLI Song No. 4879967

Let God Arise

CHRIS TOMLIN, ED CASH and JESSE REEVES

Hear the holy roar of God resound,
Watch the waters part before us now.
Come and see what He has done for us,
Tell the world of His great love,
Our God is a God who saves.
Our God is a God who saves.

Let God arise, Let God arise.
Our God reigns now and forever,
He reigns now and forever.

His enemies will run for sure,
The church will stand, She will endure.
He holds the keys of life, our Lord,
Death has no sting, no final word,
Our God is a God who saves,
Our God is a God who saves.

© 2006 sixsteps Music (admin. by EMI CMG Publishing) / worshiptogether.com Songs (admin. by EMI CMG Publishing) (ASCAP) / Alletrop Music (BMI) All rights reserved. Used by permission. CCLI Song No. xxxxxxx

Love Came Down
BEN CANTELON

When I call on Your name, You answer;
When I fall, You are there by my side.
You delivered me out of darkness,
Now I stand in the hope of new life.
Yeah, stand in the hope of new life with You.

By grace I'm free; You rescued me. All I am is Yours.

I've found a love greater than life itself.
I've found a hope stronger and nothing compares.
I once was lost, now I'm alive in You,
I'm alive in You. Thank You, Lord. I'm alive in You.

You're my God and my firm foundation.
It is You whom I'll trust at all times.
I give glory and praise, adoration
To my Savior Who's seated on high.

I'm singing: Love came down and rescued me.
I thank You, yes, I thank You.
I once was blind but now I see. I see You, yes, I see You.
And love came down and rescued me.
I thank You, yes, I thank You.
I once was blind but now I see. I see You, yes, I see You, Lord.
I see You, I see You, Lord.
By grace I'm free. You rescued me. All I am is Yours.
By grace I'm free. You rescued me. All I am is Yours.

Copyright © 2006 Thankyou Music (PRS) (adm. by EMI CMG Publishing, excluding the UK and Europe which is adm. by kingswaysongs.com) All right reserved. Used by permission. CCLI 4943316

Made To Worship
CHRIS TOMLIN, STEPHAN SHARP and ED CASH

Before the day, before the light,
Before the world revolved around the sun.
God on high stepped down into time,
And wrote the story of His love for everyone.

He has filled our hearts with wonder,
So that we always remember:

You and I were made to worship,
You and I are called to love,
You and I are forgiven and free.
When you and I embrace surrender,
When you and I choose to believe,
Then you and I will see who we were meant to be.

All we are and all we have,
Is all a gift from God that we receive.
Brought to life we open up our eyes,
To see the majesty and glory of the King.

Even the rocks cry out, even the heavens shout,
At the sound of His Holy name.
So let every voice sing out, let every knee bow down,
He is worthy of all our praise.

© 2006 worshiptogether.com Songs (ASCAP) / sixsteps Music (admin. by EMI CMG Publishing) / Alletrop Music (BMI) / Stephan Sharp Publishing Designee. All rights reserved. Used by permission. CCLI Song No. 4794118

O Church Arise
STUART KENNEDY and KEITH GETTY

O Church, arise, and put your armor on;
Hear the call of Christ, our Captain.
For now the weak can say that they are strong
In the strength that God has given.
With shield of faith and belt of truth,
We'll stand against the devil's lies;
An army bold, whose battle cry is love,
Reaching out to those in darkness.

Our call to war, to love the captive soul.
But to rage against the captor.
And with the sword that makes the wounded whole
We will fight and faith and valor.
When faced with trials on every side.
We know the outcome is secure.
And Christ will have the prize for which He died, and inheritance of nations.

Come see the cross, where love and mercy meet.
As the Son of God is stricken.
Then see His foes lie crushed beneath His feet,
For the Conqueror has risen.
And as the stone is rolled away, and Christ emerges from the grave.
This victory march continues till the day
Every eye and heart shall see Him.

So Spirit, come, put strength in every stride,
Give grace for every hurdle.
That we may run with faith to win the prize of a servant good and faithful.
As saints of old still line the way, retelling triumphs of His grace.
We hear their calls and hunger for the day,
When with Christ we stand in glory.

Copyright © 2005 Thankyou Music PRS/PRS (adm. by worshiptogether.com Songs excluding UK & Europe adm. by kingswaysong.com)
All right reserved. Used by permission. CCLI Song No. 4611992

On The Third Day
MATT MAHER and MARC BYRD

Creation brings an offering, as autumn leaves turn to gold,
The trees bow down in highest praise, now made bare before Your throne.
The western sky an amber blaze, at the end of the day,
For everything must die to rise again.

The winter's chill, a bitter cold, as sin and shame leave us to fall,
The clouds now full of newborn snow, for grace to come and save us all,
Within the darkest night of man, was found Your saving hand,
For everything must die to rise again.

On the third day, behold the King,
On the third day, death has no sting,
On the third day, we're forgiven and reconciled.

The earth it groans in labor pains, as flowers stretch to heaven above,
Your creatures sing the prophet's song, to be a gift of selfless love.
The sun is rising in the east, and Your spirit is unleashed,
For everything must die to rise again.

And so we wait in joyful hope, for You to come and take us home,
And so we join beneath the cross, in suffering from whence we go.
The greatest act of sovereign grace, In the universe displayed,
For everything must die to rise again.

On the third day, the saints rejoice,
On the third day, we lift our voice,
On the third day, united and glorified.

Resurrection Day
MATT MAHER

It's the weight of Your glory,
Brings the proud to their knees,
And the light of revelation,
Lets the blind man see.
It's the power of the cross,
Breaks away death's embrace,
And we celebrate our freedom,
Dancing on an empty grave.

Roll away the stone,
Roll away the stone.

We sing for joy, we shout Your name,
We celebrate Your resurrection day.
We sing for joy, we shout Your name,
We celebrate Your resurrection day.

You declare what is holy,
You declare what is good,
In the sight of all the nations,
You declare that You are God.
It's the power in Your Blood,
Breaks away sin's embrace,
And we celebrate our freedom,
Dancing on our broken chains.

Copyright © 2005 Thankyou Music (PRS) (adm. worldwide by EMI CMG Publishing excluding the UK and Europe which is adm. by kingswaysongs.com) spiritandsong.com Publishing (BMI) (adm. by EMI CMG Publishing) All rights reserved. Used by permission. CCLI Song No. 4669786

Shine
MATT REDMAN

Lord we have seen the rising sun,
Awakening the early dawn,
And we're rising up to give You praise.
Lord we have seen the stars and moon,
See how they shine, they shine for You.
And You're calling us to do the same,
So we rise up with a song,
And we rise up with a cry,
And we're giving You our lives.

We will shine like stars in the universe,
Holding out Your truth in the darkest place.
We'll be living for Your glory,
Jesus we'll be living for Your glory.

We will burn so bright with Your praise, oh, God,
And declare Your light to this broken world.
We'll be living for Your glory,
Jesus, we'll be living for Your glory.

Like the sun so radiantly, sending light for all to see,
Let Your Holy Church arise.
Exploding into life like a supernova's light,
Set Your Holy Church on fire, we will shine.

So we rise up with a song, and we rise up with a cry.
And we're giving You our lives, Jesus, we will shine.

© 2006 Thankyou Music (PRS) (adm. worldwide by EMI CMG Publishing, excluding the UK and Europe, which is adm. by kingswaysongs.com) All rights reserved. Used by permission. CCLI Song No. 4831435

Sound Of Melodies

LEELAND MOORING, JACK MOORING and STEVE WILSON

We who were called to be Your people,
Struggling sinners and thieves.
We're lifted up from the ashes,
And out came the song of the redeemed,
The song of the redeemed.

Can you hear the sound of melodies,
Oh, the sound of melodies rising up to You, rising up to You, God?
The sound of melodies,
Oh, the sound of melodies rising up to You, rising up to You, God?

Oh, we have caught a revelation,
That nothing can separate us from.
The love we received through salvation,
It fills your daughters and Your sons,
Your daughters and Your sons.

The sound of Your love, the sound of Your love,
Is what You're hearing.
The sound of Your sons, the sound of Your sons,
You've won Your children.
The sound of Your love, the sound of Your love,
Is what You're hearing.
Your daughters in love, Your daughters in love,
You've won Your children.

The sound of melodies, oh, the sound of melodies rising up to You.
Rising up to You, God, Rising up to You, God.
La, la, la, la, la, la, la, la, la, la, la, la.
La, la, la, la, la, la, la, la, la, la, la, la.

Copyright © 2006 Meaux Mercy (BMI) / Meaux Jeaux (SESAC) / Meaux Mercy, River Oaks Music Company (BMI)
(adm. by EMI CMG Publishing) All rights reserved. Used by permission. CCLI Song No. 4669425

Speak, O Lord

KEITH GETTY and STUART TOWNEND

Speak, O Lord, as we come to You,
To receive the food of Your holy word.
Take Your truth, plant it deep in us;
Shape and fashion us in Your likeness,
That the light of Christ might be seen today,
In our acts of love and our deeds of faith.
Speak, O Lord, and fulfill in us all your purposes,
For Your glory.

Teach us Lord full obedience,
Holy reverence, true humility.
Test our thoughts and our attitudes,
In the radiance of Your purity.
Cause our faith to rise,
Cause our eyes to see,
Your majestic love and authority.
Words of power that can never fail;
Let their truth prevail over unbelief.

Speak, O Lord, and renew our minds;
Help us grasp the heights of Your plans for us.
Truths unchanged from the dawn of time,
That will echo down through eternity.
And by grace we'll stand on Your promises;
And by faith we'll walk as You walk with us.
Speak, O Lord, till Your church is built,
And the earth is filled with Your glory.

Copyright © 2005 Thankyou Music/Adm by worshiptogether.com songs excl. UK & Europe adm by kingswaysongs.com tym@kingsway.co.uk Used by permission. CCLI Song No. 4615235

Tears Of The Saints

LEELAND MOORING and JACK MOORING

There are many prodigal sons,
On our city streets they run,
Searching for shelter.
There are homes broken down,
People's hopes have fallen to the ground,
From failures.
This is an emergency!

There are tears from the saints,
For the lost and unsaved,
We're crying for them come back home,
We're crying for them come back home.
And all Your children will stretch out their hands,
And pick up the crippled man,
Father we will lead them home,
Father we will lead them home.

There are schools full of hatred,
Even churches have forsaken love and mercy.
May we see this generation,
In its state of desperation.
For Your glory.
This is an emergency!

Sinners, reach out your hands!
Children in Christ you stand!
Sinner, reach out your hand!
Children in Christ you stand!

Copyright © 2005 Meadowgreen Music Company/ASCAP (adm. by EMI CMG Publishing) Unknown Publisher.
All rights reserved. Used by permission. CCLI Song No. ????

The Wonder Of The Cross
VICKY BEECHING

O precious sight, my Savior stands,
Dying for me with outstreched hands.
O precious sight, I love to gaze,
Remembering salvation's day,
Remembering salvation's day.
Though my eyes linger on this scene,
May passing time and years not steal
The power with which it impacts me,
The freshness of its mystery,
The freshness of its mystery.

May I never lose the wonder,
The wonder of the cross.
May I see it like the first time
Standing as a sinner lost,
Undone by mercy and left speechless,
Watching wide eyed at the cost.
May I never lose the wonder,
The wonder of the cross.

Behold the Godman crucified,
The perfect sinless sacrifice.
As blood ran down those nails and wood,
History was split in two, yes,
History was split in two.
Behold the empty wooden tree,
His body gone, alive and free.
We sing with everlasting joy,
For sin and death have been destroyed, yes,
Sin and death have been destroyed.

Copyright © 2007 Thankyou Music (PRS) (adm. worldwide by EMI CMG Publishing, excluding the UK and Europe, which is adm. by kingsway songs.com) All right reserved. Used by permission. CCLI song #4886507.

To The Only God

CHRIS TOMLIN

To the only God who is able to keep us,
Able us to keep us from falling.
To the only God be all glory and honor,
Majesty and power,
For all ages now and forevermore.

Forevermore.

Unwavering
MATT MAHER

Blessed are the poor, the kingdom is theirs.
Alive in the promise to be dead to the world.
Blessed are the meek in all of You Father,
The Word at Your right hand, spirit of truth.

Unwavering is Your voice, unwavering is Your hand,
Unwavering is the heart that bled for the sins of man.
Unwavering is Your will, unwavering is Your plan,
The fount of salvation on which we will stand.

Blessed are the righteous on bended knee,
Found in this freedom, committed to You.
Blessed are those who see the heights of glory,
Found in the valley, and suffering for You.

Send us out to be Your hands and feet,
Send us out to be Your hands and feet,
Send us out to be Your hands and feet,
Send us out to be Your hands and feet.

Copyright © 2006 Thankyou Music/PRS. (adm. worldwide by EMI CMG Publishing, excluding Europe, which is adm. by kingswaysongs.com) Spiritandsong.com Publishing (BMI) All rights reserved. Used by permission. CCLI Song No. 4669827

We Remember
MARC BYRD and LEELAND MOORING

We worship You, Lord,
In the splendor of Your holiness,
In the beauty of Your righteousness;
Holy, holy!
We offer You thanks
For the endless love You have displayed,
For the sacrifice You freely gave;
Worthy, worthy!

You are holy, precious Lamb of God.
Forever You will reign, forever You will reign.
King of glory, risen Son of God.
Forever You will reign, foever You will reign.

Father of light,
In radiance and majesty
Sent Your Son to set the captive free;
Holy, holy!
Infinite love,
On the cross You saved us from our sin,
Conquered death and will return again;
Worthy, worthy!

We remember, we remember the cross.
We remember, we remember the cost.
We remember, Lord, we remember the cross.
We remember, we remember the cost.

Copyright © 2006 Meaux Mercy/Blue Raft Music (BMI) (adm. by EMI CMG Publishing)
All right reserved. Used by permission. CCLI #4255918

Yes And Amen
MATT REDMAN, ROBERT MARVIN and JOSIAH BELL

Hear Your people saying yes,
Hear Your people saying yes to You.
Yes to anything You ask,
Yes to anything we're called to do.
Hear Your people say amen,
Hear Your people say amen to You.
Let Your kingdom come on earth,
Let it be just like we prayed to You.

Yes and amen to everything that's in Your heart,
Yes and amen to everything that You have planned.
We live to see Your will be done,
And see Your perfect kingdom come on earth, on the earth.
Yes and amen, we're taking up our cross for You.
Give us the strength to take these dreams and follow through.
We live to see Your will be done,
And see Your perfect kingdom come on earth, on the earth.

All the promises are yes,
All the promises are yes in You.
Every good and perfect gift,
Every blessing that we have was You.

© 2006 Thankyou Music (PRS) (adm. worldwide by EMI CMG Publishing, excluding the UK and Europe, which is adm. by kingswaysongs.com) / Meaux Mercy (adm. by EMI CMG Publishing) / JLCB Music (BMI) All rights reserved. Used by permission. CCLI Song No. 4835967

You Are God
CHARLIE HALL

You're closer than our troubles,
More present than any danger,
More grand than gold and silver.
You are God, You are God.
Fill our hearts with love and faith.

You're the joy of man's desire;
You are Father, Satisfier.
We are stunned with wide eyed wonder.
You are God, You are God.

Fill our hearts with love and faith.
You fight for us, You make us brave.
You are God, You are God.
You walk with us, You lead us up.
Faith, hope and love wakes up with dawn.
You are God, You are God.

And life flows from God,
It flows from God.

Copyright © 2007 worshiptogether.com Songs/sixsteps Music (ASCAP) (adm. by EMI CMG Publishing)
All right reserved. Used by permission. CCLI Song No. 4925303

You Are My God
(Like A Whisper)

BRENTON BROWN

Like a whisper, like a love song,
I can hear Your voice, I can hear Your voice.
Like a father to his newborn,
I can hear Your voice calling me:

"You are My child, you are My child, and I love you.
You are My child, you are My child, and I love you."

Like a promise, like a thank you,
I will sing this song, I will sing this song.
For the way You make my heart new,
I will sing this song to You.

You are my God, You are my God, and I love You.
You are my God, You are my God, and I love You.

There is no higher call, there's no greater reward
Than to know You, God, to be known as Yours.
There is no better goal, nothing I'm longing for
Can compare with the truth that forever more:

Copyright (c) 2005 Thankyou Music (adm. worldwide by EMI CMG Publishing, excluding the UK and Europe, which is administered by kingswaysongs.com) All rights reserved. Used by permission. CCLI Song No. 4707590

Your Glory Endures Forever
CHARLIE HALL

And You ride on wings of wind,
You are beginning and the end.
Mountains melting in Your flame,
Creation pulsing out Your name.

And You are forever,
And You are forever.

Your glory endures forever,
Your beauty outshines the heavens.
And we will declare Your wonders,
Your splendor, Your majesty.

Earth rotating in Your hand,
Galaxies in Your command.
You make and sustain the breath of man,
Your deeds go on forever.

And You are forever,
And You are forever.

Glory, and honor, and praise.

Copyright © 2005 sixsteps Music/worshiptogether.com songs/ASCAP(admin by EMI CMG Publishing)
All rights reserved. Used by permission.

how to vol. 6 — Index of Songs by Tempo

Title	Sheet Music	Chord Charts	Cut Capo Charts

Up-Tempo (above 116)

Title	Sheet Music	Chord Charts	Cut Capo Charts
Be Praised	18	200	243
Carried to the Table	38	203	246
Closer	43	204	247
Give You Glory	67	209	252
I Will Remember You	100	216	259
Let God Arise	110	218	261
Resurrection Day	134	223	266
To the Only God	164	229	272
We Remember	182	231	274
You Are God	178	233	276

Fast Mid-Tempo (93-116)

Title	Sheet Music	Chord Charts	Cut Capo Charts
A Greater Song	3	196	239
Adoration	8	197	240
Beautiful News	29	201	244
Created to Worship	62	205	248
Great God of Wonders	77	211	254
Here and Now	82	212	255
Join the Song	105	217	260

Mid-Tempo (77-92)

Title	Sheet Music	Chord Charts	Cut Capo Charts
Everything	48	206	249
Give Me Jesus	58	208	251
God of Justice	72	210	253
How Can I Keep from Singing	91	214	257
I Stand for You	96	215	258
Love Came Down	115	219	262
Made to Worship	122	220	263
O Church Arise	128	221	264
On the Third Day	130	222	265
Shine	138	224	267
Sound of Melodies	144	225	268
Tears of the Saints	152	227	270
You Are My God (Like a Whisper)	187	234	277

Slow Mid-Tempo (69-76)

Title	Sheet Music	Chord Charts	Cut Capo Charts
Be Lifted High	14	199	242
Captivated	34	202	245
Highest and the Greatest	86	213	256
Speak O Lord	150	226	269
The Wonder of the Cross	160	228	271
Yes and Amen	172	232	275

Slow (Below 68)

Title	Sheet Music	Chord Charts	Cut Capo Charts
Amazing Grace (My Chains Are Gone)	24	198	241
Forever Holy	52	207	250
Unwavering	167	230	273
Your Glory Endures Forever	190	235	278

howto vol 6 — Index of Songs by Key

Title	Sheet Music	Chord Charts	Chord Chart Capo Fret	Cut Capo Chart	Cut Capo Frets
Key of A♭					
Here and Now	82	212	1	255	4/6
The Wonder of the Cross	160	228	1	271	4/6
To the Only God	164	229	1	272	4/6
Key of A					
A Greater Song	3	196	2	239	0/2
Beautiful News	29	201	5	244	0/2
Carried to the Table	38	203	0	246	0/2
How Can I Keep from Singing	91	214	0	257	0/2
I Will Remember You	100	216	0	259	0/2
Let God Arise	110	218	0	261	0/2
Sound of Melodies	144	225	0	268	0/2
Key of B♭					
Closer	43	204	3	247	1/3
Higher and the Greatest	86	213	3	256	1/3
Love Came Down	115	219	1	262	1/3
Key of B					
Be Praised	18	200	2	243	0/2
Forever Holy	52	207	2	250	0/2
Key of C					
Everything	48	206	0	249	3/5
Give Me Jesus	58	208	0	251	3/5
I Stand for You	96	215	0	258	3/5
Made to Worship	122	220	0	263	3/5
Speak O Lord	150	226	0	269	3/5
Key of D♭					
Adoration	8	197	1	240	4/6
Key of D					
Give You Glory	67	209	0	252	5/7
O Church Arise	128	221	0	264	5/7
Key of E♭					
On the Third Day	130	222	1	265	1/3
Key of E					
Captivated	34	202	0	245	0/2
Created to Worship	62	205	0	248	0/2
God of Justice	72	210	0	253	0/2
Great God of Wonders	77	211	0	254	0/2
Unwavering	137	230	0	273	0/2
You Are My God (Like a Whisper)	187	234	0	277	0/2

how to vol 6 — Index of Songs by Key cont.

Title	Sheet Music	Chord Charts	Chord Chart Capo Fret	Cut Capo Chart	Cut Capo Frets
Key of F					
Amazing Grace (My Chains Are Gone)	24	198	3	241	1/3
Join the Song	105	217	0	260	1/3
Key of F#					
We Remember	182	231	0	274	2/4
Key of G♭					
Be Lifted High	14	199	2	242	2/4
Key of G					
Resurrection Day	134	223	0	266	3/5
Shine	138	224	0	267	3/5
Yes and Amen	172	232	0	275	3/5
You Are God	178	233	0	276	3/5
Your Glory Endures Forever	190	235	0	278	3/5
Key of G#m					
Tears of the Saints	152	227	4	270	2/4

YOUR SEARCH IS OVER...

WORSHIPTOGETHER.com®

NEW SONGS   FAVORITE SONGS
ALL IN ONE PLACE

HERE I AM TO WORSHIP

BLESSED BE YOUR NAME

FOREVER

HOW GREAT IS OUR GOD

HOLY IS THE LORD

EVERLASTING GOD

IN CHRIST ALONE

THERE IS A REDEEMER

HOW MAJESTIC IS YOUR NAME

I COULD SING OF YOUR LOVE FOREVER

For all your music resources including transposable **CHORD CHARTS, SHEET MUSIC, NEW SONG CAFÉ INSTRUCTIONAL VIDEOS** and more, visit **WORSHIPTOGETHER.com®**

WANNA PLAY?

These 5 songbooks will show you HOW TO.

*From those who play by ear to the experienced music reader...
Now everyone can play today's top modern worship songs.*

☆ Songbooks Include:

Cut Capo Instruction & Charts - Immediately enhance your guitar sound by creating unique voicings with simple chord fingerings

Demo CD - Hear the verse, chorus and bridge of each song in a simple guitar/vocal recording

☆ And Of Course...

Sheet Music - Standard notation for piano, vocal and guitar

Chord Charts - Lyric with chord names and diagrams

Overhead Masters and Key & Tempo Indexes

For these and other resources visit **WORSHIP TOGETHER.com**

WORSHIPTOGETHER.com®

for all your worship needs

Join Today!
FREE membership includes:
- New Song Café training videos
- FREE Sheet Music
- Bible Studies...and more!

also check out these great resources in our store:

Songbooks and CDs from your favorite worship leaders

NEWSONGJUKEBOX ➔ And while you browse, don't forget to click on our **NEW JUKEBOX FEATURE** to listen to brand new worship music!

visit www.worshiptogether.com